MASTERING FERMENTATION

MASTERING
Fermentation

Recipes for Making and
Cooking with Fermented Foods

MARY KARLIN

Photography by Ed Anderson

TEN SPEED PRESS
Berkeley

Some of the recipes in this book include raw eggs, meat, or fish. When these foods are consumed raw, there is always the risk that bacteria, which is killed by proper cooking, may be present. For this reason, when serving these foods raw, always buy certified salmonella-free eggs and the freshest meat and fish available from a reliable grocer, storing them in the refrigerator until they are served. Because of the health risks associated with the consumption of bacteria that can be present in raw eggs, meat, and fish, these foods should not be consumed by infants, small children, pregnant women, the elderly, or any persons who may be immunocompromised. The author and publisher expressly disclaim responsibility for any adverse effects that may result from the use or application of the recipes and information contained in this book.

Copyright © 2013 by Mary Karlin
Photographs copyright © 2013 by Ed Anderson

All rights reserved.

Published in the United States by Ten Speed Press, an imprint of the
Crown Publishing Group, a division of Random House, Inc., New York.
www.crownpublishing.com
www.tenspeed.com

Ten Speed Press and the Ten Speed Press colophon are registered
trademarks of Random House, Inc.

Library of Congress Cataloging-in-Publication Data

Karlin, Mary.
  Mastering fermentation : recipes for making and cooking with fermented foods /
Mary Karlin ; photography by Ed Anderson.
    pages cm
  Includes bibliographical references and index.
1. Fermented foods. 2. Fermentation. I. Anderson, Ed, photographer. II. Title.
  TP371.44.K35 2013
  664'.024—dc23

                          2013002413

Hardcover ISBN: 978-1-60774-438-2
eBook ISBN: 978-1-60774-439-9

Printed in China

Design by Katy Brown

10 9 8 7 6 5 4 3 2 1

First Edition

CONTENTS

INTRODUCTION

SOURDOUGH BREAD, CHEESE, YOGURT, beer, wine, sauerkraut, kimchi, sweet chile sauce, soy sauce, pickles, and even chocolate are just a few of the fermented foods that are part of our everyday diets. In the United States, we love a wide variety of savory and sweet ferments that many of us probably don't even realize are fermented.

Have you ever noticed that many cuisines serve fermented foods with their meals? In Asian cuisine, it's a small dish of pickled vegetables or spicy kimchi; in Indian cuisine, a fabulous chutney or lentil dosa; in the Mediterranean, an aromatic herbal beverage after the meal. Yes, these fermented foods and beverages are delectable players in the overall dance of flavors, textures, and tastes of a meal, but just as important as their flavor, ferments play a valuable role in the digestion of the meal and subsequent health of our digestive system. Fermentation makes those foods more digestible and therefore more nutritious. It's a bonus that fermented foods also taste great.

In many supermarkets today, overprocessed versions have replaced many foods that were traditionally fermented: processed cheese has taken the place of farmhouse Cheddar, pasteurized beers that all taste alike have overtaken regional ales and lagers, preservative-laden bread has replaced homemade loaves made with natural starters. The abundance of these foods throughout our food system makes us believe that these processed versions are safer and healthier for us. But they are not. Many ready-made foods have been robbed of many of their naturally occurring beneficial microorganisms by pasteurization and some extreme high-temperature food-safety processes such as ultra-pasteurization. Not all bacteria are bad for us. The presence of certain bacteria is essential to good health. It is important to our overall health that we get back to the practice of having *real* fermented foods as key elements of our diets. This is not a fad but a trend back to foods that are good for us, many of which we can make ourselves. Once you've tasted real fermented foods, you'll want to stick to them, if only because they simply taste *better*.

So why do fermented foods taste so good? Fermentation promotes the growth of desirable bacteria, molds, and yeasts in foods, either food-borne or through the introduction of various "starters" to create an enzymatic action that transforms the food into an elevated state of flavor and nutritive value. Acidified milk turns into creamy cheese, hard barley kernels mellow into refreshing beer, simple cabbage turns into sauerkraut.

While on this unpredictable fermentation path, you'll discover numerous unexpected gifts that the foods give you. You may start out to ferment one specific food, and in the process of doing so, be given the bonus of one or more beneficial by-products, what I call "many from one." As an example, you may start out to make a fruit vinegar or shrub and find that you have a delicious pulp by-product to turn into a marinade or use to flavor yogurt. That vinegar can become a tasty salad dressing or even flavor a carbonated beverage.

In *Mastering Fermentation*, I present a contemporary approach to fermenting popular, useful foods any cook would want in their pantry, as well as extensive tips and recipes for using these fermented foods. I'll share with you the many ways you can make delicious world-class ferments at home using safe, contemporary methods of fermentation and how to easily incorporate them into your cooking repertoire. You can't rush fermentation nor can you wield total control over it, but with proper guidance and encouragement, you can achieve a high level of success.

In addition to recipes for creating more than seventy fermented favorites are twenty-two globally inspired contemporary recipes featuring those fermented foods in chapter 9. Once you've got a pantry (or refrigerator) bursting with flavorful ferments, it's time to put them to good use.

I invite you to join me on this adventure into the intriguing world of fermentation. Together we'll explore some popular categories of cultured dairy and cheese, fermented fruits and vegetables, sourdough breads and sprouted grains, cured meats and fish, legumes and nuts, and of course fermented beverages. Beyond the pages of this book, you'll find a companion website—www.masteringfermentation.com—full of additional recipes, tips, charts, and Q & A sections designed to keep information current. It's also a way for us to keep in touch. Let's get fermenting!

CHAPTER 1

FERMENTATION BASICS

FERMENTATION IS ONE OF THE oldest forms of preservation. During fermentation, microorganisms— bacteria, yeasts, or molds—break down complex molecules into simpler substances, transforming the chemical composition of food and enhancing its nutritive value. Fermentation improves digestibility, deactivates antinutrient compounds (compounds found in foods that interfere with the absorption of nutrients during digestion) in some foods (particularly nuts and grains), and stimulates probiotic functions, which benefit gut flora development. Carbohydrates (sugar or starch) in some form must be present in order for fermentation to take place. Fermenting agents—helpers enlisted to encourage safe fermentation—come in various forms: salt, whey, a variety of brines, packaged starter cultures, wild yeast starters, and even alcohol. All types of fermentation result in the formation of preservative acids or alcohol.

Fermented foods taste better and are better for us than processed or even pasteurized foods because fermentation promotes the growth of desirable, beneficial bacteria, molds, and yeasts in foods, either food-borne or through "starters." In the fermentation process, foods are transformed texturally, aromatically, and nutritionally. Fermentation creates an environment where pathogens cannot grow and transforms the food, improving its flavor and nutritional content and breaking it down into a state that is easily digested and efficiently used by our bodies.

If fermented foods are so good for us, eating a lot of them right away might sound like a good approach. Be warned: if new to consuming fermented foods, too much all at once may produce digestive discomfort, because your body needs time to adapt to these friendly beneficial occupiers. The overall goal, from my perspective, is to incorporate a sensible amount and a variety of fermented foods into one's daily diet of healthful foods, not to adopt an extreme, all-fermented diet. Start with small 2- to 4-tablespoon portions to acclimate your body. Gradually increase to amounts that make you feel good or feel better.

Over time, you'll get to know what the right amount is for your body.

Raw ferments—those kept under 100°F—are the best source of nutrients. Sauerkraut, kimchi, pickles, and olives are some examples. When cooked (heated over 110°F), many of the beneficial organisms in foods are destroyed. However, as a cook, I look for both nutritional value and food that tastes great. To me, both raw and cooked ferments have great value. Let your palate (that includes your sense of smell) be your ultimate guide.

Note: When you ferment a food or beverage for the first time, you may experience unfamiliar aromas, flavors, and textures that develop during the food's transformation. The fermenting liquid may be slightly cloudy due to the use of whey, the color of the cured meat may not be bright red, or the texture of the pickled fish may seem soft. You may be new to that food, without a frame of reference as to how it is "supposed to" smell or taste. Or, it is likely you are unfamiliar with the changes that occur with fermentation. There's a first time for every food or drink we eat. Think of the first time you smelled sourdough bread, or fish sauce, or a "stinky" perfectly ripe cheese. Had you not experienced them previously, you might have thought they were not safe (or desirable) to eat. But, with a tiny taste, they registered as delicious. The tartness of milk kefir, the yeasty aroma of water kefir, or the vinegary sourness of kombucha may be new to your palate. Some you'll love at first sip; others may take a while longer to enjoy. It's all good. Knowing that these ferments are beneficial for us often makes it easier to venture into unfamiliar territory more courageously.

Types of Fermentation

There are two main types of fermentation: **natural**, which occurs spontaneously from bacteria, yeasts, or molds in the environment; and **starter**, in which a bacterium, yeast, or mold is introduced to a food. Both natural and starter fermentation then takes one of two forms: alcohol or acid fermentation. In alcohol fermentation, also called ethanol fermentation, yeasts convert sugars (glucose, fructose, or sucrose) into alcohol anaerobically (without oxygen). Acid fermentation involves either acetic acid or lactic acid. In acetic acid fermentation, acetobacteria convert starchy, sugary, or alcoholic substances to acetic acid. In lactic acid fermentation (also known as lacto-fermentation), yeasts and bacteria convert sugars and starches into lactic acid. In both cases, the resulting environment is too acidic for harmful bacteria to thrive or spoilage to occur.

The table on the next page is designed to give you an overview of the types of fermentation.

Fermenting Methods

A variety of methods are used to ferment foods. The primary ones include dry salting, brining, whey fermenting, and starter cultures. Two secondary methods, sprouting and soaking, enable valuable nutrients and jump-start the fermentation process.

DRY SALTING
Through osmosis, dry salting brings out moisture in foods. That liquid combines with the salt to create a natural brine and begin the development of lactobacillus bacteria. In cheese making, dry salting assists in draining moisture from curds; in some natural-rind

Fermenting Agents

TYPES OF FERMENTATION: LACTO	
Food: fruit	Fermenting Agents: salt, brine, whey, water kefir grains, water kefir, reserved fruit brine
Food: vegetables, aromatic herbs	Fermenting Agents: lactic acid bacteria activated by salt, brine, whey, packaged starter cultures, reserved vegetable brine
Food: cured meats and fish	Fermenting Agents: lactic acid bacteria activated by packaged starter cultures, used alone or in combination with salt, brine, whey
Food: legumes, nuts, grains, seeds	Fermenting Agents: water, salt, brines, whey, cultured fungi starters (miso, soy sauce)
Food: dairy	Fermenting Agents: packaged starter cultures, reserved yogurt or dairy kefir from previous batches
Food: water kefir	Fermenting Agents: water kefir grains (SCOBY—Symbiotic Colony of Bacteria and Yeast)

TYPE OF FERMENTATION: LACTO-ALCOHOL	
Food: bread and flatbreads	Fermenting Agents: yeasts, lactic acid bacteria, wild yeast starters, yogurt, buttermilk
Alcoholic Beverages: beer, wine, hard cider	Fermenting Agents: cultivated yeasts, wild yeasts

TYPE OF FERMENTATION: LACTO-ALCOHOL-ACETIC	
Food: fruit vinegars	Fermenting Agents: starter cultures (mother)

TYPE OF FERMENTATION: LACTO-ACETIC	
Food: nondairy nonalcoholic beverages, kombucha	Fermenting Agents: starter cultures (SCOBY—Symbiotic Colony of Bacteria and Yeast)

cheeses, it brings moisture in the curds to the surface of the cheese, which then evaporates to begin the formation of a rind. Similarly, when curing meat or fish, salt might be rubbed onto the surface to release internal moisture and set up a protective coating. In all cases, the salt acts as a desiccant (removing moisture), sets up a protective environment (starting the development of beneficial bacteria while curbing the development of harmful bacteria), works as a preservative, and contributes flavor.

When dry-salting produce, the salt is applied directly to the produce (for example, sauerkraut), and then the produce is tossed and gently massaged or pressed to release the inherent juices.

When used to ferment vegetables and some vegetables, the amount of salt is based on the weight of the produce being fermented, generally $1\frac{1}{2}$ percent salt by weight, or about 2 to 3 tablespoons per quart of produce.

BRINING

The first brine ever used was undoubtedly sea water. Brining generally involves a saltwater (nonchlorinated) solution in which the food is submerged. Other brines are used depending on the food being brined and the desired results. Sometimes both dry salting and brining are called for, such as when the produce has limited inherent moisture. Brine recipes are on pages 13–14.

WHEY FERMENTING

Whey is the watery liquid remaining after curds have formed in cultured dairy and cheese. Drained, uncooked whey (whey that has not exceeded 110°F) containing valuable strains of bacteria (probiotic and nutritional) starts the fermentation process in many foods and helps create a safe environment for beneficial bacteria to proliferate. It is used for fruits, vegetables, nuts, meats, and fish as noted in the table on page 5. It is especially useful with fruit, where it minimizes the salty flavor in a sweet preparation. Fresh whey from yogurt or kefir cheese is best, although whey from some cultured cheeses (such as basic chèvre) made at temperatures less than 110°F will work as well. Whey fermenting is usually used in combination with brine, where it turns the brine slightly cloudy.

Note: Though minimal, there is lactose in whey. People who are lactose-intolerant may need to limit (or avoid altogether) their intake of whey-fermented food.

STARTER CULTURE FERMENTING

Starter cultures are desirable bacteria, yeasts, or molds that are introduced into the food to start fermentation. By the nature of their composition, and as their name implies, starters contribute their properties to the fermenting environment, jump-starting the growth of beneficial organisms that are on or in the food to ensure safe and successful fermentation. Portions of previously fermented foods—mother cultures (cultures used to inoculate new batches of the same or a different fermented food or beverage; see page 37), yogurt, kefir, buttermilk, sourdough, brine from fermented produce, and whey—are often used as starter cultures for another batch or an entirely new ferment.

SPROUTING

Sprouting is an effective low-tech method for getting nutritional grains, seeds, and legumes into your diet. It neutralizes enzymes inhibitors and breaks down complex sugars. Numerous enzymes that aid digestion are produced during the germination process. Sprouting also increases many key nutrients. Some evidence shows that sprouting may also render the sprouted grains less allergenic to those with grain protein sensitivities. Sprouted items are best for us when lightly cooked or added to breads (see Sprouted Lentil Dosas, page 126).

SOAKING AND PREPARING NUTS

Tree nuts—walnuts, pecans, almonds, hazelnuts, cashews, macadamias, pistachios, pine nuts, and chestnuts—cannot be sprouted but they can be soaked in salted water to deactivate the enzyme inhibitors (which would interfere with digestion) to make them more digestible and reduce intestinal gas. Soak raw (not roasted) nuts in salted filtered water over multiple hours (overnight is best for most hard nuts such as walnuts or almonds, 6 hours is enough for raw cashews, 4 hours is enough for pine nuts). After soaking and draining, the nuts can be roasted at a low temperature (under 115°F) in a dehydrator, an oven, or a skillet on a stove until the nuts have dried further and are lightly caramelized. See photos and recipe for Toasted Nut Butter on page 78.

> To avoid cross-migration, always store cultures separated from each other by a few feet. Were cross-migration to occur, the original culture would become a hybrid, a new blend of others it has been in contact with, negatively affecting the desired results.

How to Sprout

Use any organic grains, seeds (such as sesame or chia), and legumes (such as chickpeas or lentils). Fill a glass quart jar fitted with a mesh sprouting jar lid (available in many stores and online sources that carry canning supplies) with ½ inch of seeds. Add filtered water to the shoulder of the jar and apply the mesh lid. Allow to soak at room temperature for 8 hours or overnight before pouring off the water. With the soaked seeds still in the jar, rinse them with water and set the jar at an angle to drain.

Repeat the rinsing and draining process two or three times a day. In 1 to 4 days, sprouting will be visible. Sesame seed sprouts will appear within 2 days; larger grains or legumes will be ready in 3 to 4 days. When ready, rinse them well with water, drain, and secure a solid lid on the jar. Store in the refrigerator and use within 3 days.

Sprouted chickpeas and lentils

CHAPTER 2

EQUIPMENT, INGREDIENTS, AND TROUBLESHOOTING

THE PROCESS OF FERMENTATION is sustainable, diverse, and primarily low-tech, and the number of foods and beverages one can ferment are extensive. Many fermentation processes are so simple they don't even need a heat source. (Others, such as bread making, require heat; meat curing calls for a controlled cooling source; cheese making and beer making need both.) In truth, anyone with a small clean kitchen space, basic kitchen equipment, a few jars, and refrigeration space can make delicious ferments.

The first steps to success are simple. Start with small, manageable goals, gain some confidence through experience, and then expand the scope of your fermentation projects. You don't have to go it alone. Fermenting food is fun, so do it with friends or family. Whether making cheese, bread, or jars of fermented seasonal produce, consider organizing a fermentation exchange: trade your finished ferments to diversify your fermentation pantries, while building a greater sense of community.

Building Your Skills

Here are some practices that will help you succeed.

1. MAKE SMALL BATCHES.

Choose a ferment that's easy to make and make a small batch or even one jar. These easy ferments make great starting points: Nonfat Greek-Style Yogurt (page 98) or Coconut Milk Yogurt (page 40), Crème Fraîche (page 95), a chutney or salsa (pages 49–50), sauerkraut (page 56), kimchi (page 54), Lacto-Mayonnaise (page 53), mustard (page 62), or even Gravlax (page 149). You can also easily make natural sodas (pages 166–169) or, even though they require special starter cultures, Milk Kefir (page 175), Water Kefir (page 171), or basic Kombucha (page 177).

2. SET REASONABLE EXPECTATIONS.

After initial success, make more ferments or larger batches as seasonal fruits or vegetables peak. Assess your time, work area, and storage space to determine what and how much to make. Determine the number of jars, bottles, or other fermentation vessels your space can handle. You can then figure out how best to build your fermentation pantry, having some items at room temperature and others under refrigeration. Before long, you could have multiple ferments going at the same time. The list of options is limited only by your space, time, and imagination.

> Aging cheeses and curing meats must be kept in separate environments to avoid any cross-contamination.

3. PLAN AND PREPARE.
The recipes in this book contain a start-to-finish timeline. Read through the recipes you want to make to get a sense of the pacing of the project. Fermenting certain foods involves ordering some special equipment and supplies, so factor delivery time into your schedule. Once made, the fermentation might require a series of tasks over a period of hours or days (or, for ripening tasks, weeks or months). Determine a realistic scope of work.

You should also familiarize yourself with any terms or techniques that aren't familiar to you. Refer to the Glossary (page 235) for commonly used terms.

4. KEEP IT SAFE AND SANITARY.
When using your home kitchen, it is imperative that your space is safe to work in (no clutter or pets around) and scrupulously clean. While fermentation is pro-bacteria, they have to be the right kind! These easy steps will control bad bacteria (they can ruin the batch) and keep your ferments safe to eat.

- Sanitize your work station with a commercial sanitizer or a sanitizing solution of 2 tablespoons plain household bleach dissolved in 1 gallon of water. Alternatively, distilled vinegar works as an antibacterial agent. Use paper towels to apply the sanitizer and to wipe the surface clean.

- All pieces of equipment that come into contact with food should be sanitized, rinsed, and air-dried before using. This includes any glass storage vessels. To sanitize properly, run equipment through a dishwasher. Otherwise, wash with hot soapy water, rinse thoroughly with tap water, rinse in bleach-water sanitizing solution, then rinse in clear tap water again. Allow to air-dry on a rack set on a baking sheet (do not drain in a dish drainer to minimize contact with unwanted bacteria that might live on the drainer frame).

- Equipment used solely for fermenting (as opposed to being taken from your usual kitchen equipment) should also be sanitized, rinsed, and air-dried before you put it away. If possible, store it all in one place—a lidded box is perfect—so it's organized, at the ready, and dust-free.

- Clay or porous vessels do not need to be scrubbed out with detergent if they will be reused for making the same product since they contain desirable bacteria that are valuable for the next batch of the same product. They should simply be rinsed out, very lightly cleaned with a natural bristle scrub brush, rinsed with filtered water, air-dried, and stored if not using immediately.

- Do not wear fragrance while preparing, tasting, or cooking food. It masks your ability to use your sense of smell to guide you in the process.

- Wash your hands thoroughly before starting and after handling foodstuffs or other nonsterile items. Use unscented bar soap, not antibacterial liquid soap.

- Don't prep multiple categories of food (protein and vegetables, for instance) on the same work surface or at the same time. This can cause cross-contamination and spread harmful bacteria.

- Stay focused on one category of fermentation during any one session. This, along with trying to cook while fermenting, can cause cross-contamination.

- Set up a work station with a roll of paper towels and a small trash receptacle to make cleanup easy, two clean cotton kitchen towels for drying your hands as you work, and any utensils on a baking sheet to keep them clean.

5. KEEP NOTES.
Note your observations and results so you can apply that information to future batches. Detailed checklists, worksheets, and observation forms are available as downloads at www.masteringfermentation.com.

Equipment and Supplies

Specialized equipment and supplies specific to fermenting dairy and cheese are in chapter 5 (pages 84–85); for curing meats and fish are in chapter 7 (page 144); for beverages are in chapter 8 (pages 164–165). See Resources (page 241) for recommended suppliers.

Basic equipment and supplies you'll need for most of the ferments include the following:

- Blunt meat pounder or potato masher

- Bottle-cleaning brushes (assorted sizes)

- Butter muslin or fine-weave cheesecloth (4 to 6 yards); from cheese-making supplier

- Clay fermentation crocks of multiple sizes (1 gallon smallest)

- Fermenting vessels with air locks: buckets, bottles, jars, and crocks (no reactive metals)

- Flexible-blade rubber or silicone spatulas (no wooden handles)

- Food blender

- Food-grade plastic buckets or beverage fermenting containers with lids

- Food-grade (preferably BPA-free) plastic storage containers with lids (2 cups, 4 quarts, 7.5 quarts)

- Food processor

- Funnels (wide mouth to fill jars and small to fill bottles)

- Glass clamp-top preserving jars (1 pint, 1 quart, and ½ gallon)

- Glass clamp-top (swing-top, aka Grolsch-style) beverage bottles
- Glass jars and lids ($\frac{1}{2}$ gallon, 1 gallon)
- Glass vinegar or wine bottles with stoppers
- Glass wide-mouth canning jars and lids ($\frac{1}{2}$ pint, 1 pint, 1 quart)
- Instant-read or dial kitchen thermometer
- Kitchen scissors
- Kitchen timer (two-phase)
- Ladle or slotted spoon (stainless steel or other nonreactive material)
- Mandoline slicer
- Mesh strainers (stainless steel and nylon mesh)
- Mixing bowls (glass, stainless steel, ceramic, or food-grade plastic)
- Nonreactive metal (only stainless steel, ceramic on cast iron, or enamel on steel; no aluminum or nonstick) pots and stockpots
- Repurposed ceramic Crock-Pot liners
- Stainless steel measuring spoons (including $\frac{1}{8}$ teaspoon and $\frac{1}{16}$ teaspoon)
- Tea bags (muslin or mesh)
- Weights (glass coasters, glass votive candle holders, small plates, small glass jars, washed river rocks)
- Optional equipment: dehydrators; vacuum sealer; aging or storage refrigerator; wok; electric smoker; tortilla press; stainless-steel food mill

Ingredients

Start with the freshest ingredients you can find. Know the source of the ingredients you are using; look for local producers when possible. If packaged, read labels thoroughly. Whenever possible, produce should be organic because it contains inherent bacteria useful to fermentation; meats ethically raised; fish sustainable; milk from antibiotic-free animals. If frozen food is all you have available, by all means ferment it. It (and you) will certainly benefit from the process.

SALT

The use of salt is the oldest method of fermentation, and it's the primary method for fermenting vegetables and some fruits. Salt plays a major role in preserving during fermentation, converting sugars into an acidic environment and prohibiting harmful bacteria from growing. Salt serves to firm up pectin in fruits and vegetables, keeping them crunchy.

If left submerged in a salty brine for too long, food will ultimately become dried out, having lost its moisture to the brine through osmosis. The amount of salt used to ferment can be decreased from the amount called for; however, be aware that if the level is too low, bad bacteria will have a chance to grow. Also, the resulting texture may be mushy. If you want to reduce the amount of salt, cut the salt in half and replace the deleted amount with starter to keep the ferment safe. While not enough salt is a more common problem, too much salt will inhibit the growth of the beneficial bacteria. You may need a series of trials to establish the correct amount of salt to your taste due to variables from batch to batch. Salt is also used in this book as a soaking solution for legumes, nuts, and potatoes to release antinutrients, making the foods more digestible.

The only type of salt to use for fermenting is non-iodized, unrefined fine sea salt without any additives. For cooking (as in chapter 9), kosher salt is fine, too.

STARTER CULTURES

Starters introduce specific bacteria and yeast into the fermentation environment. Their role is to jump-start the development of desirable beneficial bacteria that keep the fermenting food safe. Refer to Starter Culture Fermenting in chapter 1 (page 6) for more information.

WATER

Many fermentation processes include water. Water quality is as important to success as milk quality is in fermenting dairy. Fermentation is pro–bacterial growth; any chemicals that may be in household tap water are antibacterial and therefore detrimental to the fermentation process (they are also detrimental to the beneficial bacteria in our guts). It is best to use household or bottled filtered or spring water. If your household tap water contains chlorine, you can remove it. Simply bring the water just to a boil and let it cool, or set a pitcher of tap water at room temperature overnight; the chlorine will evaporate. Some fermentations (such as water kefir) benefit from the extra minerals that well water contains. In those cases, the minerals should not be filtered out.

RAW, UNFILTERED HONEY

Raw honey has not been cooked, pasteurized, or filtered. Wildflower is a universally useful flavor.

RAW, UNFILTERED APPLE CIDER VINEGAR

For fermenting, use homemade of any variety of apples or store-bought Bragg's with Mother.

RAW, UNREFINED CANE SUGAR

Granulated organic sugar, made from evaporated cane juice.

BASIC WHEY

Whey is the watery liquid remaining after curds have formed in cultured dairy or cheese. Use fresh whey from (ideally homemade) drained plain European-style yogurt, milk kefir, or other cultured dairy product that has not been heated over 110°F (no higher than 105°F is best).

BASIC BRINE

YIELD: 2 quarts

This creates a 5 percent brine solution that can be used unless a recipe states a different percentage.

6 tablespoons fine sea salt
8 cups filtered water

Make the brine by combining the ingredients, whisking to dissolve the salt. Place in a jar, cover, and refrigerate.

SWEET AND SALTY PICKLING BRINE

YIELD: 1 pint

3/4 cup raw, unfiltered apple cider vinegar

1 cup Basic Brine (page 13)

1 tablespoon brine from sauerkraut (optional, but preferred)

1 tablespoon raw, unfiltered honey

1/2 teaspoon Whole Grain Dijon-Style Mustard (page 63)

Combine the apple cider vinegar and brines. Whisk in the honey to dissolve, and then stir in the mustard. Place in a jar, cover, and refrigerate.

BEER BRINE

YIELD: 1 quart

2 cups flat handcrafted beer

2 cups Basic Brine (page 13)

Combine the ingredients. Place in a jar, cover, and refrigerate.

VEGETABLE BRINE

Use at least 1 tablespoon and up to 1/4 cup of the salty brine left from another batch of the same product—brine from fermented garlic, sauerkraut, or kale are good foundational vegetable brines. Vegetable brine is used in combination with Basic Brine (page 13). The amount used will be stated in the individual recipes.

Environment

It is important to maintain a proper development environment in which to ferment your food, and then store it. That includes maintaining a desirable temperature range to promote and protect healthy fermentation, a necessary amount of air circulation, and little to no direct sunlight as directed.

TEMPERATURE

Consistent ambient temperatures must be maintained to encourage fermentation. The fluctuation should stay within 5°F. The ranges of ideal temperatures differ for various styles of fermentation. The individual recipes specify required temperatures. Room temperature is 68°F to 72°F. When making cheese or curing meats, the aging or ripening environment's humidity range must also be monitored and maintained.

> Warmer temperatures speed up fermentation, resulting in shorter fermentation cycles; colder temperatures slow things down, meaning the same fermentation tends to take longer.

OXYGEN

Direct exposure to oxygen should be limited as prescribed in directions. However, good air circulation is often needed within the fermentation storage environment, especially in cheese making and meat curing, to maintain consistent ambient temperatures and humidity.

DIRECT SUNLIGHT

Not allowed. Exposure to sunlight interferes with the consistent temperatures needed during fermentation.

FOOD STORAGE

Ideal storage environments vary depending on the type of fermentation. In general, most ferments are best stored in cool to cold temperatures of between 38°F and 50°F (a home refrigerator is in the 38°F to 40°F range). Once they reach the desired state, aged cheeses and cured meats can be stored at temperatures ranging from 40°F to 50°F or in home refrigeration. A home refrigerator, wine cooler, repurposed dedicated refrigerator, subterranean basement or cellar, cool root larder, or cool pantry can be viable storage environments. Temperatures colder than recommended will retard further fermentation and freezing temperatures will suspend or halt fermentation entirely.

While you certainly can freeze fermented food, freezing reduces the vitality of the beneficial organisms over time; eventually, the probiotic benefits are lost.

Troubleshooting

If you're new to fermenting, a lot of questions may arise. What should my ferment look like? How can I tell it is going well? How should it smell and taste? Along with the troubleshooting tips below, more tips and reference photos are at the companion website, www.masteringfermentation.com.

- **Look.** If fermentation is taking place in a crock or jar:

  Bubbles may appear at the surface—this is a sign that healthy, vibrant fermentation is underway.

  If foam or scum appears, skim it off and discard it. The food underneath is safe.

  The brine or liquid level increasing (fruits and vegetables) is a sign that a natural brine is developing.

  There can be a noticeable color change to one that is less vibrant, due to the enzymatic action taking place; sometimes there's also a visible change in texture from the raw state to the fermented state.

  If a beverage is fermenting in a bottle:

  Small bubbles are signs of carbonation. When you burp the bottle to test for carbonation, you should see a misty spray given off, and hear the release of the stopper. If you don't, not enough time has passed for carbonation to have built up, or there hasn't been enough food (sugar) for the yeast to consume, then create, carbonation.

- **Smell.** You will know if a food has putrefied to become undesirable rot. The smell will permeate the pantry, kitchen, refrigerator, or ripening cave. You will want to dispose of it as quickly as you can.

- **Taste.** It should taste good to you. If it does not, throw it out and clean the vessel thoroughly.

CHAPTER 3

FERMENTED FRUITS AND VEGETABLES: Pickles, Vinegars, Juices, Sauces, and Condiments

LONG BEFORE REFRIGERATION, the use of lacto-fermentation kept fruits and vegetables perfectly preserved, although transformed. Fermentation changes textures, amplifies flavors, and heightens aromas. These treasures have enhanced digestibility and increased vitamin levels. Developed lactic acid bacteria in fruits and vegetables creates crunchy pickles, bright vinegars, zesty sauces, and useful condiments.

Take note that within this enormous category of fermentation, you can get "many from one." That is, from any given fruit or vegetable can come multiple, often surprising offshoots. In making one ferment, you might also get a juice, a sauce, a stock, or a paste. (See photo on page 23.) Look for these offshoots throughout this book as Bonus Recipes.

During fermentation, the starches and sugars in fruits and vegetables are converted into lactic acid by different strains of lactic acid–producing bacteria (lactobacilli). These bacteria are everywhere, present in abundance on the leaves, skins, and roots of all produce, and even on the surface of our skin and in the soil. Our job is to utilize the lactobacilli present, especially on organic, untreated produce, and limit any undesirable bacteria to create safe fermented food. Once the proper environment exists for safe fermentation to take place, it all occurs naturally, with little involvement on our part.

Because of their sugar levels, fruits ferment more quickly than vegetables, usually within 3 to 5 days (although citrus can often take a few weeks). After that, fermenting fruit will become alcoholic, perhaps a desirable result. After that, the alcohol will be converted to acetic acid (vinegar), which, again, may be the goal. To halt fermentation, the fruit needs to be refrigerated.

I hope the examples presented here will inspire you to venture down many delicious paths, using the bounty of the season and your own palate as a directional guide.

Basic Preparation for Fruits and Vegetables

Always begin with locally grown, preferably organic, produce. Not only is this an ethical lifestyle choice, but it is also one that supports a healthy environment necessary for the development of beneficial bacteria and safe fermentation.

Rinse all produce with filtered water and drain or air-dry before fermenting. (Tight-leafed organic produce such as cabbage does not have to be washed; remove the outer leaves until you get to the clean, untouched leaves.)

> Save the brine from batches of fermented vegetables or fruits. Use some as a starter for another batch or to season soups, make into dressings, or use in beverages. Cover and store in refrigeration if not using immediately.

Use only kosher or unrefined sea salt. Remember, in addition to enhancing flavor, salt is a purifier (it's antibacterial), a desiccant (removes moisture), and a preservative.

These are the general steps to start fermentation: Rub the cut-up produce with salt, gently massaging it to release some liquid and start a natural brine. Leave it at room temperature for at least 10 minutes, or longer if specified in recipes, to release more liquid (see photo on page 57). Then place the produce and its brine in a fermentation vessel and press down with a blunt meat pounder or potato masher to release more natural juices. Augment the natural brine with additional salt brine to cover. Apply a weight to keep the produce under the brine and limit oxygen exposure, cover the vessel, and let fermentation begin. The immediate goal is to promote the growth of beneficial bacteria to overtake any bad microbes and set up a healthy, safe environment for beneficial bacteria to prosper. Be sure to keep any clay fermentation storage vessels free of cracks and dedicated to specific ferments.

Cured Olives

YIELD: 1 pound of olives generally yields 1 pint cured (dry-cured will yield less due to the moisture loss)
START TO FINISH: Time varies depending on the curing method used: 1 hour prep postharvest + 4 to 8 weeks curing

Beautiful silvery green-leafed olive trees bear fruit that is too bitter to eat when first harvested. Whether harvested when ripe but green (very bitter), purple (more mature and less bitter), or black (fully ripe and even less bitter), olives must be fermented (cured) in order to tenderize the flesh, leach out the bitterness, and render them edible.

Olive curing at home is neither difficult nor time consuming, though as with some other fermenting processes, you have to be patient. The degree of maturity of the fruit will often dictate the best curing method. The type of olive, its oil content, and curing style determine the final taste. Olives can be salt-cured, brined, water-cured, and dry-cured. Once cured, you can smoke the olives, soaked in olive oil, for even more depth of flavors. Cured olives can be stored covered, unrefrigerated, in olive oil until ready to eat. They should be refrigerated once opened, and will keep for months. Find a recipe for water-cured green olives at this book's companion website, www.masteringfermentation.com.

Note: Exposure to air after harvesting causes the olives to begin to deteriorate, so try to cure them within 12 hours of picking. If you must store the olives before curing, store them submerged in cool water.

Always start with fresh olives that are plump, firm, and free of blemishes. If the olives are organic, check for small puncture holes in the flesh. If present, destroy these olives; the holes may indicate olive fly

continued

infestation. Pick through the saved olives to remove all stems, leaves, and any dirt. Sort the olives by size, color, and variety (if you have multiple varieties) so each group will cure evenly. Rinse the olives with water twice and drain before curing. Olives are cured and stored with their pits in.

Brine-Cured Green Olives. Make a brine of 1¾ cups unrefined fine sea salt to 1 gallon filtered water. Stir to dissolve and then cool to 50°F to 55°F. Place 1 gallon of olives in a large food-grade container and cover with the cool brine. Place a weight on top to keep the olives completely submerged. Cover with fine-weave cheesecloth and store in a cool, dark location. Every 7 to 10 days, drain and rinse the olives and replace with a fresh batch of brine. Begin to taste a sample after 30 days for bitterness. Based on your taste, you can continue to brine for another 15 days, or until they taste good to you. Drain and rinse the olives several times until they do not taste too salty. You can also soak the olives for a few hours in filtered water to remove some of the saltiness.

To finish brine-cured olives, make a fresh batch of brine for storing. This brine has a lower salinity level: 1 cup unrefined fine sea salt to 1 gallon filtered water. Stir to dissolve and then cool to 50°F to 55°F. Place the olives in a glass jar or crock and cover with the brine. Herbs or garlic can be added at this point. Again, place a weight on top to keep the olives completely submerged. Cover with fine-weave cheesecloth and store in a cool dark location or in refrigeration. Allow the olives to brine for 1 week before eating. They can be stored for up to 6 months or longer.

Dry-Cured Ripe Olives. Fully ripe black olives work best. Mission olives are preferred because of their high oil content. The ratio is approximately ½ pound unrefined fine sea salt to a 1 gallon bucket of ripe olives. Weight and volume will differ among varieties.

Use a draining box or bucket with openings for draining placed in a receptacle to catch the draining liquid. Layer the container with fine-weave cheesecloth, then a thick layer of salt. Layer alternating with olives, and finish with a layer of salt on top; completely covering the olives. Set in a warm (70°F to 72°F) place (indoors or outdoors, but out of the sun) and cover with a dish towel or cheesecloth. Using your hands, toss every day or two to help expel moisture. If all of the salt has melted, replenish once during the curing timeline. The olives are ready in 4 to 8 weeks, or when they stop dripping. The olives will taste slightly bitter at this point. Rinse the olives and then lay out on a clean dish towel to dry overnight at room temperature. Once dry, they can be finished with salt or covered with olive oil. If salting, toss them with clean salt and pack into sterilized jars. Pack with aromatics such as bay leaf, rosemary, or citrus zest, dried chiles, or peppercorns. If packing in olive oil, completely cover the olives. Aromatics can be added here as well. Store in a cool, dark location for up to 1 month. If refrigerated, they can be stored for up to 6 months.

Oil-Cured Olives. This refers to a method of finishing the olives. We see this style as Moroccan olives at retail olive bars. Dry-cured black olives are finished in salt and tossed to coat with olive oil. They are then stored in an airtight container and should be kept refrigerated.

Fruit and Vegetable Juices, Sauces, Pastes, and Stocks

Fruit and vegetable juices, sauces, and pastes are basic cooking components for every cook. Beginning with any fresh, seasonal, preferably organic produce, you can branch off in a variety of directions to get the finished products you want. You'll need a food processor or a food mill, as well as a blender and a fine-mesh strainer to prepare the fruits. Then you'll use a stovetop, oven, hot summer sun, or food dehydrator to process the prepared fruits to their desired final consistency. Rather than using a juicer that separates the juice from the pulp, I prefer to blend raw fruits into a liquid juice state, retaining the nutritious pulp. When making both a juice and a paste, I can press the pulp-filled juice through a mesh strainer to give me both.

You can create interesting flavors from specific individual fruits or from combinations of compatible ones. Once made, add layers of flavor with herbs, spices, and other aromatics of choice.

JUICE

You can liquefy fermented fruits into a juice using a blender, or first liquefy and then ferment by adding Basic Brine (page 13) or basic whey (see page 13) to the juice.

SAUCE

Over low heat, reduce the fermented juice to the desired consistency. Or pass the fermented fruits through a food mill to create a raw sauce that can be heated if desired. Stir in a small amount (about 1 teaspoon) of coconut flour, if needed, to thicken slightly. The coconut flour will add sweetness as well. If the sauce needs thinning, stir in some coconut milk (if you want a creamy sauce) or coconut water.

PASTE

Combine the pressed fruit pulp with raw, unfiltered honey and aromatics such as vanilla or cinnamon or vegetable pulp with olive oil and aromatics such as fresh parsley or thyme leaves, then puree into a paste. Place in a jar, cover with cheesecloth, and leave at room temperature for 2 days to ferment. Replace the cheesecloth with a lid and refrigerate until ready to use.

VEGETABLE STOCK

Once you have juice, you can add water or fermented vegetable brine (from sauerkraut or other compatible vegetables), reserved whey, or the delicious drained liquid from Tapenade of Herbs, Citrus, and Olives (page 77) to become a stock.

If not using vegetable juice, you can coarsely grate or chop vegetables (such as onions, leeks, celery, carrots, beets, turnips, or chard), and then toss with unrefined fine sea salt (1 pound to 5 pounds of vegetables), massage for 5 minutes, cover with fine-weave cheesecloth, then leave overnight at room temperature to release juices (the method used when making sauerkraut). Combine all of this with water to make the stock.

To add more layers of flavor: First, roast the produce spread in a single layer on a baking sheet in a 350°F oven until tender and slightly caramelized, 30 to 35 minutes, then ferment using Basic Brine (page 13) or basic whey (see page 13) and blend into a sauce or dehydrate into a paste. Make amazing pastes from fruits macerated to make shrubs (page 169), adding a sweetener such as raw, unfiltered honey, raw cane sugar, agave syrup, or smoked sugar.

Or first cold-smoke (see page 56), ferment, then blend into juice; add water to become a stock.

Vegetables fermenting in an air lock jar, vegetable paste, vegetable juice turned into stock

Tomato Ketchup

YIELD: 1 quart
START TO FINISH: 20 minutes to make + 8 to 12 hours fermenting + 2 days refrigeration

Make this fermented version once and you'll never buy another bottle of ketchup again. Spice it up by adding red pepper flakes, cayenne pepper, or even smoked paprika.

3 cups canned or homemade tomato paste
2 teaspoons unrefined fine sea salt
¼ cup Worcestershire Sauce (page 146)
½ cup raw, unfiltered apple cider vinegar
6 tablespoons robust flavored raw, unfiltered honey
    such as clover, or organic amber maple syrup
¼ cup basic whey (see page 13), Water Kefir (page 171),
    or vegetable brine (such as from sauerkraut),
    as fermenting agent

Combine all the ingredients in a bowl, making sure the salt and the honey are dissolved. Transfer to a wide-mouth 1-quart jar. Secure a piece of cheesecloth to the opening and allow to sit at room temperature for 8 hours or overnight. Remove the cheesecloth and secure an airtight lid. Refrigerate for 2 days before using. Use within 2 months.

MUSHROOM KETCHUP

YIELD: 1 pint
START TO FINISH: 20 minutes to make + 24 hours fermenting + 2 days room temperature + 2 days refrigeration

Ketchup made with mushrooms was developed by the British long before Americans created the tomato version. Somewhat related to Worcestershire sauce, this mushroom condiment can be used like tomato ketchup or steak sauce. I sometimes like to add a few pieces of chopped walnuts with the bay leaf.

½ pound fresh shiitake mushrooms, stemmed and sliced
½ pound fresh cremini or portobello mushrooms, stemmed and sliced
2 teaspoons unrefined fine sea salt
1 Roasted Shallot (page 212), mashed
1 tablespoon grated fresh ginger
¼ teaspoon crushed bay leaf
Pinch of ground white pepper
Pinch of ground allspice
1 tablespoon robust raw, unfiltered honey
2 tablespoons Worcestershire Sauce (page 146)
¼ cup raw, unfiltered apple cider vinegar
2 tablespoons basic whey (see page 13)
¼ cup Basic Brine (page 13) or vegetable brine (such as from sauerkraut)

Put the mushrooms and salt in a bowl and toss well. Cover with cheesecloth and leave in a cool place for 24 hours. Stir in the shallot, ginger, bay leaf, white pepper, and allspice to combine. Dissolve the honey with the Worcestershire sauce and vinegar and then stir into the mushroom mixture. Place the mixture in a food processor and blend thoroughly. Add the whey and half of the brine and then blend into a smooth sauce. Add more brine as needed to thin to a desired consistency. Place in a jar and secure the airtight lid. Leave at room temperature for 2 days. Refrigerate for at least 2 days for the flavors to develop before using. Flavors will deepen and be optimum after 1 week. Use within 2 months.

Clockwise from left: pickled grapes, pickled onions, pickled carrots with lovage and juniper berries, roasted jalapeños

Sweet and Salty Pickled Vegetables

YIELD: 1 pint
START TO FINISH: 15 minutes to make + 6 hours fermenting

These are one of my favorite pickles, featured in the Grilled Ahi Tuna on Pickled Vegetables and Rice Salad with Miso Dressing (page 198). This sweet-salty pickling brine can be used to make numerous tasty vegetable and fruit pickles. Pickled onions and pickled shallots are terrific when made with this brine.

2 small unpeeled carrots, cut into 1-inch-long matchsticks

3 large radishes, cut into matchsticks

4 green onions (with ½ inch of green part), quartered lengthwise

1-inch piece fresh ginger, cut into matchsticks

¼ cup steamed edamame beans

1 teaspoon unrefined fine sea salt

1 pint Sweet and Salty Pickling Brine (page 14)

1. In a bowl, combine the carrots, radishes, green onions, ginger, and edamame and toss with the salt.

2. Pack the vegetables into a pint jar and cover with the pickling brine to 1 inch from the top. Press down on the vegetables to pack tightly and release some of their moisture. Cover the opening with cheesecloth and set at room temperature for 6 hours. Remove the cheesecloth, secure with a lid, and refrigerate. Best used from 3 days to 1 week.

STEM AND STALK PICKLES

Here's a great way to utilize vegetable stems and stalks that you might otherwise toss. I like to use stems from chard (red, white, or yellow), beets, carrots, parsley, or cilantro (or both), as well as the thick ends and tender tops of celery and lovage. You may find other stems and stalks to pickle, or combinations that work for you. Cut the stems and stalks into uniform pieces, stuff them into a jar (you can add aromatics such as peppercorns, dried chiles, bay leaf, or cloves of garlic if you like), cover with Basic Brine (page 13), brine from other vegetables, the Sweet and Salty Pickling Brine (page 14), or the Beer Brine (page 14). Cover the jar with cheesecloth and leave out at room temperature for 8 hours or overnight, then store in refrigeration. *See photo on page 193.*

Bran-Fermented Vegetables

YIELD: About 2 cups
START TO FINISH: 30 minutes to mix the bran (first batch only) + 3 days bran mixture fermenting (first batch only) + 30 minutes vegetable prep + 1 to 2 days vegetable fermenting

Making pickles using rice bran—*nuka* pickles—is a traditional practice in Japan. In the past, each kitchen had its own nuka pot that sat on the counter and was fed new vegetables each day. These pots of rich, fermented bran were passed along to the next generation of women in the family. Making nuka pickles had been virtually abandoned by modern cooks, but has recently regained popularity. Here is my spin on a traditional method. It is very easy, extremely nutritious, and great fun for kids. Toasted bran, salt brine, fermented beer or wine, and miso (if using) are massaged together; along with the surface bacteria of the vegetables the mixture creates a healthy, rich lactobacillus (beneficial bacteria) community in which the vegetables, through lacto-fermentation, become crunchy, salty, earthy pickles. The transformation occurs rapidly, with some vegetables (depending on size and thickness) becoming pickled within 12 hours, while others take 1 to 2 days. With this process, to my taste, a longer burying time does not necessarily result in better tasting pickles. Traditionally, though, daikon can be buried for up to 6 months.

With their roots in Japan, these pickles are traditionally fermented with rice bran. However, wheat and oat bran are often more available in the United States and can be used as well; each will produce a slightly different flavor.

1-gallon crock

2 pounds bran (rice, wheat, or oat)
3 strips dried kelp (optional)
2½ cups nonchlorinated water
¾ cup handcrafted beer (ale or lager), at room temperature
¾ cup unrefined fine sea salt
¼ cup miso (optional)
1-inch piece fresh ginger, cut into small chunks
2 to 2½ cups vegetables (small root vegetables, pickling cucumbers, baby onions, cauliflower florets, asparagus, green beans, and ginger), for pickling
Vegetable scraps (about ½ to ¾ cup), for jump-starting the bran mixture

1. Dry-toast the bran in a large skillet over medium heat for about 5 minutes, or spread on a baking sheet and roast in a 300°F oven just until you can smell it, about 7 minutes. Remove from the heat and cool. Place in a large bowl and toss in the dried kelp, if using. In a separate bowl, combine the water and beer and stir in the salt to combine and dissolve. Stir this into the bran to incorporate; it should look like wet sand. Mix in the miso, if using, and the ginger.

2. Massage the mixture with clean hands until it is a smooth paste sort of like wet sand. For the initial batch, you'll need to get the bacteria happening a few days in advance of burying the vegetables meant for pickles. In the crock, layer the vegetables in the "sand" and then layer the vegetable scraps. Top with the rest of the "sand," set the crock on the kitchen counter, cover it with fine-weave cheesecloth, and let the fermentation party begin. Let stand for 3 days, and then remove the pieces of vegetable. The wet sand is then ready to be used for making nuka pickles.

continued

3.   Wash and trim the vegetables. Peel if the skin is not to be eaten. Small whole vegetables of about equal size are best. They will ferment at about the same pace, and they are easy to bury and then find in the sand. They can be sliced into smaller pieces postpickling.

4.   Dump out the wet sand mixture from the crock onto a baking sheet. Mix in a bit more water if the mixture has become crumbly. Taste and smell it. To me, it smells like healthy bread dough or even miso. If at any time the mixture smells sour or funky, discard it and start a fresh batch.

5.   Fill the bottom of your crock with about 2 inches of the "sand." Partially bury one variety of vegetable into the mixture, leaving space between the pieces to fill with sand. Fill with sand in between, and then place another layer of sand on top (this time about 1 inch deep), and proceed with the next vegetable. Repeat the process, finishing with a layer of sand to completely enclose the vegetables. Cover the crock with fine-weave cheesecloth and secure with a rubber band. Set it on your kitchen counter or in a cool place to ferment.

6.   Taste-test 1 piece after 12 hours. If still "raw," continue fermenting; most vegetables take 1 to 2 days. If you like it (it should still be a bit crunchy), gently dump the mixture onto a baking sheet and dig for your treasures. Brush off any bits of bran from the pickles or gently slosh them in a bowl of cool water to remove excess. The pickles are ready to consume. It is best to eat them within a day or two after pickling. Cut into slices or chunks as desired and serve.

7.   Gather up the wet sand and store in the same crock. You do not need to wash the crock, as the bacteria within will be good for the next batch. Start a new batch of pickles or plug in a few bits of veggies to keep the bacteria colony going. Cover the crock with cheesecloth and set at room temperature for a day. If not using within 24 hours, cover with plastic wrap and refrigerate. Bring to room temperature and massage with your clean hands before making your next batch of pickles. Handled properly, with salt and water replenished as needed, this bran mixture will only get better with time. You'll be able to pass it along to a loved one!

Adding water to make bran sand; hand-mixing bran sand; inserting asparagus into sand; packed bran sand

PICKLED DRIED FRUIT

YIELD: 1 pint
START TO FINISH: 10 minutes to make + 8 hours fermenting + 1 week refrigeration

Pickled dried fruits are wonderful as cocktail garnishes, in chutneys, or tossed into a salad. Use organic whole raisins (golden or dark), currants, cranberries, blueberries, cherries, or even chopped dates, figs, apples, or apricots. Try to buy local or regional dried fruit whenever possible. A good source for finding regional products is Local Harvest (see Resources, page 241). Many grocery retailers carry dried fruit from Sun Organic Farm, a brand I prefer. You might also try using plain water kefir as an alternative to the dairy whey.

¼ teaspoon yellow mustard seeds
½ cup raw unrefined cane sugar
1 cup filtered water
¼ cup raw, unfiltered apple cider vinegar
1 teaspoon unrefined fine sea salt
2 tablespoons basic whey (see page 13)
1 cup dried fruit

Combine all the ingredients, place in a pint jar, cover with cheesecloth, and let sit for 8 hours. Secure the jar with a lid and place in the refrigerator. Shake vigorously every day for 1 week before using. Drain the fruit and use as a garnish or ingredient. Save the liquid to ferment another fruit or use in a beverage.

Fruit Vinegars

True fruit vinegars are not timid; they have substance and presence. These fermented fruit vinegars are one of my favorite pantry items to use in both sweet and savory ways. Think beyond vinaigrettes to drinks and tonics! Finished, aged fruit vinegars carry the true essence of the fermented fruit, infused with bright flavors and aromas along with intense colors. Use these four methods as starting points and feel free to experiment. You'll always get the most intense flavor when you use peak-of-the-season fruit, but you can also make tasty vinegars with unprocessed sun-dried or dehydrated fruit, using the infused raw vinegar method (see page 36). Fruit has to have a high enough sugar (fructose) level to attain the needed alcohol level to then develop into good quality vinegar, which is why many methods call for additional sugars.

Vegetable Vinegars

Vegetable-based vinegars are quite different from fruit vinegars. The vegetables one might use to flavor a tasty vinegar (red bell pepper, carrot, beet, celery, garlic, shallot) do not contain enough sugar to convert to alcohol to then convert to acetic acid (vinegar). In order to make flavorful vegetable-based vinegars, you need to use the pulp method for fruit vinegars (page 34) or start with fermented vegetable juices and proceed using the pulp method. Herbs and spices can be added as well at bottling. Additionally, brines from homemade sauerkraut, kale, cucumber pickles, kimchi, fermented garlic, or shallots are delicious and can be used as the base liquid (in place of the base vinegar) to which vegetable puree or juice is added to make a tonic-style vinegar.

PINEAPPLE VINEGAR

YIELD: 8 to 10 ounces
START TO FINISH: 30 minutes prep + 6 weeks to 6 months fermenting

The following recipe involves the "let it be" method of fermentation, which happens to be the simplest. Fruit, skins, or peels are placed in a jar, sugar is added, and then it's left alone to ferment naturally, with additional sugar added over a couple of weeks.

This recipe is from Steve Sando, owner of Rancho Gordo specialty foods. Steve notes, "I've seen many techniques for making pineapple vinegar and they all seem to vary a little, making me realize that making pineapple vinegar is an easy and forgiving process." Some other fruits that work well for this method are banana, apple, melon, mango, papaya, pumpkin, and coconut. Find fun ways to use this delicious vinegar at www.masteringfermentation.com.

The peel and center core of 1 pineapple (only use the pineapple peel and not the "flesh")

½ cup raw unrefined cane sugar (or, even better, granulated or cone Mexican piloncillo sugar; see Resources, page 241)

8 cups filtered water

1. Place the pineapple peel and core in a large wide-mouthed glass jar. (A Mexican glass barrel, used mostly for making delicious agua frescas, works great for this, too.)

2. Add the sugar to the water and stir to dissolve. (If the piloncillo is in cone form, you can shave off pieces

continued

and heat them in a little water to help them dissolve and then add it to the jar.) Add the sugar water to the pineapple and stir to combine and thoroughly dissolve the sugar.

3. Once well mixed, cover with a piece of fine-weave cheesecloth and secure around the top with a rubber band. Set the jar in a dark, cool place and leave it alone for 2 weeks. Then add another 2 tablespoons of sugar or piloncillo. Repeat every two weeks until the mother (see page 37) appears on the top. Taste the vinegar; there's a good chance it's to your liking in about 6 weeks. I tend to let it go and keep feeding it for 6 months and I think it makes a superior vinegar. On the other hand, if you're impatient, you can add some organic apple cider vinegar to the mix and help it along, but I feel as if this is cheating, and it will interfere with the final pineapple flavor.

4. Strain the finished vinegar into bottles (empty tequila bottles that were too fancy to discard are great to repurpose for storing vinegar). Use leftover wine corks as stoppers. Discard the strained fruit.

> Save any fruit pulps or pressed macerated fruits left from making vinegars or shrubs. They are sensational, flavorful candidates for incorporating into marinades, spreads, and frozen ices.

PLUM VINEGAR

YIELD: 10 to 12 ounces, depending on the amount of juice in the fruit
START TO FINISH: 30 minutes prep + add more sugar after 2 weeks + 6 weeks to 3 months fermenting

This vinegar uses what I refer to as the pulp (or must) method. I prefer to use a food processor rather than a juicer to create the pulp. I find it better to control the amount and consistency of the juice extracted (pressed) manually, and the resulting pulp remains in a condition I can use to make other foods. A few of the other fruits that work well for this method are stone fruits (peaches and nectarines), table grapes, oranges, and rhubarb. These fruits require added sugar because they do not inherently contain enough to convert to alcohol to then convert into vinegar. If you use other types of fruit with this method, citrus fruits should be peeled, while other fruits should simply be cored or pitted.

2 to 4 cups of cut-up plums, pitted
1 tablespoon plus 1 teaspoon raw unrefined cane sugar or raw honey
2 tablespoons raw, unfiltered apple cider vinegar

Using a food processor or blender (not a juicer), pulverize the plums to a pulp consistency. Place a fine-mesh strainer over a bowl, and fill with 1 cup or so of fruit pulp. Using a spatula, firmly press the plums to release as much juice from the pulp as you can. Reserve the pulp for other uses such as fruit mustards or marinades. Stir in 1 tablespoon raw sugar

continued

Clockwise from left: orange-coriander vinegar, apple cider vinegar, rhubarb vinegar, ale vinegar, white wine vinegar, plum-ginger vinegar

250 mL
KIMAX®
KIMBLE

or raw honey to dissolve. Stir in the vinegar as a starter. Transfer to a wide-mouth jar and cover with fine-weave cheesecloth. Set in a dark, cool place and leave it alone for 2 weeks to ferment naturally. Add the 1 teaspoon sugar or honey at this point. Let it ferment until it converts to vinegar and you like how it tastes. This may take from 6 weeks to 3 months. Peel off and discard any surface sum. Strain into bottles, close with a stopper, and store in a cool, dark location. Once bottled, you can add dried spices or herbs such as coriander seed, rosemary, thyme, or basil.

Infused Raw Vinegar Method

This method for making vinegar takes little of your time and attention. It involves fresh, ripe seasonal fruit that is macerated in an equal volume of raw, unfiltered vinegar for 1 week. Fruit is placed in a glass jar, the vinegar is added, and the lid is tightly closed. The mixture is vigorously shaken for 10 seconds. Leave at room temperature. Repeat the vigorous shaking every day for 1 week. Strain out the fruit and reserve for other uses. Bottle the infused vinegar, and store.

Blueberries, strawberries, huckleberries, blackberries, cherries, and tomatoes work the best because they release their juices, sugars, and a bit of pulp during this short-term macerating process, infusing the base fermented vinegar. Raw, unfiltered apple cider vinegar or homemade unpasteurized Champagne vinegar are the base vinegars I use. This maceration process is also step 1 in making shrubs, one of my favorite beverage flavoring concoctions (see Ginger-Mint Shrub, page 169).

Maple-Port Vinegar

YIELD: About 4½ cups
START TO FINISH: 10 minutes to make + 10 weeks fermenting

This recipe uses alcohol (fermented port) and apple cider vinegar to jump-start the fermentation of the final vinegar. It results in a vinegar that is truly delicious, with a musky hardiness. It surpasses malt vinegar when used on fish and chips. Use it to make marinades for grilled meats, and in a vinaigrette to toss onto roasted root vegetables.

1½ cups organic maple syrup
2¼ cups raw, unfiltered apple cider vinegar
¾ cup tawny port
½ cup filtered water
¼ cup organic dark raisins

Combine all of the ingredients and place in a glass jar. Cover the opening with fine-weave cheesecloth and secure with a rubber band. Place in a cool, dark location and allow to ferment for 10 weeks or longer. Strain into storage bottles, apply stoppers, and store in a cool, dark location.

Respect the Mother

Fruit juice goes through two stages of fermentation to become vinegar. First, sugar in the juice (fructose) is converted to alcohol. Foaming and bubbling will occur. Second, bacterial activity then converts the alcohol into the sour acetic acid (vinegar). A mother—a slick, rubbery, translucent layer of bacteria—will have developed at this stage, floating in or on top of the vinegar. Her presence is a sign that all is well and signals the start of the second stage of fermentation. If the mother is found on the bottom of the vinegar, that is a sign that production has stopped. This may be due to too cold or too hot an ambient temperature (the desirable range is 70°F to 85°F) or a fluctuating temperature. Or there may be not enough oxygen. The mother is different from any moldy scum that may develop on the surface. That mold should be pulled off and discarded when ready to bottle. The mother should be left in one of the bottles of vinegar to be put into service for the next batch or to pass along to a friend. The nonharmful residue on the bottom of the fermentation crock or jar is what is left after the sugar has been converted. It can be strained out at bottling or not.

Though not a must when starting a new batch of vinegar, using a quality mother starter from a friend, store-bought, or from a previous batch of the same-flavor vinegar, will shorten the time it takes to get a finished vinegar. Vinegar can be made without a mother starter, though the process will take longer. If you have a mother, simply add it to the mixture in each recipe.

Fruit Syrups

Fruit syrups are viscous, usually sweet reductions of water, sugar, and the fresh or unpasteurized juice of fruit. When made with fresh fruits containing pectin, less sugar or other natural sweeteners are necessary to thicken the liquid. The syrups can be infused with fresh or dried herbs, crushed or toasted spices, botanical roots, or dried or fresh flower petals to create amazing concoctions. Dried fruit such as raisins, figs, cherries, or dried plums can be macerated in a simple sugar syrup (see below), in a vinegar, wine, or spirit, and then turned into syrups. Shrubs (see page 169) are one form of a syrup made with fruit or herbs muddled or macerated in vinegar, then sweetened and thickened with sugar.

Here, the syrups are allowed to ferment slightly to enhance flavors. Fruit syrups can be used in marinades, glazes, vinaigrettes, and sorbets. They are superb poured over ice cream or shaved ice, or stirred into oatmeal, smoothies, shakes, and yogurt. They can be used to create a beverage (such as wine-based vermouth) or to flavor and sweeten both alcoholic and nonalcoholic beverages and cocktails. The flavors and combinations are limitless. Syrups can be made using a number of methods as demonstrated in this recipe for pomegranate molasses.

Simple Syrup

Simple syrup is a reduction made by simply combining sugar and water, which is then boiled, reduced, and cooled to result in the desired consistency (see Heated Reduction Method, opposite). The most commonly used formula is a 1:1 ratio of sugar and water (heavy syrup); though different ratios of 1:2 (medium syrup) and 1:3 (light syrup) are also used depending on the application. Other natural sweeteners can be used in place of sugar with adjustments to the ratio of water. As applied in this book, raw unrefined cane sugar is the sugar of choice.

Simple syrups can also be made from fruit shrubs or the soaking liquid of macerated dried fruit, then employed as glazes on baked goods (Panettone Originale, page 138); they can be infused with fresh fruit pulp or zest and used as the foundation for fruit syrups (see above) or fruit preserves (Rhubarb Preserves, page 45). And of course, simple syrup can be stirred into your favorite beverage or cocktail as a sweetener.

POMEGRANATE MOLASSES

A staple in Middle Eastern and Mediterranean pantries, pomegranate molasses is a thick syrup made from the juice reduction of the pomegranate seeds. It is robust, tart, slightly sweet, and astringent. As with other fruit syrups, pomegranate molasses is used in marinades, meat glazes, and vinaigrettes. It is wonderful paired with just about anything grilled.

NATURAL EVAPORATION METHOD

YIELD: About 10 ounces
START TO FINISH: 5 minutes to make + check in daily for 4 days + 10 minutes bottling

This method thickens the juice into a syrup and ferments it at the same time.

1½ cups pomegranate juice
6 tablespoons agave syrup
1 teaspoon unsulphured molasses (not blackstrap)

Combine the ingredients in a bowl, and then pour into a shallow, 8-inch square glass cake pan or food-grade container. Cover with fine-weave cheesecloth and secure with a rubber band. Place in a warm (70°F to 75°F) location, out of direct sunlight, and allow to evaporate for 4 days or until it has a slightly thickened consistency. This syrup will be a thinner consistency than the heated version. Check development daily by smelling and tasting, as you want to bottle and refrigerate before it turns alcoholic. Bottle, close, and refrigerate before using. Refrigerate after opening. Syrup will last for up to 4 months.

HEATED REDUCTION METHOD

YIELD: About 8 ounces
START TO FINISH: 5 minutes to make + 1 hour reducing + 45 minutes cooling + 8 to 12 hours fermenting + 10 minutes bottling

This syrup is sweetened by raw cane sugar or the fruit's natural sugars, heightened by the reduction to a concentrated syrup. Though the juice is cooked to reduce to a syrup (eliminating most of the beneficial bacteria in the juice), it is then allowed to ferment slightly at room temperature before being bottled and refrigerated.

4 cups fresh or unpasteurized bottled juice
¼ cup raw unrefined cane sugar

1. Place the juice in a nonreactive pot, stir in the sugar to dissolve, and then bring to a boil over medium-high heat. Decrease the heat to a simmer, and cook, uncovered, until the juice has reduced by one-third or until it is a syrupy consistency, about 1 hour. Remove from the heat and let cool to room temperature. Place in a wide-mouth glass jar, cover with fine-weave cheesecloth, and secure with a rubber band. Place in a warm (70°F to 75°F) location, out of direct sunlight, and allow to ferment slightly for 8 hours or overnight.

2. Bottle, close, and refrigerate before using. Refrigerate after opening. Syrup will last for up to 4 months.

Coconut Milk Yogurt

YIELD: 2 pints
START TO FINISH: 30 minutes to make + 6 to 8 hours ripening + 1 to 4 hours chilling + 8 to 12 hours refrigeration

Coconut water, coconut milk, and coconut oil taste great and contain beneficial nutrients, including lauric acid, a plant-based fatty acid and powerful anti-pathogen. Making this luscious cultured fruit milk yogurt is easy. It is a fabulous alternative to yogurt made with dairy. The texture and flavor are what we like yogurt to be: creamy, soft, fragrant, and naturally sweet. It also contains probiotic cultures. Make sure the coconut milk is unsweetened and stabilizer free. Canned coconut milk works great. The label should read coconut, coconut cream, and water, or just coconut milk—nothing else. I use coconut sugar to sweeten and a small amount of coconut flour (pure ground coconut) to thicken. Add any sweetener or fruit to the finished yogurt. Your results will be more consistent—and you won't have to monitor temperature as often—if you use a yogurt maker. I use the simple, free-standing, nonelectric Yogotherm Yogurt Incubator for making all of my yogurts. Sources for vegan yogurt starter cultures (for making any nondairy yogurts) and yogurt makers are listed in Resources (page 241). Coconut sugar can be found in the natural foods section of many national grocery stores. For coconut flour, see Resources (page 241).

Yogurt incubator
4 cups coconut milk, at room temperature
1 packet (slightly less than $1/4$ teaspoon) vegan starter culture
3 tablespoons coconut sugar or raw unrefined cane sugar (optional)
2 teaspoons coconut flour

1. In a nonreactive pot over low heat, gently heat the milk to 110°F. This should take about 15 minutes. Sprinkle the starter over the surface of the milk, and let rehydrate for 5 minutes.

2. Gently whisk the culture into the milk to dissolve and distribute evenly. Place the mixture in the yogurt incubator, cover, and allow to set for 6 to 8 hours. Alternatively, set up a stovetop water-bath system (see page 191) to maintain the desired temperature. Leave the mixture in the pot, then place in the warmed water bath (120°F water temperature). Cover and wrap the entire water bath with a terry towel and set under your stove hood light for 6 to 8 hours.

3. Once set, immediately move to refrigeration to chill to below 70°F, to stop the fermentation process (the culture will remain active at 70°F or above). Once the mixture reaches 70°F, remove 1 cup of yogurt and stir in the sugar to dissolve; add the flour and stir to fully incorporate. Add this mixture to the rest of the yogurt and thoroughly combine. Divide the mixture between two 1-pint jars, cover tightly, and refrigerate for 8 to 12 hours. The yogurt will thicken as it chills. You can add more coconut flour if you like a thicker consistency.

continued

Top to bottom: orange-mint frozen coconut milk yogurt, fig frozen coconut milk yogurt

FROZEN COCONUT MILK YOGURT

Once you have finished yogurt, you can flavor with any variety of fruit pastes or preserves you've made. Or use seasonal, finely chopped fresh fruit. Perhaps you have orange paste or fig paste that you've saved from making fruit juices, shrubs, or vinegars. These are perfect as flavorings for your yogurt. Sweeten the fruit to taste, then fold into the sweetened plain coconut milk yogurt. Maybe add herbs or spices as well. You can adjust the fruit-to-yogurt ratio to your liking. I suggest 2 to 3 tablespoons paste to 1 cup of yogurt. Mix thoroughly, then place in a plastic food-grade container, cover, and freeze to the desired consistency. The texture will be icy and sherbertlike. Allow to soften, then scoop.

Clockwise
from top: Basic
Dijon-Style Mustard,
Plum-Raisin Mustard,
Whole Grain Dijon-Style
Mustard, Tomato Ketchup,
Lacto-Mayonnaise

PLUM-RAISIN MUSTARD

YIELD: 2 cups
START TO FINISH: 15 minutes to make + 3 days fermenting + 3 days refrigeration

This is one of my favorite fruity mustards—it has a lot of texture from the chunky fruit bits. Try this on a ham or salami sandwich! *See photo opposite.*

¾ cup ground mild mustard powder (milder Brassica variety powder preferable; see Resources, page 241)

1 teaspoon unrefined fine sea salt

2 teaspoons raw, unfiltered honey

¾ cup filtered water

1 tablespoon basic whey (see page 13) or brine from a fermented vegetable (such as sauerkraut)

4 teaspoons raw, unfiltered apple cider vinegar

¼ cup plum paste (from making plum vinegar; see pages 34 and 22) or store-bought unsweetened plum preserves

2 tablespoons pickled dark raisins (see page 32)

Whisk the mustard powder and salt together in a bowl. Add the honey, water, whey, and vinegar and whisk to combine. Place in a food processor, add the plum paste and raisins and blend to a thick paste. Add additional filtered water if too thick. Place in a jar, cover tightly, and ferment at room temperature for 3 days; then transfer to refrigeration. Allow the ingredients to blend together for 3 days before using. Mustard will keep for up to 2 months in refrigeration.

RHUBARB PRESERVES

YIELD: About 2 cups
START TO FINISH: 10 minutes preparation + 1 week first fermentation + 8 hours second fermentation + 1 week refrigeration

Strawberries are a classic partner with rhubarb in preserves, pie fillings, and cobblers; they contribute their sweetness as a counterpoint to the tartness of the rhubarb. When using classic canning methods for making preserves, the two fruits and sugar are cooked together into a thickened consistency; the pectin in any under-ripe strawberries supplies a natural thickening for the preserves. Here, the rhubarb is first slightly fermented using the Sweet and Salty Pickling Brine (page 14), without the mustard. After a 1-week ferment (first fermentation), the rhubarb is then sweetened with strawberry shrub (or syrup), allowed to ferment a bit longer, then stored in refrigeration to finish until soft. The fermented preserves can then be used as a filling for a pie or the Seasonal Fruit Tart (page 227). The rhubarb will soften further in baking.

Note: If you don't already have it in your refrigerator, you'll need to prepare a strawberry shrub (using the method on page 169) 1 week before fermenting the rhubarb.

1 pound trimmed rhubarb stalks, red part only

2 cups Sweet and Salty Pickling Brine (page 14); omit the mustard

¾ cup strawberry shrub or syrup (see page 169)

continued

1. Cut the rhubarb stalks into lengths to fill a quart jar outfitted with an air lock. Pack the stalks standing up into the jar to fill. Pour in the brine to cover to 1 inch from the top. Secure the jar lid and air lock. Set in a dark, cool place and allow to ferment for 1 week.

2. After 1 week, drain the rhubarb and cut diagonally into ¾-inch pieces. Place the rhubarb pieces in a bowl and toss with the strawberry shrub. Place the mixture in a pint jar, cover the opening with cheesecloth, secure with a rubber band, and set at room temperature for 8 hours or overnight. Remove the cheesecloth, secure with a lid, and refrigerate for 1 week or longer to soften before using. Best used within 1 month.

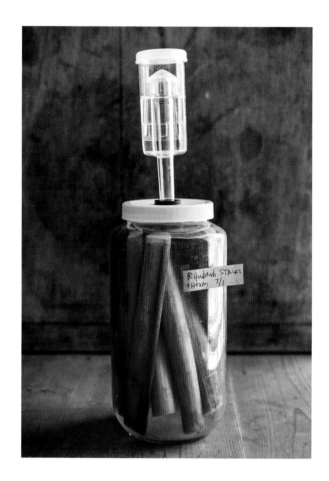

Technically a vegetable (though treated like a fruit), rhubarb is a beautiful plant with large ruffled leaves at the ends of fibrous pink-to-red stems. Its curled-up leaves are the first of the plant to peek through the soil in late spring. The bright or dark red stems (referred to as the stalks) are the part of the plant we can eat (once cooked); the leaves are poisonous to humans. When full size and fully ripe and deep in color, the stalks are harvested from the base of the plant. Any green ends and the leaves are removed and discarded. Rhubarb stalks are typically cut into bite-size pieces, sweetened, and cooked to a softened state to become chewable. The sweetening thickens and counters the natural bitterness of the fruit.

APPLE BUTTER

YIELD: 1 quart
START TO FINISH: 25 minutes to make + 55 minutes roasting + 20 minutes cooling + 8 to 12 hours fermenting + 1 week refrigeration

Buttery-smooth fruit spreads or purees are known as butters. Apple butter is probably the most popular in the category, though butters can be made from a number of different fruits, such as pears, stone fruits, or even pumpkin. Sometimes the fruits are used raw; other times the fruit is roasted or smoked before pureeing and fermenting. For a smoky-sweet flavor, replace the honey with smoked brown sugar (see Resources, page 241).

4 medium (about 1½ pounds) seasonal baking apples (such as Braeburn, Gala, or Fuji), peeled, cored, and cut into chunks
1 cup raw, unfiltered honey
¼ cup raw apple cider
1 tablespoon freshly squeezed lemon juice
½ teaspoon ground cinnamon
Pinch of freshly ground nutmeg
2 tablespoons basic whey (see page 13)
2 sprigs fresh thyme, for the jar

1. Preheat the oven to 350°F. Toss the apples with ¼ cup of the honey and spread out in a single layer on a baking sheet. Roast the apples until tender, about 55 minutes.

2. Place the apples in a bowl to cool for 20 minutes. Combine the remaining ¾ cup honey with the cider and lemon juice and then whisk in the cinnamon and nutmeg. Puree the apples in a food processor until chunky and then add the honey-seasoning mixture. Continue to puree until smooth. Blend in the fermenting agent (whey) and then place in a jar.

3. Tuck sprigs of thyme into the butter, push down to remove any air bubbles and space, secure a lid, and ferment for 8 hours or overnight at room temperature. Refrigerate for 1 week before using. Butter will keep for up to 1 month, refrigerated.

Sweet Tomato-Jalapeño Salsa

YIELD: About 3 cups
START TO FINISH: 20 minutes to make + 8 to 12 hours fermenting + 12 hours refrigeration

The bright colors and flavors of salsa are great complements to grilled and slow-roasted foods. This one partners well with pork and fish. Due to the sweetness of the fruit, this salsa is fermented for a short period and then moved to refrigeration. Taste a tiny bit of a jalapeño before you begin to prep. If too hot, add more honey and more mangoes to this recipe, or reduce the number of jalapeños you use. You can also toss in more cut tomatoes and chopped cilantro just before serving to add a bit more bright color and fresh flavor. Serve with Grilled Buttermilk–Black Bean Flatbread (page 124). *See photo on page 218.*

2 cups red or mixed cherry tomatoes, halved

3 small or 2 large jalapeño chiles, stemmed, seeded, and chopped (option: fermented, seeded, and chopped)

3 cloves garlic, thinly sliced

½ cup chopped fresh mango

1 tablespoon minced or finely grated fresh ginger

1 teaspoon cumin seed, toasted

½ teaspoon coriander seed, toasted and crushed

¼ teaspoon ground white pepper

½ teaspoon unrefined fine sea salt

2 tablespoons raw, unfiltered apple cider vinegar

¼ cup raw, unfiltered orange blossom honey

1 teaspoon grated lime zest

Juice of 1 lime

2 tablespoons fermenting agent (basic whey, water kefir, or brine from fermented vegetables like jalapeño chiles)

1 sprig fresh cilantro, for the jar (optional)

Gently combine the tomatoes, chiles, garlic, mango, ginger, cumin, coriander, white pepper, and salt in a bowl. Combine the vinegar, honey, lime zest, and lime juice and stir into the mixture. Stir in the fermenting agent last. Place in a jar or crock and push down slightly to remove any air pockets. Secure the opening with cheesecloth. Ferment at room temperature for 8 hours or overnight. Add the sprig of cilantro just before refrigerating. Cover with an airtight lid and refrigerate overnight for the flavors to come together. This salsa will keep for up to 2 weeks.

BONUS RECIPE

This salsa creates some lovely juice. You can drain it a bit before serving and drizzle the juice on grilled fish or shellfish, use it to make ceviche, whisk in some fruity olive oil to create a vinaigrette, or reduce it to make a syrup to add to cocktails or fizzy beverages.

Apricot-Date Chutney

YIELD: About 2 cups
START TO FINISH: 20 minutes to make + 8 to 12 hours fermenting + 3 days refrigeration

Chutneys are sweet-tangy chunky condiments to accompany meat, fish, or cheese made with fresh or dried fruit, vinegar, sugar, and spices. They can be mild or spicy, cooked or fermented raw as this chutney is. Serve at room temperature over Saffron Yogurt Cheese (page 99) garnished with pistachios or on your favorite grilled or roasted meat. See Grilled Lamb Stuffed with Apricot-Date Chutney and Saffron Yogurt Sauce (page 213).

1 cup (about 6 ounces) dried Mediterranean or Turkish apricot halves, slivered

½ cup (about 3 ounces) chopped dried dates

¼ cup (about 1½ ounces) dried cranberries or fresh pomegranate seeds

½ small white onion, diced (about ⅓ cup)

2 teaspoons tamarind paste or concentrate

Grated zest of 1 small orange

2 teaspoons natural date sugar or unrefined cane sugar

1 teaspoon unrefined fine sea salt

2 tablespoons raw, unfiltered apple cider vinegar

1 teaspoon yellow mustard seeds

¾ teaspoon garam masala

Pinch of freshly ground black pepper

4 tablespoons basic whey (see page 13) or Water Kefir (page 171)

Filtered nonchlorinated water (as needed)

¼ cup salted, roasted pistachios, coarsely chopped, for garnish (optional)

1. In a bowl, combine the dried apricots, dates, and cranberries and then stir in the onion. In a separate bowl, combine the tamarind paste, orange zest, sugar, salt, and vinegar and stir it into the fruit mixture to moisten. Sprinkle in the mustard seeds, garam masala, and pepper, and stir to combine. Stir in the whey and place the entire mixture in a pint jar. Push down gently to remove air bubbles. Add a small amount of water if needed to moisten the mixture.

2. Cover the jar with cheesecloth and secure. Place the jar in a pantry or out of sunlight, at room temperature, for 8 hours or overnight. At this time, stir once, replace the cheesecloth with a seal and lid, and refrigerate for 3 days before using. Chutney will last for up to 1 month covered, in refrigeration.

Agrodolce Onion Marmalade

YIELD: 1 quart
START TO FINISH: 20 minutes to roast + 15 minutes to make + 8 to 12 hours fermenting + 1 week refrigeration

Agrodolce means "sweet and sour" in Italian. Think eggplant caponata or even ketchup. Use this jam as a topping for pizza, the filling for a tart, or piled on a burger. It's great in combination with blue cheese or any creamy, melty cheese. Pulse into a paste and use it to fill ravioli. If available, use Walla Walla, Maui, or other sweet onions in place of standard white onions. Add anchovy paste for an earthier, robust flavor. The onions are roasted slightly just to soften before fermenting.

1 pound white onions, cut into 1/8-inch-thick wedges

1/2 pound red onions, cut into 1/8-inch-thick wedges

1 tablespoon unrefined fine sea salt

1/2 cup raw, unfiltered apple cider vinegar

2 tablespoons balsamic vinegar

1 tablespoon smoked brown sugar (see Resources, page 241) or dark brown sugar

1 teaspoon anchovy paste (optional)

1/8 teaspoon ground white pepper

2 teaspoons fresh thyme leaves

1/4 cup fermenting agent (basic whey or brine from a fermented vegetable)

1. Preheat the oven to 350°F. Put the onion wedges on a lightly oiled baking sheet and roast just until softened, about 20 minutes. Place the onions in a bowl, toss in the salt, and massage them to release some moisture.

2. In a small bowl, combine the vinegars and sugar. Stir to dissolve the sugar. Stir the pepper and thyme into the onions, add the vinegar mixture and the fermenting agent, and stir to combine.

3. Place the mixture in a 1-quart wide-mouth jar and push down to remove any air pockets and release some liquid. Fill to 1 inch from the top of the jar. Add filtered water to cover the onions if needed. Secure a piece of cheesecloth to the opening and allow to sit at room temperature for 8 hours or overnight. Remove the cheesecloth and secure an airtight lid. Refrigerate for 1 week before using for the flavors to develop. Use within 2 months.

LACTO-MAYONNAISE

YIELD: About 3 cups
START TO FINISH: 30 minutes to make + 6 hours fermenting

This fermented version of mayonnaise is a bit thinner than store-bought. You can adjust the amount of mustard to your liking and even add other flavorings such as pureed red bell pepper, curry powder, chipotle powder, or herbs. Make a Provence-style aïoli version by adding 4 cloves of minced garlic with the eggs and salt. *See photo on page 44.*

2 large whole eggs, at room temperature
2 egg yolks, at room temperature
1/4 teaspoon unrefined fine sea salt
2 teaspoons Basic Dijon-Style Mustard (page 63)
3 tablespoons freshly squeezed lemon juice
2 tablespoons cool basic whey (see page 13)
1 1/2 to 2 cups mild extra-virgin olive oil

1. Using a food processor or blender, whisk together the eggs, egg yolks, and salt. Blend in the mustard, lemon juice, and whey. With the motor running, very slowly drizzle in the oil to make the emulsion.

2. Place in jar, cover with a lid, leave at room temperature for 6 hours, then refrigerate.

3. The mayonnaise will keep for 4 to 6 weeks refrigerated.

PREPARED HORSERADISH

YIELD: 1 1/2 cups
START TO FINISH: 30 minutes to make + 5 to 7 days fermenting + 2 days refrigeration

Horseradish is a naturally piquant condiment perfect on prime rib, roast beef, and ham or in sauces and dressings. Most commonly only pickled, this version has whey added as a fermenting agent for increased flavor and other benefits. If you can't find raw horseradish root in the market, use raw turnips (the larger, the spicier) and a pinch of wasabi powder to get the bite and heat of fresh horseradish. Add crème fraîche for a creamier version.

2 cups peeled and coarsely chopped fresh
    horseradish root (about 3/4 pound)
2 teaspoons unrefined fine sea salt
2 tablespoons raw, unfiltered apple cider vinegar
2 teaspoons raw, unfiltered honey
2 tablespoons basic whey (see page 13)
Filtered water
1/4 cup Crème Fraîche (page 95; optional)

Place the horseradish, salt, vinegar, honey, and whey in a blender and pulse until finely chopped. Add a few tablespoons of water and blend until smooth. Add more water as needed to create a spreadable consistency. Stir in crème fraîche if you want a creamier horseradish. Transfer to a wide-mouth pint glass jar and cover with an airtight lid. Ferment at room temperature for 5 to 7 days and then transfer to refrigeration for 2 days before using. Store for up to 3 months.

KIMCHI

YIELD: 1 quart
START TO FINISH: 20 minutes prep + 3 hours draining
+ 30 minutes packing + 5 hours at room temperature
+ 3 days fermenting + 3 days refrigeration

Made with cabbage, kimchi (kimchee) is a pungent, spicy pickle originating in Korea, mostly used as a condiment with Asian foods but also used to season soups and rice dishes. Knowing that fermentation will tenderize and increase the flavors of any leafy green, think outside the cabbage crate and create some fun combinations of your own (see Kimchi Variations, following, for some ideas).

Note: The amount of salt used is 3 percent of the weight of the cabbage and other vegetables.

1 head (about 2½ pounds) napa cabbage, outer leaves trimmed off

2 tablespoons plus 2 teaspoons unrefined fine sea salt

½ pound daikon radish or turnips, peeled

½ pound carrots, peeled

1-inch piece fresh ginger, peeled

4 green onions

4 cloves garlic

4 teaspoons Chile-Garlic Paste (page 75, or store-bought)

1 teaspoon Asian Fish Sauce (page 145, or store-bought)

Basic Brine (page 13), as needed

1. Quarter the cabbage and cut out any thick core. Salt between the leaves (using all of the salt). Put the quarters in a large bowl to sit while the cabbage releases some of the moisture. Leave for 3 hours to allow draining.

2. When the cabbage has fully drained, coarsely grate the radish, carrots, and ginger. Cut the green onions into ¾-inch-long pieces. Cut the garlic into thin slices. Toss all together in a bowl with the Chile-Garlic Paste and the Asian Fish Sauce.

3. Using filtered water, rinse the salt off the cabbage leaves and cut the leaves into chunks or leave in quarters.

4. If quartered, pack some of the chile mixture between the cabbage leaves. If cut into chunks, toss the chunks in with the chile mixture. Pack the cabbage into a 1-quart jar along with the juices and press down to release more moisture. Add a small amount of Basic Brine, if needed, to cover the cabbage. Place a weight on top to keep the cabbage submerged, and then cover. Keep at room temperature for 5 hours, then move to a cooler (60°F is best) location for at least 3 days, then cover and refrigerate. This kimchi will be ready after 3 days, and gets stronger while fermenting for up to 1 month.

KIMCHI VARIATIONS

Use unrefined fine sea salt and Basic Brine (page 13) with these other leafy vegetables and herbs for stunning variations on classic kimchi. Note that leaves can be left whole, coarsely chopped, shredded, or sliced into ribbons.

ASIAN-INSPIRED: bok choy, Thai basil, whole green onions, fresh ginger, garlic, chiles

ITALIAN-INSPIRED: escarole, radicchio, fresh flat-leaf parsley, arugula, golden raisins, garlic, capers

SPANISH-INSPIRED: spinach, fresh flat-leaf parsley, arugula, fresh mint, fresh oregano leaves, capers, salted anchovies

MEDITERRANEAN-INSPIRED: spineless kale leaves, fresh dill, fresh mint, lemon zest, oil-cured olives, garlic, fennel seeds

NORTH AFRICAN-INSPIRED: fresh flat-leaf parsley, carrots, green olives, fresh cilantro, fresh mint, garlic

MOROCCAN-INSPIRED: Swiss chard, fresh flat-leaf parsley, fresh cilantro, garlic, harissa, cumin, red wine vinegar

INDIAN-INSPIRED: napa cabbage, jalapeños, fresh cilantro, brown mustard seeds, garlic, coriander

If you want to use other brines, try these combinations:

SWEET AND SALTY PICKLING BRINE (PAGE 14): shredded red cabbage, beets, turnips, sweet onions

BEER BRINE (PAGE 14): shredded brussels sprouts, endive, shallots, yellow mustard seeds, coriander, orange zest

Or try this refreshing fruit combination—I liken fruit kimchi to salsas and uncooked chutneys—using salt and the Basic Brine or the Sweet and Salty Pickling Brine: fresh pineapple chunks, mango wedges, coconut pieces, green onion stalks, cilantro sprigs, grated fresh ginger, jalapeño rings, garlic cloves, raw cane sugar.

SMOKED SAUERKRAUT

YIELD: 1 quart
START TO FINISH: 15 minutes smoking setup + 30 to
35 minutes smoking + 10 minutes packing + 2 weeks to
1 month fermenting

This is a basic sauerkraut recipe embellished with a
kiss of smoke before being fermented. Consider this
process for other leafy greens, too. Cold-smoking
is not cooking the food, but imparting flavor. It can
be done in an outdoor smoker, indirectly in a cooling wood-fired oven, or indirectly on a grill. Indoor
stovetop smoking using a wok works great and is
very easy. What you choose as a smoking wood is up
to you. On cabbage I like alder or apple wood chips.
Of course, you can omit the smoking, but I love the
essence it adds to the fermented cabbage. If you like
smokiness but don't want to go through the smoking
process, you can toss the cabbage with a smoked sea
salt before packing it into the jar.

Wok
Steamer basket
Quart jar with air lock
Weight(s)

$\frac{1}{2}$ cup smoking chips (such as alder or apple wood)
1 head (about 2$\frac{1}{2}$ pounds) napa cabbage, quartered
4 teaspoons unrefined fine sea salt
$\frac{1}{2}$ teaspoon alder-smoked fine sea salt (optional)
Filtered water

1.   To smoke the cabbage: Line a wok with aluminum foil, fitting tightly around the inside of the pan.
Add the smoking chips.

2.   Put ice cubes in a pan or pie tin slightly smaller
in diameter than the smoking rack or basket and set
the pan in the bottom of the wok, between the smoke
source and the rack. This pan acts as a barrier to
the heat but allows for smoke to get to what you are
smoking. Place the quartered cabbage in a bamboo
steamer basket or on a mesh pizza rack to fit the wok
set about 2 inches above the ice. Keep space between
the pieces of cabbage so the smoke will hit all surfaces
evenly.

3.   With the cabbage in place, heat the wok over
moderate heat until the chips begin to smoke.

4.   Cover immediately and decrease the heat to low;
smoke for 10 to 12 minutes. Turn off the heat and
allow to smoke for another 3 to 5 minutes. Test a small
piece of cabbage for smokiness. If needed, smoke a
few minutes longer. Wrap up the smoking ingredients
in the foil and discard.

5. To ferment the cabbage: Coarsely chop the smoked cabbage, place it in a bowl, and toss with the salt. Massage the cabbage to release enough liquid to reduce it to one-third the original quantity. Place the cabbage and the liquid in a 1-quart jar equipped with an air lock, pushing down to release moisture and eliminate any air bubbles. Leave 1 inch of space at top. If needed, add filtered water to submerge the cabbage. Use a weight to keep the cabbage submerged. Secure the lid and air lock.

6. Place the jar in a cool location (60°F is best). Ferment for 2 weeks to 1 month. Replace the top with an airtight lid. Refrigerate for up to 6 months.

APPLE-CARAWAY SAUERKRAUT

YIELD: 1 quart
START TO FINISH: 20 minutes to make + 2 weeks fermenting + 1 month refrigeration

This recipe adds the sweetness of apples as a counterpoint to the salty, earthiness of the cabbage. I love this combination in Cider-Braised Duck and Apple-Caraway Sauerkraut and Potatoes (page 209).

Quart jar with air lock

8 cups coarsely chopped napa cabbage (1 head, about 2½ pounds
4 teaspoons unrefined fine sea salt
2 medium apples, peeled, cored, and chopped (about 4 cups)
½ teaspoon brown mustard seeds
½ teaspoon caraway seeds
1 cup raw apple cider
Filtered water

Place the cabbage in a bowl and toss with the salt. Massage the cabbage to release the liquid until reduced to one-third the size. Toss in the apples, mustard seeds, and caraway. Place in a 1-quart jar and add the cider. Push the mixture down into the jar, leaving 1 inch of space at the top. Cover the mixture with filtered water. Secure the lid and air lock. Place in a cool, dark location. Ferment for 2 weeks, then remove the air lock, submerge the mixture, cover with an airtight lid, and refrigerate for up to 1 month. It is ready to consume after 1 week in refrigeration but will last for up to 2 months when refrigerated.

CHAPTER 4
LEGUMES, NUTS, SEEDS, AND AROMATICS: Spreads, Sauces, and Soy

IN THIS CHAPTER, we'll delve into the world of legumes, dried beans, nuts, seeds, and their aromatic partners to build our fermented foods pantry. Legumes cover a family of seedpods that includes beans, peas, lentils, peanuts, and soybeans. Nuts are the edible shelled fruits from nut trees.

Legumes can be transformed into sauces, spreads, butters, tapenades, salads, soups, and stews. When ground into a flour, they can be creatively woven into breads, flatbreads, cakes, crusts, and other desserts. These plant-based seedpods are high in vegetable protein, as well as other vitamins, minerals, and the important omega-3 and omega-6 fatty acids.

Legumes and nuts should not be eaten in large quantities (multiple cups) in their raw state. Doing so can result in gastric discomfort. Soaking in water or salt water is one process that makes them more digestible; taking them even further into a fermented form with a range of processes and combinations—as we do with the recipes here—is even better.

SPROUTED CHICKPEA HUMMUS

YIELD: 4 cups
START TO FINISH: 30 minutes

Hummus is a versatile, delicious Mediterranean condiment. This version features a combination of sprouted and cooked chickpeas to get a bit of fermentation started. You can make this hummus chunky or smooth, or add fresh, peeled fava beans with the chickpeas. For a smoky flavor, add a bit of smoked paprika or drizzle with some smoked olive oil (see Resources, page 241).

1 cup sprouted chickpeas (see page 7)
1¼ cups cooked chickpeas
1 cup tahini paste
6 large cloves Fermented Garlic (page 75)
1 to 1½ teaspoons unrefined fine sea salt
¼ teaspoon Aleppo pepper or cayenne pepper
½ teaspoon cumin seed, toasted
Juice of 1 to 2 lemons
2 tablespoons Basic Brine (page 13)
⅓ cup extra-virgin olive oil (peppery flavor preferable)

In a food processor, combine the chickpeas, tahini, and garlic, and pulse to a chunky consistency. Add the salt, pepper, and cumin and blend. Add the juice of 1 lemon and the brine, combine, and taste. With the food processor running, drizzle in the olive oil. Taste again and add more lemon juice if desired or add a few drops of water to thin, if necessary. Adjust salt and pepper and adjust lemon again to taste. Place in a jar, cover, and refrigerate. Hummus will keep for 3 weeks or longer.

Mustard

It is simple to make your own mustard, and these two basic flavors will get you started (fruit-based mustards are on pages 45). Mustard powders vary in hotness and flavor from one brand to another. It is most cost effective to purchase the powder in bulk from a quality spice purveyor such as Frontier Natural Products (see Resources, page 241). Coleman's, a staple for many cooks, carries a lot of heat, so I like to use a milder Brassica type of mustard powder. Once you have a favorite mustard recipe as your foundation, you can add horseradish, wasabi, chipotle, dried herbs, sun-dried tomatoes, citrus zest, honey, or even chopped olives to put your own spin on this popular condiment. Have fun with it!

Basic Dijon-Style Mustard

YIELD: About 1½ cups
START TO FINISH: 10 minutes to make + 3 days fermenting + 3 days refrigeration

¾ cup mustard powder (milder Brassica powder preferable)

1 teaspoon unrefined fine sea salt

⅛ teaspoon garlic powder

2 teaspoons raw, unfiltered honey

½ cup filtered water

1 tablespoon basic whey (see page 13) or vegetable brine from a fermented vegetable (such as sauerkraut)

2 tablespoons raw, unfiltered apple cider vinegar

Whisk the mustard powder, salt, and garlic powder together in a bowl. Add the honey, then the water and brine, and whisk to combine. Place in a jar, cover tightly, and ferment at room temperature for 3 days. The mustard will thicken, so stir in more water or brine after 1 day to create a consistency you like. Transfer to refrigeration. Allow the ingredients to blend together for 3 days before using. Mustard will keep for up to 2 months in refrigeration. *See photo on page 44.*

Whole Grain Dijon-Style Mustard

YIELD: About 1¾ cups
START TO FINISH: 3 hours soaking + 20 minutes to make + 1 day fermenting + 3 days refrigeration

¾ cup mixed yellow and brown mustard seeds

1 cup Basic Brine (page 13)

1 teaspoon unrefined fine sea salt

⅛ teaspoon garlic powder

2½ teaspoons raw cane sugar

1 tablespoon vegetable brine from a fermented vegetable (such as sauerkraut)

3 tablespoons raw, unfiltered apple cider vinegar

Soak the mustard seeds in Basic Brine for 3 hours. Drain and discard the brine. Place the mustard seeds in a food processor, and pulse 10 times to break open about half of the seeds. Add the salt, garlic powder, and sugar, then pulse 4 times to combine. Add the 1 tablespoon vegetable brine and 2 tablespoons of vinegar and then process for 2 minutes to combine and create a thick, chunky paste. Place in a jar, cover tightly, and ferment at room temperature. After 1 day, stir in the remaining tablespoon of vinegar. Transfer to refrigeration. Allow the ingredients to blend together for 3 days before using. Mustard will keep for up to 2 months in refrigeration. *See photo opposite.*

Soy Milk

YIELD: 6 to 8 cups
START TO FINISH: 8 to 12 hours soaking + 10 minutes draining + 20 minutes cooking + 15 minutes draining + 15 minutes squeezing process

Fine-weave cheesecloth or butter muslin as used for cheese making (see page 84)

6 ounces (about 1 cup) whole dried soybeans
Filtered water

1. Place the soybeans in a large glass bowl and cover with filtered water so the water level is 3 inches above the beans. Cover the bowl with plastic wrap and soak at room temperature for 8 to 12 hours or overnight. Set a fine-mesh strainer over a heat-resistant food-grade container.

2. Drain the beans and place them in a blender (not a food processor) with 2 cups of filtered water. Puree at a high speed into as smooth a mash as possible. You may find some bits of bean still visible.

3. In a nonreactive pot, boil 3 cups filtered water over high heat, then add the soybean puree. Rinse out the blender jar with $\frac{1}{2}$ cup more filtered water and add that liquid to the pot. Bring the mixture to a boil over medium-high heat and cook the mixture until a frothy foam is formed and begins to rise, 4 to 6 minutes; stir frequently to prevent scorching and sticking. You are looking for a foamy layer like lightly whipped egg whites. When the foam rises, remove from the heat. Let the mixture sit for 5 minutes.

4. Line the strainer with dampened fine-weave cheesecloth, leaving enough excess hanging over the sides of the strainer to fully cover the pureed beans. Carefully pour or ladle the mixture into the cheesecloth-lined strainer, capturing any bits of bean left in the pot. Let the mixture drain until most of the milk has passed through and the bean mash in the strainer is just cool enough for you to handle. Gather up the ends of the cloth, hold the sack of mash over the strainer, and twist and squeeze the mash to extract as much milk as possible. Open the sack, add another $\frac{1}{2}$ cup filtered water, close up the sack, and repeat the squeezing process. The liquid you have captured is soy milk. Skim off any foam. Place in a covered container and refrigerate. Soy milk will keep for up to 1 week.

BONUS RECIPE

Save the bean mash! There's still protein there. Refrigerate it in a closed container or resealable plastic bag and use for thickening soups, turning into fritters, or adding to your favorite meatloaf.

TOFU

YIELD: One 8- to 8½-ounce block
START TO FINISH: 10 minutes preparation + 15 minutes cooking + 15 minutes coagulant and curd formation + 25 minutes draining + 2 hours cooling

Tofu is a bean curd traditional to many Asian cuisines. It is high in protein and is often used to replace meat in dishes. It can be marinated, grilled, braised, stir-fried, or even whisked into a salad dressing. It is often added to soups, such as Hot-and-Sour Tofu Soup with Shrimp and Pickled Vegetables (page 202), and noodle dishes. Basic tofu is not a fermented food per se, but the soaking of the beans for multiple hours starts the germination process (the beginning of fermentation), which begins to make the soybeans more digestible.

To make tofu, soybeans are mashed and cooked, and then the soy milk is cooked before coagulating into curd. Making tofu is much like making a fresh cheese; the method is like a blend of making ricotta, with the draining and shaping of feta. Rather than citric acid or rennet as the coagulant for cheese, nigari flakes are used. They are available in natural food stores and online from Cultures for Health (see Resources, page 241). For draining and shaping the tofu, I use a feta cheese basket to get the perfect block of solid curd. The method used in this recipe is adapted from recipes by my colleague Andrea Nguyen, in her book *Asian Tofu*. As a shortcut to making your own soy milk (to then turn into tofu), you can use quality fresh soy milk purchased from the refrigerated section of a reputable Asian market.

Note: The texture of the tofu is best when you begin with hot milk, fresh from pressing. However, I have made tofu successfully from soy milk that I have refrigerated overnight. As I do with dairy milk when making cheese, I bring the milk to room temperature before heating. The amount of milk listed for this recipe is based on the yield from one batch made according to the method on page 64.

1 feta cheese basket
Fine-weave cheesecloth or butter muslin as used for cheese making (see page 84)

1½ teaspoons coagulant (packaged nigari flakes)
½ cup filtered water
6 to 8 cups Soy Milk (amount depends on the beans and how much is extracted; page 64) or store-bought fresh soy milk

1. In a glass measuring cup, thoroughly dissolve the coagulant in the ½ cup water; set aside. Set a draining rack on a rimmed baking sheet. Place the feta cheese basket mold on the draining rack, and line with dampened fine-weave cheesecloth, leaving enough excess hanging over the sides of the mold to fully cover the curds.

2. Place the soy milk in a nonreactive pot and bring to a simmer over medium-high heat. Stir frequently with a spatula to prevent scorching and sticking. When the mixture starts to bubble, decrease the heat to medium and gently cook until it has reached 185°F, about 5 minutes, stirring constantly. If a skin forms, remove it (this is tofu skin, which is sometimes used as a wrapper).

3. Once the milk has reached 185°F, remove it from the heat and stir once to blend the soy. Using a spatula, making an N pattern, stir in one-third of the coagulant. Let the milk settle, then pour another

continued

one-third over the surface and repeat the incorporation. Cover the pot and let sit for 3 minutes.

4. Add the last of the coagulant, stirring into only the top ½ inch of the curds. Cover and wait until the curds are a mass in the pot or separated from the clear pale yellow or tan whey, 3 to 5 minutes.

5. Ladle off some of the whey until the surface of the curds is exposed. Then scoop the curds into the lined cheese mold.

6. Cover the curds with the cheesecloth and allow to gravity drain (without any additional weight applied) for 15 minutes, then lift the sack of curds out of the mold, flip the curds over back into the mold, and remove the cheesecloth. Drain for another 10 minutes.

7. Place the block of tofu in a covered container and refrigerate for 2 hours (or until cool) before using. Tofu will keep for up to 1 week.

Note: I find this method works well for creating a soft tofu. You can add up to 1 pound of weight to the wrapped tofu to get a firm result.

FERMENTED WHITE TOFU

YIELD: About 8 ounces, depending on desired firmness
START TO FINISH: 10 minutes combining ingredients
+ 30 minutes draining + 2 hours pressing + 4 days
fermenting + 4 to 5 weeks refrigeration

Pungent, spicy, and slightly sweet, fermented tofu is a traditional Chinese ingredient used as a condiment or broken up and added to stir-fried vegetables. White fermented tofu is considered the most versatile version of the many variations made throughout Asia. This recipe, adapted from Andrea Nguyen's book *Asian Tofu*, is quite easy to create. It is simply seasoned with salt, red pepper flakes, and rice wine, though you can add other Asian seasonings such as toasted sesame oil or toasted garlic or both, after fermenting, or toss with chopped fresh cilantro or green onions. The finished texture is much like that of the smooth Indian cheese, panir, and is used in similar ways. The tofu-fermenting process is similar to aging a wine-soaked firm cheese. To ferment successfully, it is best to use very firm, pressed tofu.

Bricks or heavy skillets, for weights
Two 8-inch square food-grade containers
(preferably glass) with lids
Fine-weave cheesecloth or butter muslin as used
for cheese making (see page 84)

8- to 8½-ounce block firm or extra-firm Tofu
(page 65), cut into 1-inch cubes
6 teaspoons unrefined fine sea salt
½ teaspoon red pepper flakes
¼ to ½ cup Shaoxing rice wine
½ cup filtered water, plus more as needed

1. Set a fine-mesh strainer over a bowl. Line a rimmed baking sheet with a double layer of paper towels. Put the tofu cubes in a bowl and toss to coat with 2 teaspoons of the salt. Allow to rest for 10 minutes to expel some moisture.

2. Transfer the cubes in a single layer to the strainer and let drain, unweighted, for 30 minutes to remove more of the moisture.

3. Lay the cubes out in a single layer so they do not touch on the prepared baking sheet.

4. Cover the tofu with a second baking sheet; apply 1½ to 2 pounds of weight to the sheet.

5. Press for 30 minutes at room temperature to remove moisture. Remove the tofu to a bowl; replace the wet paper towels with dry towels. Lay out the cubes in a single layer on the towels and apply weight again. Allow to drain for 1½ hours at room temperature. Tofu should be very firm to the touch and only slightly moist as this point. If not, continue for another 30 minutes. Blot off any additional moisture from the tofu with paper towels.

continued

6. Transfer the tofu to one of the food-grade containers (you will use the second later on) in a single layer, leaving at least ½ inch of space around each piece. Cover the container with cheesecloth and secure with a rubber band. Lay the container's lid askew over the opening of the container to allow for air circulation and slow down evaporation.

7. Move the container to a spot in your kitchen, out of direct sunlight, where the temperature is between 68°F to 72°F (room temperature).

8. After 3 to 4 days, the tofu will have fermented to the point of having a pungent aroma. Some mold will appear on the surface. Wipe off any mold with a dry paper towel. Turn the tofu over.

9. At 4 days, drain the tofu and transfer it to a clean container. Combine the remaining 4 teaspoons of salt and the red pepper flakes. Toss the tofu in the seasoning to thoroughly coat.

10. Combine the wine and water and pour over the tofu so it is covered with liquid (add more water, if necessary, to cover the tofu). Secure the airtight lid and refrigerate for 4 to 5 weeks before using. Test a sample at 3 weeks for desirable flavor development.

11. Tofu will keep for up to 4 to 6 months in refrigeration. Drain pieces of tofu as you use them, and bring to room temperature before using. Combine with additional flavorings if desired at this point.

MISO

YIELD: ½ gallon or more
START TO FINISH: 8 hours soaking + 2 hours cooking
+ 30 minutes cooling + 30 minutes mixing + 6 months to
1 year fermenting

This fermented soybean paste is a staple in Japanese cuisine, used to flavor sauces, soups, marinades, dressings, glazes, dipping sauces, and even to make pickles. Miso is made from cooked soybeans combined with either barley, rice, or more soybeans, and then mixed with a dried koji (the fermenting culture that has been inoculated with *Aspergillus oryzae*), then traditionally allowed to ferment naturally for 6 months to 3 years. Once you have the few ingredients at hand, it takes only a short amount of time and simple steps to get the miso mixed. From there you will periodically monitor its progress but basically leave it alone to quietly ferment until it reaches the desired flavor. Refrigerate the finished miso.

Miso comes in three basic varieties: white, yellow, and red. Sweet white miso is delicate in flavor. Mellow or mild miso is golden yellow and considered the all-purpose miso. Red miso is saltier with deeper flavors. White and red misos are most commonly used in recipes. They are typically found refrigerated near tofu in Asian markets or grocery sections. Barley and brown rice koji can be purchased in many natural food stores or online from Cultures for Health (see Resources, page 241). This recipe makes a big batch. You'll definitely have enough to share. Koji and miso both can be used to make fermented pickles (see chapter 3).

1-gallon crock or food-grade container
Bricks or water-filled plastic milk containers, for weights (total 1 pound)

10½ ounces whole dried soybeans
Filtered water
1 (17.6-ounce) bag barley koji
7½ ounces (about 11 tablespoons) unrefined fine sea salt

1. Place the soybeans in a bowl and cover enough with filtered water so the water level is 2 inches above the beans. Cover with plastic wrap and let the beans soak for 8 hours or overnight.

2. Drain the beans, put them in a large pot, and cover with enough filtered water so the water level is 3 inches above the beans. Cover with a lid and cook the soybeans over medium-low heat until soft, about 2 hours.

3. Drain the beans, reserving 13½ ounces of the cooking liquid.

4. Spread the cooked soybeans on a baking sheet to cool until they reach room temperature.

5. Place the beans in a large bowl, and mash with a potato masher or wooden spoon to break up the beans. Stir in the koji, 7 ounces of the sea salt, and the reserved cooking liquid, and mix well to incorporate.

6. Place the mixture in a clean crock and push down to remove any air pockets. Sprinkle the remaining ½ ounce of sea salt on the surface to cover. Place plastic wrap directly onto the surface of the mixture to eliminate exposure to air.

continued

7.   Place a 1-pound weight on top to maintain pressure on the mixture. Cover with a lid and place in a cool, dark location. Allow the mixture to ferment until ready (see Note, below).

8.   Divide the miso into small covered food containers and refrigerate until ready to use. Miso will keep for 6 months or longer.

Note: The fermentation period will be shorter during warmer months and warmer ambient temperature, with a total period of approximately 6 months if fermentation is started in the spring and 10 to 12 months if fermentation is started in the fall.

SOY SAUCE

YIELD: 4 to 5 cups
START TO FINISH: 24 to 36 hours starter + 24 hours soaking + 1 hour steaming + 10 minutes packing time + 2 months to 1 year fermenting

Ranging from light to dark in color, flavor intensity, and saltiness, soy sauce is an essential ingredient in every Asian pantry. The variety we in the United States see most is from Japan (shoyu), which is made using the traditional method of fermentation, taking one to three years to age; with fine grades of soy sauce aged even longer. In addition to soy (either ground cooked beans or soy flour), the combination includes roasted wheat or barley. The version here uses a wild yeast made from bran, water, and raw apple cider as a starter. You can use barley koji, an inoculated starter culture traditionally used containing the bacteria *Aspergillus oryzae*, if you choose (see Resources, page 241).

The toughest part of making your own soy sauce is having the patience to wait until it's ready. I find the results are best when you use a jar outfitted with an air lock. Make a big batch once a year and bottle it on the anniversary date.

Fine-weave cheesecloth or butter muslin as used for cheese making (see page 84)
Half-gallon jar with air lock

STARTER
3 tablespoons wheat bran
3 tablespoons filtered water
1 teaspoon raw apple cider

2 cups whole dried soybeans (organic, if possible)
2 cups wheat or oat bran, toasted
2 cups cool filtered water
3 tablespoons unrefined fine sea salt

1. To make the starter: Combine the 3 tablespoons untoasted wheat bran, 3 tablespoons water, and apple cider in a small bowl. Stir together *using your clean fingers*. (The bacteria on the surface of your skin are valuable to the development of the starter.) Cover with fine-weave cheesecloth and leave at room temperature until the starter appears active and slightly bubbly, 24 to 36 hours.

2. Combine the soybeans and toasted bran in a bowl. Cover with filtered water and soak for 24 hours.

3. Drain and transfer the beans to a rice cooker or steaming basket, and steam until the beans are soft, about 1 hour; let cool.

4. Toss the cooled beans in the sea salt, and blend in a food processor or blender until only slightly chunky (like tapenade).

5. Stir in all of the starter. Pack the mixture into a $\frac{1}{2}$-gallon jar with an air lock, pushing down to compress, and pour in enough water so the water level is 1 inch from the top of the jar. Secure the lid.

6. Fill the air lock with water to the designated level on the lock, and secure into the air hole on lid.

7. Place in a pantry or other room-temperature location away from direct light. Taste after 1 month. Ferment for 2 to 6 months, or even longer, up to 1 year. When you like how it tastes, strain and bottle. Store when bottled in a cool location for up to 4 months.

Ponzu Sauce

YIELD: 1¼ cups
START TO FINISH: 20 minutes to make + 2 to 6 months fermenting

Here's another better-than-store-bought item that is very easy to make. Ponzu is a citrusy-soy Japanese pantry ingredient used in soups and noodle dishes as soy sauce would be. To best duplicate yuzu, the fruit traditionally used, this recipe calls for both lemon and lime. Yuzu juice is sometimes found bottled in Asian markets—if you can find it, use that instead. I also love the combination of sour Seville orange and lime. The staple Japanese soup stock ingredients of bonito flakes and kombu (seaweed) lend earthy, salty, fishy flavors. You can use instant dashi-no-moto soup powder or make the simple dashi yourself. Dashi is best when used fresh so if you can, make it just before making the ponzu (cool it before adding).

⅓ cup Soy Sauce (page 71) or good quality store-bought soy sauce

⅓ cup Dashi (following)

2 tablespoons freshly squeezed lemon juice

4 tablespoons freshly squeezed lime juice

1 strip lemon zest

1 strip lime zest

2 tablespoons unseasoned rice vinegar

1 tablespoon mirin

2 tablespoons raw unrefined cane sugar

2 tablespoons Water Kefir (page 171) or basic whey (see page 13)

1. Combine all the ingredients in a bowl and stir to dissolve the sugar.

2. Place in a 1-quart glass jar equipped with an air lock.

3. Fill the air lock with water to the designated level on the lock, and secure into the air hole on the lid of the jar.

4. Place in a pantry or other location at room temperature and away from direct light.

5. Taste after 1 month. Ferment longer, if desired, 2 to 6 months. Strain into a pouring vessel and bottle. Store in a cool, dark pantry or other similar location. Refrigerate after opening. It will last for up to 4 more months.

DASHI

To make about 4 cups: Place 1 sheet (about 5 by 4 inches) of kombu (kelp) in a saucepan and cover with 4¾ cups filtered water. Bring to just below a boil over medium-high heat, and then remove from the heat. Stir in ⅓ cup bonito flakes and let it stand for 2 to 3 minutes. Remove the kelp and strain immediately. Cool uncovered, then cover and refrigerate, or use freshly made.

Note: Dashi should not be boiled; it may be covered and refrigerated but when reheated do not bring to a boil. Reserved dashi will keep for up to 2 weeks.

Smoky Chipotle in Adobo

YIELD: About 2 cups
START TO FINISH: 45 minutes to make + 8 to 12 hours fermenting + 2 days refrigeration

Adobo is a piquant paste or thick sauce used in Mexican cuisine made from ground chiles (often chipotles), herbs, garlic, and vinegar, used as a marinade or sauce for poultry or meat. Chipotles are smoked jalapeños. Other dried chiles can be used or you can roast and smoke fresh chiles. Sometimes the sauce is used separately from the chipotles; other recipes use the chipotles and the sauce. For extra smokiness, I've used smoked brown sugar (see Resources, page 241). You can use a natural brown sugar in its place.

¾ pound red jalapeños, smoke-roasted, liquid reserved (see page 74)

½ cup julienned dry-packed sun-dried tomatoes

2 tablespoons dark raisins

¼ cup tomato paste

3 cloves Roasted Garlic (page 212), peeled

2 shallots, roasted and peeled

1 teaspoon cumin seeds, toasted and ground

1 teaspoon coriander seeds, toasted and ground

2½ teaspoons dried Mexican oregano

1 teaspoon ground cinnamon

2 tablespoons smoked brown sugar (see page 241) or natural brown sugar

2 teaspoons unrefined fine sea salt

4 tablespoons raw, unfiltered apple cider vinegar

6 tablespoons balsamic vinegar

2 tablespoons fermenting agent (basic whey; Water Kefir, page 171; or brine from pickled vegetables)

1. Cut a slit down the side of each of the smoked chiles, and remove the stems and most of the seeds. Remove the skins from 5 of the chiles and set aside to stir in whole. Reserve any liquid from this process.

2. In a blender (preferably) or a food processor, combine all the chiles but the 5 whole chiles (chipotles), any reserved liquid from the peppers, sun-dried tomatoes, raisins, tomato paste, garlic, shallots, cumin, coriander, oregano, cinnamon, brown sugar, and salt with 2 tablespoons of the apple cider vinegar; blend to create a thick paste. Add the remaining 2 tablespoons of the cider vinegar along with the balsamic vinegar and puree into a smooth, soft paste.

continued

SMOKE-ROASTED CHILES

3. Place the paste in a bowl and stir in the fermenting agent. Starting with the paste, spoon into a pint jar in layers, alternating with the smoked jalapeños, being careful not to break them up. Finish with a layer of paste; secure a piece of cheesecloth to the top of the jar and ferment at room temperature for 8 hours or overnight. Cover with an airtight lid and refrigerate for 2 days before using. Store, refrigerated, for up to 2 months.

Using the method described for tea-smoking on page 214, line a wok snugly with aluminum foil.

Place a handful of aromatic wood chips in the bottom of the wok, then insert a mesh pizza rack sized to fit the wok, raising about 2 inches above the chips. Line the rack with a single layer of fresh or dried chiles of your choice. Leave room between the pieces so the smoke will cover the surfaces evenly. Heat the wok over moderate heat until the chips begin to smoke.

Cover, decrease the heat to low, and smoke for 10 to 12 minutes. Turn off the heat and allow to smoke for another 3 to 5 minutes. Remove the chiles, portion into food-storage containers, and refrigerate until ready to use. The smoked peppers can also be packed in olive oil and stored in refrigeration. The bonus here is a smoky, peppery olive oil.

CHILE-GARLIC PASTE

YIELD: About 2 cups
START TO FINISH: 45 minutes to make + 3 days fermenting

The spicy combination of chiles and garlic finds its way into many cuisines around the globe: Asian, Latino, Middle Eastern, African, Mediterranean, and Southwestern American. This version is a basic Asian-inspired paste that you can play with and adjust to your liking or application. Add more liquid to turn it into a sauce. For added depth of flavor, toast some or all of the chiles for 5 minutes in a dry skillet before making the sauce.

1 ounce small dried Thai or Mexican chiles, stemmed
Hot water
8 cloves garlic, coarsely chopped
2 teaspoons raw unrefined cane sugar
1 tablespoon unrefined fine sea salt
3 tablespoons raw, unfiltered apple cider vinegar
2 tablespoons Asian Fish Sauce (page 145)
3 tablespoons liquid reserved from hydrating the chiles

1. Place the chiles in a bowl and cover with about 1 cup of hot water. Allow to rehydrate until soft, about 20 minutes. Drain and reserve the liquid to thin the paste.

2. Place the hydrated chiles, garlic, sugar, salt, vinegar, and fish sauce in a blender and puree into a chunky paste. Add the reserved liquid and puree at high speed until smooth. Add water, if needed, to create a smooth paste.

3. Place in a wide-mouth pint glass jar, cover tightly, and set at room temperature for 3 days. Transfer to refrigeration after that primary fermenting stage. Set for 3 days before opening; best if used within 2 months after opening, though it will last longer.

FERMENTED GARLIC

Blanched, fermented garlic is a staple in my kitchen. Bring a pot of water to a boil, add the cloves from 1 head of garlic, and cook for about 1 minute; drain. Peel the cloves, place them in a small jar to within 1 inch of the top, and cover with Basic Brine (page 13). Cover and refrigerate for up to 2 weeks.

FERMENTED MIXED BEAN SALSA

YIELD: About 4 cups
START TO FINISH: 8 to 12 hours soaking + 30 minutes cooking + 45 minutes to make + 8 hours at room temperature + 2 days refrigeration

Fermenting this delicious and nutritious bean salsa makes the flavors more vibrant. It's a great accompaniment to flatbreads and chips, or as a side to grilled meat or fish. You can use any combination of dried beans. Be sure to buy beans from a reliable source, one you know is replenishing the supply frequently and where the beans are not old and wrinkly (yes, they show signs of aging, too). My favorite supplier is Rancho Gordo (see Resources, page 241) for beans that are heirloom varieties, seasonal, and fresh.

For this recipe, the beans are soaked overnight for a number of reasons: to reduce the cooking time, to break down the amino acids so the beans are more digestible, and to start the fermentation process. If you do not have access to dried beans, you can use canned beans if they are not salted and they are packed in water. However, the resulting salsa will be mushy. The brine and the raw pineapple vinegar will assist in promoting further fermentation. I love to use a vegetable brine such as one from sauerkraut or kale.

¾ cup dried black beans
¾ cup dried red or pinto beans
Filtered water
1 cup cooked corn kernels
½ cup diced red bell pepper
¼ cup diced white onion
3 cloves garlic
1½ teaspoons cumin seed, toasted
2 teaspoons unrefined fine sea salt
¼ cup brine (Basic Brine, page 13, or from another vegetable)
¼ cup Pineapple Vinegar (page 33)

1. Place each variety of beans in a separate bowl; add enough filtered water to cover the beans by 2 inches. Cover and soak overnight.

2. Pour off the soaking water, place each variety of beans in a separate saucepan, add water to cover the beans by 1 inch, and cook over medium heat until the beans are soft but not mushy, about 30 minutes. Drain the beans, combine them in a large bowl, and toss with the corn, bell pepper, onion, garlic, cumin, and salt. In a measuring cup, combine the brine and pineapple vinegar.

3. Fill 2 pint jars with the bean mixture, leaving 1 inch of space at the top. Pour in the brine mixture to cover the beans. Cover each jar with fine cheesecloth and secure with a rubber band. Leave at room temperature for 8 hours, then replace the cheesecloth with a lid, close tightly, and refrigerate for 2 days before using. The salsa can be refrigerated for up to 4 weeks; 2 weeks after opening.

Tapenade of Herbs, Citrus, and Olives

YIELD: 2 cups
START TO FINISH: 40 minutes to make + 3 days fermenting

Consider this recipe a foundational one, presented as an example of the combinations and techniques you can employ. You can make this with any proportion of herbs you prefer, as long as you get 2 cups packed herb leaves, chopped or whole. I often keep the leaves whole to use this tapenade as a salad. Make in small batches, packed in pint or half-pint jars, so the amounts are reasonable and the jars are easy to store in refrigeration once opened.

Small weight(s)
Pint jar with air lock

1 cup packed fresh flat-leaf parsley leaves, chopped
1/2 cup packed arugula leaves, chopped
1/4 cup packed fresh mint leaves, chopped
1/4 cup packed fresh basil leaves, chopped
1 1/2 teaspoons unrefined fine sea salt
1 small fennel frond or 1/2 teaspoon fennel seeds
1/4 cup oil-cured olives, pitted and chopped
2 tablespoons thin strips orange zest
4 cloves garlic
1 1/2 tablespoons raw, unfiltered apple cider vinegar or orange vinegar
Filtered water
Olive oil
1 cup cooked lentils (optional)

1. In a bowl, toss the chopped greens with salt, fennel, olives, and zest. Allow to release liquid for 30 minutes. Pack one-third of the greens into a pint jar; poke in 2 cloves garlic; pack in more greens; poke in the remaining 2 cloves garlic. Pour in the released liquid and the vinegar, then press down to compress the greens. If needed, add just enough water to cover. Add a small weight to keep the mixture submerged in the liquid. Attach a lid with an air lock. Place in a cool, dark location for 3 days.

2. Once the ingredients have fermented, drain off any excess liquid (this is good stuff to save for adding to soups, stocks, or making vinaigrettes), then stir in olive oil to coat. (Option: At this point you can add in a cup of cooked lentils.) Secure with an airtight lid and refrigerate until ready to use. Portion off the amount being used and bring to room temperature. Refrigerate for up to 3 weeks.

Toasted Nut Butter

YIELD: 2 cups
START TO FINISH: 6 hours soaking + 30 minutes drying + 20 minutes toasting + 20 minutes to make + 6 hours fermenting

Use any of your favorite nuts to make delicious butters. A personal favorite is toasted cashew butter. Melt nut butters into a sauce, toss into hot pasta, stuff into ravioli, stir a spoonful into hot oatmeal, spread on toast, slather on fish or meat to roast, add to moles, or even make into frostings. Coconut oil smoothes out nut butters and renders them suitable for cooking. Nut butters can be sweet or savory, sweetened with raw honey, flavored with dried herbs, or given a little heat from ground chiles.

2 cups raw cashews, almonds, pistachios, peanuts,
    or walnuts
5$\frac{1}{2}$ teaspoons unrefined fine sea salt
Filtered water
$\frac{1}{3}$ cup coconut oil
2 tablespoons raw honey

1.   Place the nuts in a bowl and toss in 4$\frac{1}{2}$ teaspoons of the salt to combine. Cover with filtered water and soak for 6 hours (see more about soaking nuts on page 6).

2.   Drain the nuts, pat dry with paper towels, and spread out on a small baking sheet to dry for 30 minutes. Spread a single layer of the nuts in a skillet and toast over medium heat for about 10 minutes, stirring

continued

occasionally, until the nuts have dried further and are lightly caramelized. Remove from the heat and let cool.

3.   Place the nuts in a food processor. Add the coconut oil, honey, and the remaining 1 teaspoon salt. Blend into a smooth or slightly chunky paste. Divide the mixture into two $\frac{1}{2}$-pint jars, cover the openings with fine-weave cheesecloth, and secure with rubber bands. Leave at room temperature for 6 hours, then replace the cheesecloth with lids and securely fasten.

4.   Refrigerate until ready to use. Bring to room temperature 20 minutes before using. The butter will last for 3 weeks or longer.

SAVORY WALNUT-THYME BUTTER

YIELD: 2 cups
START TO FINISH: 6 hours soaking + 30 minutes drying + 20 minutes toasting + 20 minutes to make + 6 hours fermenting

This is a great example of a savory nut butter—use it to coat fish or to toss into pasta.

2 cups walnut halves
5$\frac{1}{2}$ teaspoons unrefined fine sea salt
Filtered water
$\frac{1}{3}$ cup coconut oil
1 teaspoon dried thyme

1.   Place the nuts and 4$\frac{1}{2}$ teaspoons of the salt in a bowl and toss to combine. Cover with filtered water and soak for 6 hours.

2.   Drain the nuts, pat dry with paper towels, and spread out on a small baking sheet to dry for 30 minutes. Spread a single layer of the nuts in a skillet and toast over medium heat for 10 minutes, stirring occasionally, until the nuts have dried further and their surface is lightly caramelized. Remove from the heat and let cool.

3. Place the nuts in a food processor. Add the coconut oil, dried thyme, and salt. Blend into a smooth or slightly chunky paste. Divide the mixture into two ½-pint jars, cover the openings with fine-weave cheesecloth, and secure with rubber bands. Leave at room temperature for 6 hours, then replace the cheesecloth with lids and securely fasten.

4. Refrigerate until ready to use. Bring to room temperature 20 minutes before using. The butter will last for 3 weeks or longer.

Sprouted Tahini Paste

YIELD: About 4 cups
START TO FINISH: 2 days sprouting + 30 minutes to make + 3 days fermenting

Tahini is a smooth sesame seed paste (essentially a seed butter) used extensively in Middle Eastern cuisines. It is an ingredient in Sprouted Chickpea Hummus (page 61) and other seed or vegetable spreads, and is also used in delicious sauces to serve with falafel (see page 203). This version calls for sprouted sesame seeds as well as toasted ones, creating both a color and slight textural contrast. Because the sesame seeds are so small, you won't actually see much evidence of sprouting, but germination will have occurred. Tahini is typically unflavored but I like to use the brine from fermented garlic for extra flavor.

2 cups white sesame seeds, toasted
2 cups white sesame seeds, sprouted for 2 days
    (see page 7)
2 tablespoons coconut oil
1 teaspoon unrefined fine sea salt
2 tablespoons Basic Brine (page 13) or brine from
    Fermented Garlic (page 75)

Place the seeds, coconut oil, and salt in a food processor and blend until smooth. Drizzle in the brine and combine. Place in a jar, cover the opening with fine-weave cheesecloth, and secure with a rubber band. Set at room temperature for 3 days and then replace the cheesecloth with a lid, close, and refrigerate until ready to use. The paste will last for months in refrigeration.

CHAPTER 5

FERMENTED DAIRY: Cultured Butter, Yogurt, Crème Fraîche, and Cheese

WE HUMANS LONG AGO figured out that when milk is fermented, not only is it transformed into something delicious—like cheese, yogurt, butter, and crème fraîche—but it also keeps longer and is easier to transport. As a bonus, it's more nutritious and digestible, too.

This chapter will demystify and give a hands-on view of how fermented milk almost magically becomes cheese, or yogurt, or butter (kefir, a fermented dairy drink, is presented in chapter 8 with other beverages). These recipes are a mix inspired by cheeses or cheese makers I admire, adaptations from old favorites, and new contributions from cheesemaker friends. This chapter is structured to let you develop your skills progressively. We'll start with the easiest fresh-cultured dairy and add complexity. As you work through the progression, you'll be building your skills and confidence while gaining an understanding of the processes.

Be sure to read through the following descriptions of the equipment, ingredients, and techniques to get a sense of the cheese-making process before diving into the recipes. More recipes, forms, charts, and ripening and aging information as well as storage information are available in my book *Artisan Cheese Making at Home*, and on its companion website, www.artisancheesemakingathome.com. Check there for regular updates, to make contact, or to learn more about my cheese-making classes.

Equipment and Supplies

The basic equipment and supplies you'll need for nearly all the recipes in this chapter include the following:

- Butter muslin (4 to 6 yards) and fine-weave cheesecloth (4 to 6 yards)

- Curd-cutting knife or 10-inch cake-decorating spatula

- Disposable vinyl or food-service gloves

- Draining bowl or bucket: a large, nonreactive, food-grade vessel for catching up to 2 gallons of whey

- Flexible-blade rubber spatulas

- Flexible wire stainless steel whisk with a long handle

- Instant-read kitchen or dairy thermometer

- Ladle or skimmer (stainless steel or other nonreactive material) for removing curds from whey

- Paper towels

- Ripening boxes: food-grade storage boxes with lids (see photo on page 94)

- Spoons: large nonreactive metal, wood, or plastic spoons for stirring; one slotted and one not

- Stainless steel pots: a 6-quart pot for working with 1 gallon of milk; a 10-quart pot for working with 2 gallons; a 12-quart pot for making a water bath for indirect heating

- Stainless steel measuring spoons that include the very important $1/8$-teaspoon measure

- Strainer or colander (made of plastic or another nonreactive material) for draining curds

Clockwise from left: 5-inch Tomme mold with follower, mini-Camembert mold, chèvre mold, Saint-Marcellin mold, feta basket, $4^1/2$-inch hard cheese mold with follower

- Wrapping materials: resealable plastic storage bags, plastic wrap, and aluminum foil

For a few of the cheeses, you will also need some of the following:

- Cheese mats (plastic): to drain molded curds

- Draining rack: nonreactive material, to sit inside draining tray

- Draining trays: food-grade plastic trays or rimmed quarter-sheet or half-sheet baking pans

- Hygrometer: a tool for measuring relative humidity; very helpful for monitoring the environment in which cheeses ripen

- Molding and shaping devices (see photo opposite)

- pH strips or pH meter: used to measure the acidity of curds in some recipes

- Specialty wrapping materials: cheese paper

- Weights: such as foil-wrapped bricks, heavy skillets, or empty milk containers filled with water

Ingredients

As with any food preparation, your final results when culturing dairy or making cheese begins with using the highest-quality ingredients you can source. It starts with milk.

MILK

Milk always has a fuller flavor when the animals are fed their natural diet. Find a reputable source for locally produced, high-quality milk. You'll need raw or pasteurized milks; ultra-pasteurized milk will not form curds. Always read the labels for processing procedures and sell-by dates, and always buy the freshest milk available and keep it refrigerated at 40°F. Avoid milks or creams that have stabilizers or thickeners added, as these additives can inhibit proper coagulation and curd development. More information on milk and home pasteurization is at www.artisancheese makingathome.com. Here are a few labels you'll need to be familiar with:

Raw. Not processed at all, raw milk contains all of its natural flora. Cheeses made with raw milk have complex and layered flavors. Raw milk curdles and separates when left at room temperature, as lactic bacteria in the air produce a culture. So, when you're using raw milk, the amount of starter culture needed may differ. Also, the character of raw milk cheese will differ from that made with pasteurized milk inoculated only with laboratory-produced cultures. Importantly, if you use raw milk when making cheese, omit any calcium chloride called for in the ingredient list. If using raw milk, observe a few precautions. Unless you know your animal, pasteurize raw milk to kill any harmful pathogens before consuming; however, it can safely be used to make cheese if aged to 60 days or more. Note: Raw milk is not available to many home cheese makers because it is illegal to sell in a number of states. Check for availability in your area; where legal, look for local cow or goat herd shares (see Resources, page 241).

Pasteurized (Nonhomogenized). If you're not using raw milk, this is the best choice for cheese making Pasteurized milk coagulates better than homogenized milk, and even curdles and separates if left at room temperature, as lactic bacteria in the air produces a culture in the milk. Pasteurization destroys dangerous pathogens, including salmonella and *E. coli*. However, it also destroys, to a degree, vitamins, useful enzymes, beneficial bacteria, texture, and flavor.

Pasteurized and Homogenized. Most milk available at retail is in this form. Homogenization breaks up the fat globules and forces them into suspension in the liquid. Meant to prohibit the separation of milk and cream, this process changes the molecular structure of the milk and renders it incapable of producing a culture if left out at room temperature. Homogenized milk sours more quickly than nonhomogenized milk. Some calcium chloride and valuable bacteria are destroyed with each of these processes (homogenization and pasteurization) and in cheese making must be replaced with added calcium chloride and bacteria. In the recipes in this chapter, it is assumed that the milk used is pasteurized or both pasteurized and homogenized.

Ultra-Pasteurized (UP) or Ultra-High Temperature (UHT). These milks are exposed to extreme heat and cold shocks to denature the milk and make it shelf stable, allowing it to last longer in transport and in the dairy case. This process is used for many brands of organic milk because they may sell more slowly at retail. Unfortunately, ultra-pasteurized milk and cream do not work at all for setting proper curds in making cheese and should be avoided.

STARTER CULTURES

When added to warm milk, starter cultures kick off the development of desirable bacteria. Specific strains in a given culture help the desired flavors, textures, and aromas to develop in the finished cheese. Culture companies put together specific blends depending on the style of cheese being made. Most of the blends are standard and can contain anywhere from two to six different strains of cultures in varying ratios. Before making a cheese in this chapter, look at which types of cultures are required. See the Culture Chart on pages 88–89, and for information on more starter and secondary cultures, refer to the charts at www.artisancheesemakingathome.com. In creating the formulas, I list both general and specific preferred cultures that I trust and that are readily available in small quantities from cheese-making supply companies (see Resources, page 241).

Note these important reference terms regarding cultures:

- **Acidifier.** Lactic acid producer

- **Proteolysis.** An important process that refers to the breakdown or fermentation of milk proteins

- **Proteolytic (protein-degrading) enzymes.** Components that contribute to development of desirable flavor and texture in aged cheeses

- **Diacetyl.** A fermentation compound that contributes a desirable buttery aroma to a cheese

- **Gas production.** Term referring to cultures that produce carbon dioxide

SECONDARY CULTURES: MOLDS, BACTERIA, AND YEASTS

These are molds, bacteria, and yeasts that do their jobs during the ripening phase of certain cheeses. Working independently or in combination with other cultures and enzymes, they are responsible for the white fuzzy surface on bloomy-rind cheeses such as Coastal Breeze (page 111), the smeared or washed rinds on stinkers such as Wild and Creamy Muenster (page 109), as well as the tracks of blue in blue cheeses such as Blue-Eyed Jack Cheese (page 114). Depending on the style of cheese, they are added directly to the milk, added between layers of curds, or sprayed or rubbed onto the surface of the cheese.

COAGULANTS

Coagulants solidify milk protein (casein) to form curds. Some acidifiers such as lemon juice, vinegar, or buttermilk work at high temperatures to create curds in simple direct-acid cheeses such as ricotta, queso blanco, or panir. The chief coagulant in cheese making is rennet, which does its job in milk that is heated to a moderate temperature and then maintained for a period of time until a solid mass of curds is created.

RENNET

Animal rennet (containing the enzyme rennin or chymosin) is naturally found in the stomachs of calves, kids, or lambs. Calf rennet is generally the rennet of choice for cheese makers. It is the only animal rennet a home cheese maker will need and is available from cheese-making suppliers (see Resources, page 241). Non-animal rennet (often identified as vegetarian rennet) is a microbial enzyme used by those who may be concerned about using an animal-based enzyme.

Rennet comes in liquid or tablet form. Liquid rennet is easier to measure, dissolve, and distribute into the milk than tablets, and the recipes in this chapter call for it. Half a tablet is equivalent to $\frac{1}{4}$ teaspoon of regular-strength liquid rennet; to use tablet rennet, crush the tablet and dissolve in the same amount of water called for in the recipe. Liquid rennet often comes in double strength, so read the label to know the ratio of dilution needed. Rennet should always be diluted in nonchlorinated water because chlorine will kill the enzyme and make it ineffective. Liquid rennet will keep for 3 months, refrigerated. Tablets may be stored in the freezer for up to 1 year.

SALT

Noniodized salt (typically kosher salt) is used in cheese making and is almost always introduced into the process after some or all of the whey is drained and at the beginning of or during the ripening process, depending on the style of cheese. Cheese salt is available from cheese supply companies; for the recipes in this chapter you may use kosher salt (preferably Diamond Crystal brand) or unrefined fine or flake sea salt. Never use iodized salt.

WATER

Always use cool (50°F to 55°F) nonchlorinated water to dissolve rennet, calcium chloride, or other additives to ensure their effectiveness. Chlorine not only has an undesirable flavor and odor but will also make a coagulant ineffective. Bottled or filtered water is your best option for this and for making brines. If the only water available is chlorinated tap water, boil it first, cool to 50°F to 55°F, then use at the temperature designated in the recipe.

Culture Chart

NAME	TYPE	ACTIVE INGREDIENTS	SUPPLIERS	NOTES AND USES
Meso I	Mesophilic starter culture	*Lactococcus lactis* ssp. *lactis*	Glengarry Cheese-making and Dairy Supply	Low-level acidifier. Cheddars and Jacks.
MA 011	Mesophilic starter culture	*Lactococcus lactis* ssp. *lactis* *Lactococcus lactis* ssp. *cremoris*	The Cheesemaker, Glengarry Cheese-making and Dairy Supply, New England Cheesemaking Supply	Moderate to high acidifier with no gas or diacetyl production. Creates a clean flavor and very closed texture, and is proteolytic during aging. Cheddar, Colby, Monterey Jack, feta, chèvre.
MM 100	Mesophilic starter culture	*Lactococcus lactis* ssp. *lactis* *Lactococcus lactis* ssp. *cremoris* *Lactococcus lactis* ssp. *lactis* biovar. *diacetylactis*	The Cheesemaker, Glengarry Cheese-making and Dairy Supply, New England Cheesemaking Supply	Moderate acidifier with some gas production and high diacetyl production. Brie, Camembert, Edam, feta, Gouda, Havarti, and other buttery, open-textured cheeses, including blue cheeses and chèvre.
MA 4001 Farmhouse	Mesophilic starter culture	*Lactococcus lactis* ssp. *lactis* *Lactococcus lactis* ssp. *cremoris* *Lactococcus lactis* ssp. *lactis* biovar. *diacetylactis* *Streptococcus thermophilus*	The Beverage People, The Cheese-maker, Glengarry Cheesemaking and Dairy Supply, New England Cheese-making Supply	Moderate acidifier with some gas and diacetyl production; similar to the bacteria balance in raw milk. Creates a slightly open texture. The culture used for most types of cheese. Caerphilly, Brin d'Amour, Roquefort.
Aroma B	Mesophilic starter culture	*Lactococcus lactis* ssp. *lactis* *Lactococcus lactis* ssp. *cremoris* *Lactococcus lactis* ssp. *lactis* biovar. *diacetylactis* *Leuconostoc mesenteroides* ssp. *cremoris*	The Beverage People, The Cheese-maker, Glengarry Cheesemaking and Dairy Supply	Moderate acidifier with some gas production and high diacetyl production. Cream cheese, crème fraîche, cottage cheese, cultured butter, fromage blanc, sour cream, Camembert, Havarti, Valençay.
C20G	Mesophilic starter culture	*Lactococcus lactis* ssp. *lactis* *Lactococcus lactis* ssp. *cremoris* *Lactococcus lactis* ssp. *lactis* biovar. *diacetylactis* Rennet	The Beverage People, New Eng-land Cheesemaking Supply	Premeasured blend chèvre starter containing rennet. Used for mak-ing chèvre and other fresh goat cheeses.
Thermo A	Thermophilic starter culture	*Streptococcus thermophilus*	The Beverage People	Fast-growing lactic acid producer. Used in fresh mozzarella and some alpine-style cheeses.
Thermo B	Thermophilic starter culture	*Streptococcus thermophilus* *Lactobacillus delbrueckii* ssp. *bulgaricus*	The Beverage People, The Cheese-maker, Glengarry Cheesemaking and Dairy Supply	More proteolytic than *S. thermo-philus* alone. Italian-style cheeses including mozzarella, Parmesan, Provolone, Romano, and various soft and semisoft cheeses.

NAME	TYPE	ACTIVE INGREDIENTS	SUPPLIERS	NOTES AND USES
Thermo C	Thermophilic starter culture	*Streptococcus thermophilus* *Lactobacillus helveticus*	The Beverage People, The Cheesemaker, Glengarry Cheesemaking and Dairy Supply	Used in Italian and farmstead-type cheeses. More proteolytic than *S. thermophilus* alone. Emmental, Gruyère, Romano, Swiss.
Bulgarian 411 yogurt starter	Nondairy culture	*Streptococcus thermophilus* *Lactobacillus delbrueckii* ssp. *Bulgaris*	The Beverage People	For making yogurt.
Brevibacterium linens	Secondary culture	*B. linens*	The Beverage People, The Cheesemaker, Glengarry Cheesemaking and Dairy Supply, New England Cheesemaking Supply	High pH is required for growth of this bacteria. Used to create red or orange rinds on smeared-rind or washed-rind cheeses including Muenster.
Geotrichum candidum	Secondary culture	*G. candidum*	The Beverage People, The Cheesemaker, Glengarry Cheesemaking and Dairy Supply, New England Cheesemaking Supply	Rapid-growing mold that prevents unwanted mold growth in moist cheeses, for use in cheeses made with *P. candidum* or *B. linens*. Several varieties are available. Geo 13 produces intermediate flavors, Geo 15 is mild, and Geo 17 is very mild.
Penicillium candidum	Secondary culture	*P. candidum*	The Beverage People, The Cheesemaker, Glengarry Cheesemaking and Dairy Supply, New England Cheesemaking Supply	Produces fuzzy, white mold on the surface of bloomy-rind cheeses including Brie, Camembert, Coulommiers, and a variety of French goat cheeses. Various strains are used to produce a range of flavors from mild to very strong. Strains available include ABL, HP6, Niege, SAM3, and VS.
Penicillium roqueforti	Secondary culture	*P. roqueforti*	The Beverage People, The Cheesemaker, Glengarry Cheesemaking and Dairy Supply, New England Cheesemaking Supply	Creates colored veins and surfaces and is a major contributor to flavor in blue cheeses including Gorgonzola, Roquefort, and Stilton. Various strains are used for a range of colors, with variations of gray, green, and blue. Strains available include PA, PJ, PRB18, PRB6, PV Direct, and PS.

CALCIUM CHLORIDE

Pasteurization and homogenization change the structure of milk, removing some of the calcium and destabilizing it slightly. When using other than raw milk to make cheese, add calcium chloride (before the coagulant) to increase the number of available calcium ions and help firm up the curds. Purchase calcium chloride from a cheese-making supplier (see Resources, page 241) and store it in the refrigerator according to the supplier's directions, generally up to 12 months.

LIPASE POWDER

Lipase is an enzyme found in raw milk that breaks down fat into aromatic short-chain fatty acids; it is often added in powder form to processed cow milk to impart a stronger, tangy flavor to the cheese along with a distinctive aroma (see Crumbly Feta, page 105). If using, add lipase powder diluted in cool water to the milk before adding the rennet. It can be purchased from cheese-making suppliers (see Resources, page 241); store in the freezer and use within 12 months.

VEGETABLE ASH

The finely ground powdered ash used in cheese making is a food-grade charcoal available from cheese-making suppliers (see Resources, page 241). It is mixed with salt and sprinkled or rubbed on the surfaces of some soft, primarily goat, cheeses to encourage desirable mold growth and discourage unwanted bacteria. The ash neutralizes the surface acidity, allows moisture to be drawn out, protects the exterior, firms up the cheese, and allows the interior (paste) to ripen and stay soft. Ash is very messy to apply and stains on contact, so use disposable gloves and work carefully. Transfer some of the ash powder to a dedicated salt shaker and add the amount of salt called for in the recipe you are using. To apply ash, place the cheese in the bottom of a plastic tub and sprinkle the surface to be coated with the ash and salt, patting with your hands to distribute and adhere the mixture to the surface of the cheese.

Preparation and Techniques

The formulas for individual cheeses will teach variations on these techniques, but the same basic set of processes applies across the spectrum of cheese making, from the simplest fresh cheeses to the fussiest long-aged washed-rind cheeses: ripening milk; coagulation and curd finishing; draining, shaping, and pressing; salting; drying; affinage, or cheese ripening; and storage.

In cheese making, preparation has several components:

- Read the recipe through carefully and familiarize yourself with any terms or techniques that aren't familiar to you.

- Think about timing: cheese making requires a series of tasks over a period of hours or days, and ripening tasks can require you to focus on the cheese for weeks or months.

- Assemble your equipment, ingredients, and supplies and make sure everything is squeaky clean. Sterilize all your equipment before you use it and sanitize your work surfaces as described on page 10. Whichever pieces of your equipment are solely used for cheese making (as opposed to being taken from your usual kitchen equipment) should be sanitized and air-dried before you put them away. If possible, store them all together in one place—a lidded box is perfect—so they're collected and dust free next time you make cheese.

If you catch the cheese-making bug, be sure to keep good records of your observations and results to retain valuable information that you can apply to other sessions. You can use the charts and forms available on my website (www.artisancheesemaking athome.com).

The following techniques are used in most of the recipes in this chapter. Read through them to get a sense of some of the actions and pacing of cheese making.

RIPENING MILK

For every recipe in this chapter, the first step is to prepare the milk for acidification by warming it to a specified temperature. The general range is from 86°F to 92°F. A slow, steady increase in temperature is crucial to proper milk ripening: too much heat too fast can destroy the proteins you are depending upon to build your curds and can create a hostile atmosphere for the microflora you're trying to foster.

Always begin with a sterilized, nonreactive stockpot or pan equipped with a dairy thermometer and milk that has been left at room temperature (68°F to 72°F) for 1 hour. For many cheeses, the milk is heated directly and slowly over low heat until the desired temperature is reached. Most of the recipes in this book instruct you to heat the milk directly in this manner. A good general rule to follow for slowly heating milk over low, direct heat is to raise the milk temperature 2°F per minute. For example, if the milk is 50°F when added to the pot and the specified temperature to reach before adding the culture or bacteria

is 86°F, it should take no less than 18 minutes to reach temperature.

HEATING WITH WATER-BATH METHOD

Sometimes it's desirable to heat the milk using a water bath (if your stove burners are not easily kept at a very low heat, you may prefer using this indirect method for all of your cheese making) to heat the milk more quickly yet more gently and evenly. To make a water bath, nest a 4- to 10-quart stockpot (depending on the quantity of milk you are heating) inside a larger pot and pour water into the larger pot to come as far up the side of the smaller pot as the milk level will be (for example, if you are heating 1 gallon of milk in a 6-quart pot, the water should come two-thirds of the way up the inner pot). Remove the smaller pot and place the larger pot over low heat. When the water reaches a temperature 10°F warmer than you want

Cultured Dairy Sauces

Whether savory or sweet, warm or cold, you can make delicious sauces from cultured dairy. Compound butters (page 97) and some high-butterfat cheeses (such as creamy blue, soft chèvre, or nutty Gruyère) can be whisked into wine or spirit reductions to create silky sauces. Both crème fraîche and yogurt can be flavored by infusing them with an aromatic, such as lavender or saffron (see Saffron Yogurt Cheese, page 99), or stirring in ground herbs, spices, or blends like curry powder, garam masala, or chipotle powder. Used chilled or at room temperature, both crème fraîche and yogurt are indispensable ingredients for dressings or dips. Crème fraîche also makes a miracle white sauce since it can be heated to boiling without curdling or separating (see Yogurt-Cardamom Ice Cream with Goat Crème Fraîche Caramel Sauce, page 230).

the milk to be, put the smaller pot back in the water to warm slightly, then pour the milk into the smaller pot and slowly warm to temperature over the period of time specified in the recipe. If the milk is heating too fast, adjust the burner heat, add cool water to lower the water-bath temperature, or remove the pot of milk from the water bath.

MAINTAINING MILK TEMPERATURE

In different phases of cheese making, you will allow the mixture to sit while maintaining the milk at a particular temperature. There are several ways to accomplish this:

- In order to best maintain the temperature of milk or curds, use the water-bath method to heat the milk. The residual heat will dissipate more slowly.

- Always cover the pot.

- Use ceramic-coated cast-iron Dutch ovens or stockpots; these hold the heat better and longer than stainless steel pots.

- If using a thin-bottomed stainless steel pot, also use a cast-iron simmer plate as a buffer to the heat and to maintain temperature more efficiently.

- A towel wrapped around the sides of the pot will help hold in the heat.

- If temperatures under 95°F are required, setting the pot under the light of your stove hood should be sufficient to maintain the temperature.

- If you live in a very cool or cold environment, place the pot on a warmed heating pad to maintain the needed temperature.

UP-AND-DOWN WHISKING

After adding any culture or coagulant to the milk, you need to mix it in well, using a long-handled whisk in a vertical up-and-down motion at least twenty times, or for the time period specified in the recipe. At a minimum, rennet should be stirred in using an up-and-down motion for 30 seconds to fully distribute it throughout the milk. This technique is a valuable one: using an up-and-down rather than a circular motion draws the additives down into the milk for more even distribution. It also allows the milk to settle in a shorter period of time and contributes to a more even consistency in the developing curds.

TESTING FOR A CLEAN BREAK

The ripened milk begins its turn toward becoming recognizable cheese when a coagulant is added and the milk coagulates or curdles, separating into liquid whey and solid curds that are firm and give what is called a clean break. Use a sanitized long-blade curd cutting knife, chef's knife, bread knife, or cake decorating spatula to make a short 1-inch test cut at the edge all the way down to the bottom and observe the firmness of the curds. If the cut edge is clean, the two sides of the cut remain open, and there's some accumulation of light-colored whey in the cut area, the curds are ready to be cut into their proper size. If the cut edge is soft and the curds are mushy, the curds are not ready. Allow them to sit 15 minutes longer before testing again.

Top to bottom: cutting curds, lightly stirred curds

CUTTING CURDS

Curds are cut into varying sizes, from slabs down to rice-size pieces, depending upon the style and desired moisture content of the finished cheese. To cut the curds into uniform pieces (rather than into the large slices or slabs suitable for some soft cheeses), use a 10-inch cake-decorating spatula or curd-cutting knife to make vertical parallel cuts of the designated size all the way down through the curds from surface to bottom. Repeat this across the entire mass of curds. Turn the pot 90 degrees and repeat the process to create a checkerboard of square, straight cuts. Then, using the straight cuts as a guide, cut down through the curds at a 45-degree angle, from one side of the pot to the other. Then turn the pot 45 degrees and make angled cuts down through the curd, working in diagonal lines across the squares of the checkerboard. Turn the pot 45 degrees two more times for two more sets of angled cuts. You will now have cut the curds in six directions total: two vertical and four at a 45-degree angle. Your goal is to cut them quickly and with as much uniformity as possible throughout. Using a rubber spatula, gently stir the curds to check for larger curds below those at the surface. Cut any larger curds into the proper size. Note that the cuts should be of similar size but will not be exact.

RIPENING (AGING)

Ripening the cheese—also called aging or affinage—is the final, and for many cheeses the most critical, step of the cheese-making process that involves holding a cheese to develop its flavor, texture, and final personality. A controlled combination of temperature, humidity, and air circulation is needed for the proper ripening of any given style of cheese. For the home-based cheese maker, this important final stage can also be the most challenging. The cheese will indeed ripen, but not always at the pace or with the results anticipated. This is where the craft of cheese making takes its place alongside the science. Refer to www.artisancheesemakingathome.com for aging charts by style of cheese.

CONTROLLING UNWANTED GROWTHS

Mold and bacteria will grow on your cheeses, but you want to control their development. During the ripening process, the surface will show a bit of fuzz or can become slightly slimy from bacteria, especially if the ripening environment is too moist. Any black fuzz, blue or greenish molds, or yellow-colored growth other than what is described or desired in the development of the surface is undesirable and should be removed. Remove it by rubbing with a small piece of cheesecloth dipped in a vinegar-salt solution (a 1-to-1 solution of distilled vinegar and salt), then wiping clean with a piece of washed, dry cheesecloth. Hand-wash and rinse out the cheesecloth, dry, and store in a jar in refrigeration along with your stored washes and brines. Reuse this rag for the same function on the same cheese.

USING RIPENING BOXES

Ripening boxes are used to provide the perfect controlled environment. They can be as simple as a food-storage vegetable keeper with adjustable vent holes (see photo, adjacent). As a general rule, choose a ripening box that's more than twice as big as the cheese it will contain to provide for good air circulation and inhibit mold. You will also need a rack or tray on which the ripening mat and cheese can sit for drainage and a piece of moistened natural sponge or

paper towel to introduce moisture as a humidity contributor. Understand that this ripening system has many variables. It is up to you to monitor the progress of the ripening daily. Being able to properly ascertain by sight, smell, and touch what is going on with the cheese takes practice. Use your senses from the very beginning, and you will learn from each session.

CRÈME FRAÎCHE

YIELD: 1 quart
START TO FINISH: 30 minutes to make + 12 to 48 hours ripening

A soft cultured cow-milk cream, crème fraîche is similar to sour cream but more delicate in flavor. You can make it overnight in glass canning jars. I recommend using two pint jars so that when one jar has been opened, you have another unopened one as backup. Use it plain or sweetened on desserts instead of whipped cream. Since it doesn't curdle when heated, it's a bit of a miracle cooking ingredient you can whisk into sauces and soups. This method uses a culture to turn fresh cream into crème fraîche, but you can use 2 tablespoons crème fraîche, plain yogurt with active cultures, or buttermilk in its place if you like. *See photo on page 148.*

1 quart heavy cream, at room temperature
¼ teaspoon mesophilic starter culture (preferably Aroma B)

1. Sterilize two glass pint jars with lids and a stockpot or roasting pan, and air-dry.

2. In a nonreactive pot over medium-low heat, slowly heat the cream to 86°F. This will take about 15 minutes. Turn off the heat.

3. Sprinkle the starter over the warm cream and let it rehydrate for 5 minutes. Whisk the starter into the milk, using an up-and-down motion to distribute thoroughly.

4. Pour the cream into the two pint jars; place the jars in the stockpot with warm water halfway up the sides of the jars. Place the lids loosely on the jars and leave in the warm water bath to ripen overnight. If your kitchen is cool, cover the pot with a terry towel.

5. Take the jars out of water bath, tighten the lids, and continue to ripen at room temperature (70°F to 72°F) for up to 48 hours total. The cream should be the thickness of creamy yogurt at this point. It will thicken further in refrigeration.

6. Refrigerate to increase the flavor and thicken further. Store for 2 weeks up to 2 months. Use within 2 weeks after opening.

GOAT MILK CRÈME FRAÎCHE

Since goat milk is naturally homogenized, there is little cream that separates out easily. It would take gallons of goat milk to get the amount of cream called for to then culture into crème fraîche. But don't give up! There is a way to get close to the real deal. Make a half batch using goat milk. At the same time make a half batch using cow-milk cream. Place in separate jars and ripen according to the recipe. When the cow milk has thickened, remove them from the warm bath. Gently whisk the two together and place back into the two jars. Refrigerate until they thicken to the consistency of soft sour cream. This mixed-milk crème fraîche is less thick than the all–cow milk version, but it is delicious.

CULTURED BUTTER

YIELD: About 12 ounces
START TO FINISH: 15 minutes to make + 12 hours ripening + 12 hours refrigeration + 1 hour for bringing to temperature + 30 minutes churning + 30 minutes kneading + 6 hours to firm

Most butter is made from fresh cream. Cultured butter, however, is made from cream that has been ripened with lactic bacterial culture, or raw cream that has been left out at ambient temperature to allow its natural lactic acid to ripen it into cultured cream (see note), or crème fraîche. Use pasteurized, but not homogenized, cream to make butter. Choose the freshest cream with the highest fat content you can find. The ingredients list should read pasteurized cream—period! If the cream contains any additional ingredients, such as gums or other stabilizers, they will inhibit the bacterial activity needed to make the butter.

Once you make butter, you also have real buttermilk to use in other recipes such as cultured dairy sauces (see page 91), Grilled Buttermilk–Black Bean Flatbread (page 124), and as a tenderizer in baking. Cultured butter can also be made into a delicious compound butter (see opposite).

1 quart pasteurized, nonhomogenized cream
⅛ teaspoon mesophilic starter culture (preferably Aroma B)

1.   Pour the cream into a 2-quart nonreactive pot over low heat and bring to 68°F. This should take 5 to 7 minutes if starting with refrigerated cream. Take off the heat.

2.   Sprinkle the starter over the cream and let it rehydrate for 5 minutes. Whisk the starter into the cream, using an up-and-down motion to distribute thoroughly. Cover and set aside for 12 hours in a warm spot (70°F to 72°F).

3.   Still covered, refrigerate the ripened cream for 12 hours to firm the butterfat. Using a skimmer, remove the cream layer from the top of the milk. This will become the butter. Bring the cream to 54°F before churning.

4.   Fill the bowl of a food processor or stand mixer fitted with the paddle attachment not more than halfway with the cream and start churning. Do not overload the bowl because the cream needs room to expand. First, you are whipping the cream, then the whipped cream becomes very stiff and yellowish in color. Keep churning. Gradually the volume of the cream will reduce and the texture will be grainy as small flecks of butter form.

5.   The contents will become more liquid and the flecks of butter will separate out. Do not overchurn. Stop when there's a light splashing sound from the liquid buttermilk that is expelling from the cream.

6. Place the strainer over a bowl and pour the mixture into it. Reserve the captured buttermilk, which is real cultured buttermilk, not low-fat milk with cultures added like commercially sold versions, for another use.

7. Rinse the butter under very cold running water to wash off any milk residue.

8. Have a bowl of ice water nearby to cool down your hands while handling the butter as well as a chilled bowl for kneading the butter. (The butter is sticky and hard to handle while a bit warm). Occasionally drop the ball of soft butter into the bowl of ice water to both rinse it and firm it up a little, making the kneading much easier.

9. Place the butter into the second chilled bowl and quickly knead the butter with your fingertips to remove any excess water.

10. Form the butter into a ball or log, wrap tightly in plastic wrap, and refrigerate. Consume within 1 month.

Note: If starting with raw cream, no added culture is needed. Pour the cream into a shallow stainless steel bowl and cover with cheesecloth. Place in a warm part of your kitchen to stand and ripen for 24 hours, then continue from step 3 to make the butter.

Clockwise from left: fines herbs compound butter, smoked sea salt compound butter, apple cider–maple compound butter

Compound Butters

Compound butters are creamed (by hand or in a food processor) with other ingredients such as finely minced shallots or herbs and then snugly rolled into a smooth log in plastic wrap and chilled to firm. This butter will keep refrigerated for up to 4 weeks, and can be kept frozen for up to 3 months. Consider both savory and sweet additives for your compound butters. Slice off a bit of savory version to add to sauces, place on a grilled steak, or toss into pastas. Sweet compound butters can top your pancakes, waffles, or a slice of grilled pound cake. It is lovely to have a little crunch from coarse or flaked salts (fleur de sel, Himalayan, Hawaiian) or sugars (raw turbinado, maple). Citrus zest, fresh herbs, minced garlic, grated horseradish, red pepper flakes, blue cheese, chèvre (in goat butter), and even a splash of wine, beer, or cider are all tried-and-true options. You can even cold-smoke butter (see page 57). Have fun with this!

Nonfat Greek-Style Yogurt

YIELD: 1½ pints
START TO FINISH: 1 hour cooking and setting +
5 to 8 hours ripening + 20 to 30 minutes draining

Greek-style yogurt is typically richer than plain whole milk yogurt due to the fat content of the milk used: either whole cow milk with half-and-half added or, in Greece, sheep milk. Due to the popularity of low or nonfat yogurts in the United States, I made this version with nonfat milk (it works with 1 percent and 2 percent milks, too). Powdered skim milk is added to make the yogurt thick and creamy. It can be left out if you like a softer yogurt. Bulgarian 411 culture (see page 89) contains some skim milk powder as well as the beneficial bacteria that turns milk into yogurt. You can also use a premade plain, unsweetened yogurt with live active cultures and no stabilizers as the starter. There are interesting heirloom strains of yogurt cultures (Matsoni and Filmjölk) available from Cultures for Health (see Resources, page 241), which create different styles of yogurt, made at 70°F to 77°F, similar to those for making crème fraîche. With these varieties you can develop mother cultures that can then be used to make unlimited batches of the same yogurt. Filmjölk can be used with alternative nondairy milks. Matsoni is great for making frozen yogurt.

1 quart pasteurized nonfat milk, at room temperature
3 tablespoons skim milk powder (optional)
1 teaspoon Bulgarian 411 yogurt starter culture, or ½ cup plain, unsweetened yogurt with active cultures

1. Sterilize a large pot, whisk, measuring cup, rubber spatula, ladle, mesh strainer, and container for storing the yogurt and allow to air-dry. Have an ice bath ready.

2. Place the milk in a stockpot, whisk in the skim milk powder (if using), and slowly heat the milk over medium-low heat until 180°F, about 30 minutes. Quickly chill the milk by placing the pot in the ice bath; whisk the milk to cool to 110°F to 115°F.

3. Remove about 1 cup milk, add the culture, and whisk to dissolve. Evenly distribute this milk back into the main pot and use an up-and-down motion with a whisk to incorporate.

4. Cover with a lid and then a terry towel; move to a warm location to prevent the temperature from going below 98°F. You can place the pot in a warm water bath to maintain the temperature (see page 91). Allow to ripen for 5 to 8 hours. A solid mass of curds will have formed. Note that if left to ripen too long, the curds will taste sour.

5. Line a mesh strainer with fine-weave cheesecloth, set over a bowl, and have ready. Gently stir with a rubber spatula for 20 seconds to slightly break up the mass of curds into large chunks. Cover and let set for 10 minutes. This step will release some of the whey.

6. Gently ladle the curds into the prepared strainer and allow them to drain for 20 to 30 minutes. Reserve the whey for other purposes, if you like, by refrigerating or freezing it.

7. Transfer the yogurt to a container, cover, and store refrigerated for up to 1 week. The yogurt will firm up when refrigerated.

Saffron Yogurt Cheese

YIELD: One 8-ounce round or two 4-ounce rounds
START TO FINISH: 5 minutes to combine + 8 hours or overnight to infuse + 8½ hours draining

Yogurt cheese is simple to make. By first infusing the yogurt with an aromatic, such as saffron or dried mint, before draining to become cheese, the dimensions of flavor are expanded. Here, the saffron threads give off some of their vibrant color and distinctive aroma to the yogurt, resulting in a golden-tinted spreadable cheese. For a richer flavor, use full-fat yogurt (though you could also use a nonfat yogurt like the recipe at left). For a real explosion of flavors, serve with Apricot-Date Chutney (page 50) and crackers. *See photo on page 51.*

2 cups plain Greek or European-style yogurt
20 saffron threads
1 teaspoon unrefined fine sea salt

1. Combine the yogurt, saffron, and salt in a bowl. Cover and refrigerate for 8 hours or overnight. Stir a few times over that time period to distribute the saffron, allowing it to bleed into the yogurt.

2. Place a strainer lined with dampened butter muslin or cheesecloth over a bowl deep enough to capture the draining whey (keep the strainer about 2 inches above the bottom of the bowl). Place the infused yogurt in the strainer and drain for 30 minutes and then tie the cheesecloth into a sack and hang (suspended by a long-handled spoon) to drain over a bucket or other food-grade container.

3. Cover the strainer with a clean kitchen towel and allow to drain for 8 hours or overnight at room temperature. Reserve any captured whey and refrigerate for future use.

4. Open the sack of drained yogurt (now cheese), and place the cheese into one or two small food-grade containers or into cheese molds to shape and contain.

5. Place the molds on a small plate to catch any additional draining whey, cover, and refrigerate until ready to use. Cheese will keep in refrigeration for up to 10 days. Bring it to room temperature before serving.

CLOTTED CREAM

YIELD: 4 to 6 ounces
START TO FINISH: 12 hours ripening at room temperature + 2 hours heating and holding + 12 hours up to 4 days refrigeration

A specialty curdled sweet cream from Devonshire, England, clotted cream (known also as Devon Cream) is a British teatime favorite used to top biscuits, scones, bread, or fruit. Though made in England with very rich raw whole cow milk, you can easily make it using good-quality pasteurized whole cow milk with the highest fat content available. The process is simple: high-fat milk is gently heated until a layer of cream forms on the surface. After cooling, the cream is removed and stored for up to 4 days. Use the widest skillet you have; it allows for more surface area on which the layer of cream can form.

2 quarts pasteurized, nonhomogenized whole cow milk, at room temperature

1.   Place the milk in a wide, nonreactive, straight-sided skillet or wide saucepan with a lid and cover with cheesecloth. Set aside in a warm spot (70°F to 72°F) for 12 hours to allow the lactic bacteria to develop.

2.   Over low heat, slowly warm the milk to 190°F (just under boiling). This should take about 20 to 25 minutes. You should see movement under the surface of the milk and tiny ripples on the surface. Do not boil the milk.

3.   Turn off the heat, cover with a lid, cover with a terry towel to help keep it warm, and hold for 1 hour at this temperature.

4.   Take off the covers and let cool, about 30 minutes. Once cool to the touch, place in the refrigerator until chilled.

5.   Skim off the cream that has formed on top. Keep the cream covered and chilled, for up to 4 days. Bring to room temperature before serving.

6.   The remaining milk, now skimmed of its cream, can be used for making Nonfat Greek-Style Yogurt (page 98) or Farmhouse Cream Cheese (page 102).

BASIC FRESH GOAT CHÈVRE

YIELD: 1½ pounds
START TO FINISH: 30 minutes cheese making + 12 hours ripening + 6 to 12 hours draining

Chèvre is the common name for spreadable goat cheese. It often has dried herbs or spices blended into or coating it. This version uses a premixed, premeasured blend of culture and rennet designed for making chèvre: C20G. This is the simplest method for any novice cheese maker and is a great entry point into making cultured cheeses.

1 gallon pasteurized goat milk, at room temperature for 1 hour
1 packet C20G direct-set mesophilic starter culture
1 teaspoon unrefined fine sea salt

1. In a nonreactive stockpot, gently heat the milk over low heat to 86°F. This should take 25 to 30 minutes. Turn off the heat.

2. Sprinkle the starter over the milk and let it rehydrate for 5 minutes. Whisk the starter into the milk, using an up-and-down motion to distribute thoroughly.

3. Cover and maintain a temperature of no lower than 72°F, allowing the milk to ripen for 12 hours. Wrap with a terry towel to keep warm. (Either ripen during the day to drain at night or ripen overnight to drain the next morning.)

4. The curds are ready when they have formed one large, solid mass in the pot with the consistency of thick yogurt, surrounded by clear whey.

5. Place a strainer over a bowl or plastic bucket large enough to capture the whey. Line the strainer with a single layer of dampened butter muslin or cheesecloth, leaving excess cloth hanging over the sides of the strainer. Gently ladle the curds into it. After draining for 5 minutes, gently toss the curds with the salt. Tie the corners of the cloth together to create a draining sack, slip a wooden spoon handle through the knot, and hang over a deep cooking pot or bucket to drain at room temperature (68°F to 72°F) for 6 to 12 hours (see Option). The longer the curds drain, the drier the finished cheese will be.

6. Remove the cheese from the cheesecloth or molds and store refrigerated in a covered container for up to 1 week.

Option: Rather than gravity draining in bulk in a sack, you can fill four chèvre molds that sit on a draining rack to drain for the same amount of time. Flip the curds once during the draining process.

Tip: If you want a soft, creamy consistency, drain for 6 or so hours. If you want to create a log of chèvre, let the curds drain for up to 12 hours so the cheese can be formed more easily and hold the desired shape. When adding dried herbs, mix in after salting and draining for 5 hours, and then continue to drain until the desired consistency is achieved.

Farmhouse Cream Cheese

YIELD: Approximately 1 pound
START TO FINISH: 30 minutes cheese making + 12 hours ripening + 6 to 8 hours draining

Real, homemade cream cheese is extraordinarily delicious. Most folks have no idea it can taste so good. Much of what is marketed as cream cheese in the United States is factory-made with curds that are heated to a high temperature, centrifuged to release whey, and then mixed with salt and various stabilizers to create a firm cheese that has an extended shelf life. That's not the real deal, but this one is. Once you make your own cream cheese, you'll never want store-bought again.

1 quart pasteurized whole, 2 percent, or 1 percent cow milk, at room temperature for 1 hour

1 quart pasteurized heavy cream, at room temperature for 1 hour

¼ teaspoon mesophilic starter (preferably MA 4001)

2 drops calcium chloride, diluted in 2 tablespoons cool nonchlorinated water

3 drops rennet, diluted in 2 tablespoons cool nonchlorinated water

1 teaspoon kosher salt (preferably Diamond Crystal)

1. Step up a water-bath system with nonreactive 4-quart and 6-quart pots (see page 91); warm the water to 80°F to 85°F.

2. In the 4-quart nonreactive pot, heat the milk to 75°F over low heat. This should take 10 to 15 minutes. Take off the heat.

3. Sprinkle the starter over the milk and let it hydrate for 5 minutes. Whisk the starter into the milk, using an up-and-down motion to distribute thoroughly. Add the diluted calcium chloride and gently whisk in, using an up-and-down motion, for 1 minute, then add the rennet in the same way.

4. Cover the smaller pot and take the entire water bath off heat. Leave at room temperature until the curds are firm, about 12 hours. The milk protein will coagulate into solid curds; the liquid whey will be almost clear and light green in color.

5. Line a strainer with dampened fine-weave butter muslin or cheesecloth, leaving excess cloth hanging over the sides of the strainer. Gently ladle the creamy curds into the prepared strainer. Tie the corners of the cloth together to create a draining sack, slip a wooden spoon handle through the knot, and hang over a deep cooking pot or bucket to drain until the desired consistency is achieved, 6 to 8 hours.

6. Remove the curds from the sack, place in a bowl, and toss with the salt. Stir or knead to combine. Form into a brick or roll into a log, wrap with plastic wrap or store in a covered container, and keep refrigerated for up to 2 weeks.

CRUMBLY FETA

YIELD: 1 pound
START TO FINISH: 3½ hours cheese making
+ 9 to 12 hours draining + 5 days salt curing + 21 to
30 days brining

Known for its crumbly texture and salty flavor, feta is great in salads where there is a presence of acidic tomatoes or lemony vinaigrette to balance its briny nature. Although often associated with Greece, many Balkan countries make it, too. It is traditionally made with sheep milk, goat milk, or a combination. This version is made with goat milk (though you can substitute cow or sheep milk) and a small amount of the enzyme lipase added to emulate the deepened flavor of sheep milk. I like to dry-salt this cheese for 5 days—this allows the expelling whey to create a natural brine.

2 (4-inch square) feta cheese molds or 2 plastic square
    mesh tomato baskets

1 gallon pasteurized whole goat milk
⅛ teaspoon mild lipase powder, dissolved in ¼ cup cool
    nonchlorinated water *20 minutes before using*
¼ teaspoon direct-set mesophilic starter (preferably
    MM 100 or MA 011)
¼ teaspoon liquid calcium chloride, diluted in ¼ cup cool
    nonchlorinated water
½ teaspoon liquid rennet, diluted in ¼ cup cool
    nonchlorinated water
2 to 4 tablespoons kosher or flake sea salt

BRINE

10 ounces kosher salt (preferably Diamond Crystal)
    dissolved in ½ gallon cool nonchlorinated water and
    chilled to 55°F (optional)

1. In a nonreactive stockpot, combine the milk and the diluted lipase. Gently heat over low heat to 86°F. This should take 25 to 30 minutes. Remove from the heat.

2. Sprinkle the starter over the milk and let it rehydrate for 2 minutes. Whisk the starter into the milk, using an up-and-down motion to distribute thoroughly. Cover, maintaining 86°F, and allow the milk to ripen for 1 hour.

3. Add the diluted calcium chloride and gently whisk in, using an up-and-down motion, for a few minutes, then add the rennet in the same way.

4. Cover and allow to sit at 86°F for 1 hour. The curds will be a sold mass at this point and the light yellow whey will float at the top. The curds should show a clean break when test-cut with a knife; if there is no clean break at this point, let the curds set for another 10 minutes, then test again.

5. Cut the curds into ½-inch cubes. Maintaining 86°F, allow to sit undisturbed for 10 minutes.

6. Using a flexible rubber spatula, gently stir the curds for 20 minutes, raising the temperature to 90°F. This action will release more whey and keep the curds from matting together. The curds will look more pillowlike in shape at the end of this process.

7. Let the curds rest for 5 minutes, undisturbed. They will settle to the bottom of the pot.

8. Line a strainer with dampened cheesecloth or butter muslin, leaving excess cloth hanging over the sides of the strainer. Using a slotted spoon, spoon the curds into the prepared strainer.

continued

9.   Tie the corners of the cloth together to create a draining sack, slip a wooden spoon handle through the knot, and hang over a deep cooking pot or bucket to drain for 10 minutes. Transfer the curds from the cheesecloth to a square feta cheese mold, press them into the corners, generously salt the surface, and allow to finish draining. After 1 hour, flip the cheese over, return to the mold, and generously salt the surface again. This will help even out the texture and firm the cheese. Cover the molds with cheesecloth and allow to drain at room temperature for 8 hours or overnight.

10.   Cut the cheese into slices that are 1¼ inches thick, and then cut again into cubes. Sprinkle the chunks with salt, making sure all the surfaces are covered. Loosely cover the bowl with a lid or plastic wrap and allow to age in the salt for 5 days in the refrigerator. The cheese can be covered with brine at this point for 21 to 30 days to further cure and add saltiness. If the finished cheese is too salty for your taste, set the cheese in nonchlorinated water for 1 hour then drain before using.

GOAT FETA MARINATED IN HERB OLIVE OIL

YIELD: 1 pint
START TO FINISH: 12 hours draining + 20 minutes to make + 1 to 2 hours setting + 1 week refrigeration

Marinating fresh, salty goat and sheep milk cheeses is common practice in the Mediterranean. This version has chunks of goat feta marinated in olive oil infused with some of the herbs and spices from the region: thyme, bay leaf, peppercorns, small hot chiles, and garlic cloves. You can feature other herbs and substitute walnut oil or smoked olive oil for the olive oil. Use on an antipasti plate, in salads, on pasta, or even on pizza. Definitely use the delicious flavored oil to drizzle or in a vinaigrette.

6½ to 7 ounces Crumbly Feta (page 105), cut or
    broken into ¾-inch chunks
4 cloves Fermented Garlic or Roasted Garlic (pages 75
    and 212)
3 whole dried red chiles
2 bay leaves
2 sprigs fresh thyme
⅛ teaspoon whole white peppercorns
5 or 6 whole pitted kalamata olives (optional)
1½ cups extra-virgin olive oil

1.   Drain the feta chunks on a paper towel overnight in the refrigerator to remove any excess brine. Layer the ingredients (except for the oil) in a sterilized pint jar, pack to fill in spaces. Pour in the olive oil, filling to ½ inch from the top of the jar, and cover tightly with a lid. Leave at room temperature for 1 to 2 hours and then refrigerate. The olive oil will preserve the

continued

Top row, from left: Scooping curds into cloth-lined strainer; draining curds in cloth-lined strainer; hanging curds to finish draining. Middle row: Placing drained sack of curds in mold. Bottom row: Distributing curds into mold.

cheese, add its own flavor, and carry the flavor of the herbs. Note that the olive oil will solidify in refrigeration but will return to liquid at room temperature.

2. Age for 1 week to allow the flavors to develop; best used within 4 weeks.

CRUMBLED FETA IN GRAPE LEAVES

YIELD: 2 cups
START TO FINISH: 30 minutes to make + 1 week refrigeration

Crumbled feta or leftover feta bits make a superb cheese-herb spread to be served separately, dolloped on grilled fish, used as the filling for stuffed chicken, or rolled in grape leaves that are then marinated. Cooked rice or sun-dried tomatoes can also be added to this mixture when used as a filling.

8 to 10 grape leaves (store-bought or fresh), fermented overnight in Basic Brine (page 13)

1/2 cup chopped fresh flat-leaf parsley

1/4 cup chopped fresh mint leaves

2 tablespoons chopped fresh oregano leaves

3 cloves fresh garlic or Fermented Garlic (page 75), minced

2 teaspoons grated lemon zest

Juice of 1 small lemon

1/2 teaspoon unrefined fine sea salt

1/4 teaspoon ground white pepper or red pepper flakes

6 ounces Crumbly Feta (page 105), drained and crumbled

1/4 cup goat yogurt (optional)

MARINADE

2 bay leaves

2 sprigs fresh thyme

4 cloves Fermented Garlic or Roasted Garlic (pages 75 and 212)

3 whole dried red chiles

1/8 teaspoon whole white peppercorns

About 1 1/2 cups extra-virgin olive oil

1. Rinse the grape leaves and pat dry.

2. In a bowl, combine the parsley, mint, oregano, garlic, lemon zest, lemon juice, salt, pepper, and feta. Add the yogurt, if using (it will add a creamy texture). Adjust salt and pepper as needed.

3. Lay out the grape leaves on a baking sheet. Place 1 1/2 tablespoons or so of the feta mixture in the center of each leaf, fold the sides in over the filling, and roll up to enclose.

4. Place the rolls in a sterilized wide-mouth pint jar, standing up to fill. Tuck in the bay leaves, thyme sprigs, and the other marinade ingredients and cover with the olive oil, filling to 1/2 inch from the top of the jar. Cover tightly with a lid and refrigerate. The olive oil will preserve, add its own flavor, and carry the flavor of the herbs. Note that the olive oil will solidify in refrigeration but will return to liquid at room temperature. Age for 1 week to allow the flavors to develop; best used within 4 weeks.

WILD AND CREAMY MUENSTER

YIELD: Three 7-ounce cheeses
START TO FINISH: 2 hours cheese making + 24 hours draining + 2 days ripening + 14 days to 3 months aging

Muenster is a washed-rind cheese originating in Alsace (where it is spelled Munster). Much of this cheese we see at retail in the United States is a mere shadow of the real deal. This version is inspired by the notable triple-crème Red Hawk, created by Cowgirl Creamery. As with many artisanal cheeses, Cowgirl cheeses are greatly influenced by their Northern California coastal terroir. Washed rind cheeses (often affectionately called "the stinkers") can be washed with a number of different ingredients, including a brine or bacterial solution (as here), buttermilk, or alcohol such as beer, wine, brandy, cider, or whiskey.

In this recipe, the stage of ripening the curds at room temperature allows some wild yeast from the environment to influence the final cheese. If you don't have homemade crème fraîche (page 95) available, a high-quality, store-bought cultured one (such as from Bellwether Farms or Kendall Farms) can be used. *See photo on page 115.*

3 round Saint-Marcellin molds (3½ inches diameter by 3½ inches high)

½ cup cool nonchlorinated water
1⅓ teaspoons unrefined fine sea salt
Brevibacterium linens powder
14 cups (3½ quarts) pasteurized whole cow milk
2 cups cultured Crème Fraîche (page 95)
⅛ teaspoon mesophilic starter culture (preferably MA 011)

¼ teaspoon calcium chloride, diluted in ¼ cup cool nonchlorinated water
¼ teaspoon animal or veal rennet, diluted in ¼ cup cool nonchlorinated water

BRINE SOLUTION FOR WASHING

1½ teaspoons kosher salt (preferably Diamond Crystal) dissolved in 1 cup nonchlorinated water, cooled to 50°F to 55°F

1.   Twelve hours before starting, combine ½ cup cool nonchlorinated water and 1 teaspoon salt in a jar and mix to dissolve. Add a pinch of *B. linens* powder, cover tightly with a lid, and agitate for 5 seconds to combine. Remove the lid and cover the jar opening with cheesecloth; secure with a rubber band. Set aside at room temperature to rehydrate and activate the bacteria. Store at 50°F to 55°F.

2.   In a nonreactive stockpot, combine the milk and crème fraîche and gently heat over low heat to 90°F. This should take about 30 minutes. Remove from the heat.

3.   Sprinkle the starter culture, followed by a pinch of *B. linens* powder, over the milk mixture and let rehydrate for 5 minutes. Whisk the starter into the milk, using an up-and-down motion to distribute thoroughly.

4.   Cover the pot and maintain 90°F, letting the milk ripen for 30 minutes.

5.   Add the diluted calcium chloride and mix in, using the same up-and-down motion. Gently mix in the rennet in the same way.

continued

6. Cover and, maintaining a temperature of 90°F, ripen until you have a clean break, about 40 minutes. If not clean, wait 10 minutes more and test again.

7. Cut into ½-inch cubes, then cover and rest for 30 minutes.

8. Set a draining rack over a tray, and place the Saint-Marcellin molds on the rack.

9. Line a strainer with dampened butter muslin or fine-weave cheesecloth set over a large pot. Ladle the curds into the prepared strainer and drain for 10 minutes, then gently spoon the curds into the cheese molds.

10. Cover the molds lightly with cheesecloth (not a lid), and let them drain at room temperature for 12 hours. Flip the cheese after 12 hours, and return to the molds to drain for another 12 hours (24 hours total). Remove the whey that collects as needed.

11. Remove the cheeses from the molds onto the rack and salt each cheese with ¼ teaspoon unrefined fine sea salt. Place on a mat in a ripening box (see page 94). Ripen at 55°F and 85 percent relative humidity, turning daily until no more whey is released, usually 2 days.

12. On the third (following) day, apply the *B. linens* bacterial wash on all surfaces, using a small piece of cheesecloth dipped in the solution. Place the cheese back in the ripening box, on a clean mat. Discard the cloth. Unused *B. linens* wash can be stored in a jar in the refrigerator for future use.

13. Two days after the first wash with the *B. linens* bacterial wash, to aid rind formation and bacteria activation, wash the cheeses with cheesecloth dipped in the brine solution and rung dry.

14. Continue to wash with the brine solution and turn the cheese every other day for 2 weeks. After 10 to 12 days, the surface will have developed an orange coating from the *B. linens*. The surface should be soft and moist, but not sticky.

15. The cheese can be ready at 14 days. Wrap in cheese paper at this point and refrigerate. Consume within 4 weeks from the beginning of the ripening stage, or age up to 3 months.

COASTAL BREEZE

YIELD: Two 4-inch rounds
START TO FINISH: 30 minutes cheese making + 12 to
18 hours ripening + 4 hours initial draining + 48 hours final
draining + 3 weeks aging

This ash-coated bloomy rind goat cheese was inspired
by Cypress Grove's signature Humboldt Fog and Blue
Ledge Farm's Lake's Edge. The line of ash through the
middle defines where the separately ripened curds
joined to become the finished cheese. I've added a
pinch of *Penicillium roqueforti* for just a hint of blue
tang without visible blue mold. Lightly gray on the
bloomy surface due to the vegetable ash peeking
through the *Penicillium candidum* bloom, this cheese is
firm in the interior, yet creamy or even oozy just under
the thin edible rind. It is aged for only a few weeks,
making it a cheese you'll want to craft on a regular
basis.

4 mini Camembert cheese molds (3.9 inches top by
    3.6 inches base by 3 inches high with bottom)
Disposable gloves, for applying ash

1 gallon pasteurized goat milk
¼ teaspoon Meso I or Aroma B mesophilic starter culture
1/16 teaspoon *Penicillium candidum* mold powder
1/16 teaspoon *Geotrichum candidum* 17 mold powder
Tiny pinch of *Penicillium roqueforti* mold powder
¼ teaspoon calcium chloride, diluted in ¼ cup cool
    nonchlorinated water
¼ teaspoon liquid rennet, diluted in ¼ cup cool
    nonchlorinated water
1 teaspoon unrefined fine sea salt
⅛ cup vegetable ash powder (see Resources, page 241)
    mixed with 1 teaspoon fine sea salt

1. In a nonreactive stockpot, gently heat the milk
over low heat to 72°F. This should take 15 to 20 minutes. Take off the heat.

2. Sprinkle the starter culture and the mold powders
over the milk and let rehydrate for 5 minutes. Whisk
the starter and mold powders into the milk, using an
up-and-down motion to distribute thoroughly.

3. Cover the pot and maintain 72°F, letting the milk
ripen for 30 minutes.

4. Gently add the dissolved calcium chloride with
a whisk using an up-and-down motion for 1 minute,
then add the rennet in the same way. Cover, maintaining 72°F, and ripen until the curds are a firm, solid
mass and clear whey is floating around the sides, 12 to
18 hours.

5. Prepare a draining box with a rack and the Camembert cheese molds (see page 94).

6. Ladle thin slices of the curds into the molds in the
draining box to fill each equally. Remove the captured whey as you go. Let the curds drain to half the
amount (about 4 hours) and then salt the top of each
with a pinch of unrefined fine sea salt.

7. Wearing disposable gloves and using a fine-mesh
strainer, dust the tops of two of the cheeses with a
thin layer of the salted vegetable ash, covering to just
inside the edge. You will not need all of the ash mixture for this step. Gently pat the ash into the curds.

8. Carefully flip the remaining two molds of curds
on the tops of the two ash-covered ones, creating a
sandwich. Gently pat the curds down into the mold to
remove any spaces.

continued

9. Cover the molds with cheesecloth and let the cheese drain for 48 hours at room temperature. Remove any collected whey a few times while draining. Wipe out the draining box with a paper towel each time you drain it of excess whey.

10. Flip the cheeses in their molds when they are firm enough to handle, after about 12 hours, then twice more during the remaining 36 hours. This will aid in a uniform formation of the cheeses and the development of the bacteria. Once the cheese has stopped draining and the curds have compressed to below the halfway point of the mold, remove the molds.

11. Again wearing disposable gloves and using a mesh strainer, dust the top, bottom, and sides of the cheeses with vegetable ash, coating lightly but completely. Gently pat the ash into the surfaces.

12. Place the cheeses at least 1 inch apart on a clean mat in the ripening box. Cover with cheesecloth and let stand at room temperature for 24 hours to start the bacterial action. Drain and wipe out any moisture from the box, cover with the lid, and then ripen at 50°F to 55°F and 85 percent humidity for 3 weeks. For the first few days, adjust the lid to be slightly open for a portion of each day to maintain the desired humidity level. Too much humidity will create an undesirable wet surface and a wrinkly rind. The surface of the cheese should appear moist but not wet. Pay attention to any moisture that may collect on the draining rack. Moisture has to be allowed to drain for the cheese to ripen properly.

13. Continue to turn the cheeses daily. After about 5 days, the first signs of white fuzzy mold will appear through the ash. After 10 to 14 days, the cheese will be fully coated in white mold. As it continues to age, the surface will turn a very light gray from the combination of ash and *P. candidum*. Wrap in cheese paper and return to the ripening box. The cheese will begin to soften within a week or so. After a total of 2 weeks from the start of ripening, store the cheeses in the refrigerator.

14. Consume within 2 weeks of storing.

BLUE-EYED JACK CHEESE

YIELD: Two 1-pound cheeses or one 2-pound cheese
START TO FINISH: 4 hours cheese making + 8 hours pressing + 12 hours drying + 2 months aging

Jack cheese is an American original. It's moist, creamy, and very versatile. Recipes for making delicious plain Jacks can be found in *Artisan Cheese Making at Home*. There are also a few Jack-style cheeses from notable cheese makers with just a bit of blue in the crevices. That small amount of tangy blue mold in contrast to the mild paste makes for a subtle, but delicious, lightly flavored blue. To make my blue version, *Penicillum roqueforti* mold is added between layers of curds before pressing in a cheese mold. As an alternative, the cheese can be pressed in its cheesecloth sack. By pressing with only 2 pounds of weight, some desirable small crevices are left in the pressed curds for the blue mold to develop. No piercing, as is the practice with many blue cheeses, is needed.

2 (4½-inch) hard cheese molds with followers, or 1 (7-inch) tomme mold with follower
2 (2-pound) bricks

2 gallons pasteurized whole cow milk
½ teaspoon MA 4001 Farmhouse starter culture
½ teaspoon calcium chloride, diluted in ¼ cup cool nonchlorinated water
½ teaspoon liquid rennet, diluted in ¼ cup cool nonchlorinated water
2½ tablespoons kosher salt (preferably Diamond Crystal)
⅛ teaspoon *Penicillium roqueforti* mold powder
½ teaspoon kosher salt, dissolved in 1 tablespoon cool nonchlorinated water

1. In a nonreactive stockpot, gently heat the milk over low heat to 86°F, 25 to 30 minutes. Remove from the heat.

2. Sprinkle the starter over the milk and let rehydrate for 5 minutes. Whisk the starter into the milk, using an up-and-down motion, to distribute thoroughly.

3. Cover, maintaining 86°F, to ripen the milk for 1 hour.

4. Add the dissolved calcium chloride and gently whisk in, using an up-and-down motion, for 1 minute, then add the rennet in the same way.

5. Cover and let set at 86°F, until the curds give a clean break when cut with a knife, 30 to 45 minutes. If no clean break, wait a few minutes more.

6. While maintaining 86°F, cut the curds into ¾-inch cubes and let set for 5 minutes.

continued

Clockwise from top: Wild and Creamy Muenster, Blue-Eyed Jack Cheese, Tomme-Style Table Cheese

7.   Over low heat, bring the curds to 102°F, increasing the temperature slowly over a 40-minute period. Using a rubber spatula, gently stir continuously to keep curds from matting together. The curds will be releasing whey, firming up slightly, and shrinking to the size of a small dried bean.

8.   Once the desired temperature has been reached, remove from heat and let the curds rest undisturbed for 30 minutes. They will sink to the bottom and the whey will cover them.

9.   Set up the draining box and cheese molds lined with dampened cheesecloth.

10.   Using a measuring cup or ladle, remove enough whey to expose the curds. Using a rubber spatula, gently stir continuously until the curds are matted and cling together when a small sample is pressed in your hand, about 15 minutes. Ladle out half of the remaining whey. Gently toss in 1 1/2 tablespoons of the salt with your hands and mix thoroughly. Allow the curds to rest for 5 minutes to absorb some of the salt.

11.   Working quickly, while the curds are still slightly warm, ladle one-third of the curds into each of the cheesecloth-lined molds (or the one larger mold). Using the back of your hand, gently press the curds evenly into the molds, so they take the shape of the mold. Sprinkle with half of the *P. roqueforti* mold powder, then top with another one-third of the curds and lightly press again in the same fashion. Sprinkle the remaining *P. roqueforti* mold powder over the top and cover with the last of the curds. Press again, smooth out any wrinkles in the cloth, and then draw up one of the tails to cover the top of the curds. Place the followers on top and apply the weight.

12.   Press with 2 pounds of weight for 8 hours at 70°F to 72°F. After 4 hours, remove the cheesecloth, flip the cheese, return to the mold(s), apply the follower, and continue with the same weight for the remaining 4 hours. It is important to leave some small crevices in the pressed curds as places for the blue mold to develop.

13.   Remove the cheeses from the molds, dry-rub the entire surface with the remaining 1 tablespoon of salt, and place back on the draining rack to air-dry. Lightly cover with dry cheesecloth and let air-dry at room temperature until the surface is dry to the touch, about 12 hours. Turn once during this drying stage for even removal of moisture.

14.   Place the cheese in a ripening box, at 50°F to 55°F in 85 percent relative humidity for 1 week, turning the cheese daily for even ripening. Open the box once daily for 1 hour at a time so the cheese can breathe. Rub off any undesirable surface mold with a piece of cheesecloth dipped in the salt water and rung dry. Remove any excess moisture that may collect in the box or on the cheese. Desirable blue mold should start to peak through the crevices in 8 to 10 days.

15.   Continue to ripen at 50°F to 55°F and 90 percent relative humidity until the desired ripeness is reached, 2 months or longer. Vacuum-seal or wrap well in aluminum foil and refrigerate until ready to eat. Cheese is ready to consume at 2 months.

Whey-Based Sauces

The whey is the liquid part of the milk left after making curds, the part that is not cheese. This leftover has lots of flavor and can make amazing pan sauces without much effort. Think of whey as a stock that has acidity and some sweetness from the lactose it contains. Whey used to cook a starch such as potatoes or rice will function as a thickener, similar to what is known in classical cooking as a "blond roux." The flavors of whey vary, so taste it and decide if it is one you'd enjoy using as a sauce ingredient. The easiest to cook with come from direct-acid cheeses (such as ricotta, mascarpone, panir) or cultured dairy and cheeses (such as those presented in this chapter) that do not contain a secondary culture or mold (such as *P. candidum* in bloomy-rind cheeses, or *P. roqueforti* in blues). Remember to refrigerate fresh whey within a few hours. If not using within a day, portion and freeze. A basic method for making these sauces follows.

Sauté minced shallots or onions in a small amount of butter. Add about 1 cup heated whey and aromatics such as peppercorns or bay leaves. Over medium-high heat, reduce by about half. Stir in minced fresh herbs, if you like, and salt and white pepper to taste. Whisk in some chilled butter, add a splash of lemon juice or white wine (flavored vinegars work, too), heat through, and serve.

See Potato-Herb Gnocchi with Creamy Whey Reduction Sauce (page 207) for more information.

Tomme-Style Table Cheese

YIELD: One 1½-pound wheel
START TO FINISH: 3 hours cheese making + 3 hours pressing + 5 to 6 hours ripening + 4 to 5 months aging

The masterful cheese maker Kuba Hemmerling of Point Reyes Farmstead Cheese Company, located north of San Francisco in Marin County, contributed this recipe. The Giacomini dairy family started Point Reyes Farmstead by making Original Blue. Now they are firmly committed to making other delectable farmstead cheeses, some blue, some not, but all from the gorgeous milk of their happy coastal cows. This cheese, inspired by their Toma, is a smooth, tomme-style, "everyday" cheese. The steps to make this cheese are easy, but the management of the cheese takes a certain amount of cheese-making skills, equipment, and a proper aging environment, making it the most advanced cheese in this book. For those wanting to make a distinctive aged cheese, the results are well worth the time and patience required. You can double this recipe and use a larger mold if desired. In that case, aging needs to be increased to 7 months. *See photo on page 115.*

1 large tomme mold with bottom and follower
pH meter
Weights

2½ gallons pasteurized whole cow milk
¼ teaspoon mesophilic starter culture (preferably MM 100)
¼ teaspoon thermophilic starter culture (preferably Thermo A)
⅛ teaspoon thermophilic starter culture (preferably Thermo C)
¼ teaspoon calcium chloride, diluted in ¼ cup cool nonchlorinated water
⅛ teaspoon double-strength animal rennet, diluted in ¼ cup cool nonchlorinated water

NEAR-SATURATED BRINE
28 ounces kosher salt (preferably Diamond Crystal) dissolved in 1 gallon cool nonchlorinated water

1. Using the water-bath method (see page 91), gently heat the milk to 88°F. This should take about 20 minutes. Remove from the heat.

2. Sprinkle the starter cultures, one by one, over the milk and let them rehydrate for 5 minutes. Whisk the cultures into the milk, using an up-and-down motion to distribute thoroughly. Cover and ripen for 50 minutes. Add the dissolved calcium chloride and gently whisk in, using an up-and-down motion, for 1 minute, then add the rennet in the same way.

3. Cover, maintaining a temperature of 88°F, and ripen until you have a clean break, 30 to 40 minutes. If not clean, wait 10 minutes more and test again.

4. Cut into ½-inch cubes, cover, and rest for 3 minutes. Using a whisk, cut the curds again into smaller (¼-inch) pieces and stir for 5 minutes.

5. Start heating (cooking process) the curds to 98°F. Increase the temperature slowly, 1°F every 2 minutes. Agitation during cooking should be gentle until the temperature reaches 95°F; from that point, agitation can be more vigorous. Hold at this temperature for 15 minutes while agitating.

6. Allow the curds to rest for 10 minutes and then start draining off the whey, using a ladle, to expose the curds.

7. Gently fill the cheese mold. Apply the follower and press the cheese for 3 hours. During the first hour, press with twice the weight of the cheese. After 1 hour, turn the cheese in the form and increase the press to four times the weight of the cheese, for another 2 hours.

8. Remove the weight, and let the cheese ripen overnight at room temperature. The next day the curds should have a pH of 5.2 to 5.4 before placing the cheese in the brine.

9. Remove the cheese from the mold and soak the cheese in the near-saturated brine at 50°F to 55°F for 5 to 6 hours.

10. Remove the cheese from the brine, pat dry, and place on a mat in its ripening box (see page 94). Place in its aging environment at 53°F and 86 to 90 percent relative humidity for 4 months. During aging, the cheese needs to be turned and cleaned at least twice a week to prevent rind damage. The cheese is ready to eat at 4 to 5 months.

Two Favorite Ferments: Cheese + Beer = Beer Cheese

I find regional Americana food fun and inspirational. Beer cheese, a spreadable concoction of grated (often sharp) Cheddar and beer (lager or ale) blended together, dates back to the 1940s in Winchester, Kentucky. Many believe it was first made for Johnny Allman's restaurants along the Kentucky River by his cousin, Joe Allman. The spread was presented when you sat down—even before drinks came—to be slathered on carrot sticks, celery stalks, or crackers. Because it was complimentary, people often consumed a fair amount of it before dinner, on occasion even making it their whole meal—for just the cost of a few beers.

Like many regional specialties, recipes abound from cooks claiming to have the best or most authentic version. Regional claims of origin fly around as well. Did the beer come from Kentucky? Was the cheese from Wisconsin? It is still served in restaurants, at picnics, Derby parties, tailgates, and just about any place people gather in the region. Beer cheese is so adored that there is even an annual festival held in Winchester in its honor, the Beer Cheese Festival (www.beercheesefestival.com).

As a cook, I consider beer cheese sort of a cheese version of compound butter. Why not try combining a regional cheese and beer from your part of the world? From my location (Northern California), I love the combination of Point Reyes Farmstead Toma (or homemade tomme, page 118) with Hop Stoopid Ale (page 188) from Lagunitas Brewing Company. It's a heavenly match.

Here's how I make my beer cheese (you can adjust as you like, just be sure to make it 2 days before you plan to serve it): Combine 1 ounce of beer and 1 pound coarsely grated firm or semihard cheese in a food processor; add another 1 to 2 ounces of beer if needed to make a spreadable cheese (be careful—you don't want to add so much that you end up with a dip). Add a pinch of cayenne, mustard powder, or garlic powder, and perhaps a little pureed garlic or a splash of Worcestershire. Don't overdo the spices. Maybe you don't need any at all. You want to taste the cheese in the end product. Refrigerate for 2 days and up to 3 months and then bring to room temperature before serving.

CHAPTER 6

FERMENTED GRAINS, BREADS, AND FLATBREADS: Wild Yeast, Leavened, and Sprouted Grains

WITH SO MANY DELICIOUS, INSPIRING BREADS and flatbreads from around the world, this category could have been a book unto itself. This chapter, however, is meant to be a sampler. The recipes here span an assortment of styles and flavors to entice and encourage you to find and fuel your inner baker.

The yeasted breads use fermented ingredients such as whey, buttermilk, yogurt, cornmeal, rice, or sprouted grains; the sourdoughs are wild yeast breads with the doughs themselves fermented. Some of the flatbreads are wheat free and gluten free. Some of the recipes use measurements by weight (the most accurate system, used by professionals), while others are in standard volumetric measurements. A digital kitchen scale with multiple systems of measurement, and a low ($1/8$ ounce) to high (up to 5 pounds, at least) range is a valuable tool in all kitchens.

In chapter 9, there are additional flatbread and sourdough recipes to enjoy: Falafel-Stuffed Whey Flatbread (page 203), Grilled Yogurt Naan (page 205), and Chocolate Sourdough Cupcakes (page 224).

SOURED CORNBREAD

YIELD: One 10-inch cornbread
START TO FINISH: 24 hours making lime water + 7 hours soaking + 17 to 23 hours fermenting + 10 minutes mixing + 50 to 55 minutes baking + 20 to 30 minutes resting

I have fond childhood memories of eating corn when I visited my grandparents in Nebraska each summer. This cornbread revives those flavor memories because I can *taste* the corn. Though this recipe requires a bit of planning, the results are aromatic, slightly chewy, and moist. Soaking the cornmeal in lime water releases nutrients, starts enzymatic action, and enhances flavor. Fashioned after recipes of times gone by, where milk was left out to sour (ferment) before being added to the batter, here buttermilk is the main activator and tenderizer. The batter is also left out at room temperature to ferment a bit before the final incorporation of ingredients. Pickling lime is available from Cultures for Health (see Resources, page 241).

LIME WATER

1/3 cup powdered pickling lime
4 cups filtered water

CORNBREAD

2 cups stone-ground medium-grind cornmeal
1 cup cultured buttermilk (see page 96, or store-bought) or yogurt
1 cup unbleached all-purpose flour
3 large eggs, lightly beaten
1/3 cup raw, unfiltered honey or agave syrup
1 1/4 teaspoons unrefined fine sea salt
2 teaspoons baking soda
1/4 cup melted unsalted butter, plus 1 tablespoon for the pan

1. To make the lime water: In a quart jar with lid, dissolve the powdered pickling lime in the filtered water; set in a cool place to settle for 24 hours before using. The clear liquid is the lime water to use for the bread.

2. To make the bread: Soak the cornmeal in 1 1/2 cups lime water for 7 hours. Add the buttermilk, cover, and ferment at 70°F to 72°F for 5 hours. Stir in the flour, cover, and ferment further at 70°F to 72°F for 12 to 18 hours.

3. Preheat the oven to 325°F. Set a dry 10-inch cast-iron skillet in the oven to heat it.

4. In a small bowl, whisk together the eggs and honey. To the flour batter, mix in the salt and baking soda. Mix in the egg mixture and then the 1/4 cup melted butter.

5. Carefully (it's hot!), remove the hot skillet from the oven, quickly coat with the 1 tablespoon remaining butter, and pour in the batter.

6. Bake until the bread is a deep golden brown and a toothpick inserted in the center comes out clean, 50 to 55 minutes. Though hard to resist, cool for 20 to 30 minutes before cutting. It will taste best then.

Sprouted Corn Tortillas

YIELD: 12 tortillas
START TO FINISH: 7 to 12 hours soaking + 15 minutes mixing + 1 hour resting + 20 minutes shaping + 20 minutes cooking

Tortillas, perhaps the most cherished food in Mexico, are made with different grains and grinds of flours—primarily corn and wheat. Traditionally, corn tortillas are made with masa harina—flour made from lime-soaked corn kernels that are drained, dried, and ground into a fine meal. The lime-soaking releases the corn's nutrients, making it more flavorful and nutritious. In place of masa harina, I use readily available stoneground fine-grind cornmeal and soak it in a pickling lime (food-grade calcium hydroxide powder) solution for 7 hours. For more texture I've added sprouted corn kernels that are soaked in filtered water overnight and then pulverized into medium-grind meal the following day (see page 6 for more on the benefits of sprouting). You can replace the sprouted corn with fine cornmeal for a smoother texture. Sprouted grains and pickling lime are available from Cultures for Health (see Resources, page 241).

½ cup sprouted corn kernels, soaked in filtered water overnight

2 cups fine cornmeal, soaked in 2 cups lime water (see opposite) for 7 hours and drained

1 teaspoon unrefined fine sea salt

4 tablespoons cold-pressed corn oil, plus more for the pan

Cool filtered water, as needed

1. Drain the soaked corn, place in a food processor or blender, and pulverize into a medium-grind meal. Pulse in the cornmeal and salt, and then drizzle in the oil to combine. Drizzle in a small amount of water, if needed, to make a stiff, smooth dough. Cover and let the dough rest at room temperature for 1 hour to allow the corn to hydrate slightly. Portion into golf ball-size pieces (about 2 tablespoons each).

2. Heat a cast-iron skillet, griddle, or Mexican comal over medium-high heat.

3. Have a cloth-lined basket or a towel ready to keep the tortillas warm for serving.

4. Lightly oil the skillet. One by one, press each ball of dough in a tortilla press or roll out to ⅛ inch thick between two sheets of plastic wrap. Immediately place the shaped tortilla in the hot skillet and cook until it begins to brown and blister on the bottom, about 5 minutes. Flip and cook the other side to the same color.

5. Place the finished tortillas in the basket or towel, and wrap to keep warm until all are made. Serve warm.

GRILLED BUTTERMILK–BLACK BEAN FLATBREAD

YIELD: 6 small flatbreads
START TO FINISH: 20 minutes to make dough +
1½ hours first rise + 20 minutes to make filling + 30
minutes second rise + 20 minutes shaping + 20 minutes
grilling

This is my favorite rustic bean flatbread, especially when topped with Slow-Roasted Pork in Adobo (page 219) and a dollop of Sweet Tomato-Jalapeño Salsa (page 49). It is slightly chunky, dotted with black beans and tomato bits. You can replace the black bean flour with white bean flour or try a version with garbanzo bean (chickpea) flour in combination with cooked chickpeas instead of black beans. The buttermilk powder acts as a culturing agent and tenderizer. You can use liquid buttermilk to replace some of the water, but I like powdered buttermilk because it is made from real cultured buttermilk—the by-product of cultured butter. If you make your own cultured butter (page 96), by all means use your own buttermilk here. Bean flours and buttermilk powder are available in many natural foods stores or online from Bob's Red Mill (see Resources, page 241). You can use canned or dried black beans for the filling. *See photo on page 218.*

DOUGH

1 tablespoon raw, unfiltered honey

1½ cups warm water, or more as needed

2 teaspoons active dry yeast

3½ cups unbleached all-purpose flour

½ cup black bean flour

4 tablespoons dry buttermilk powder

1½ teaspoons unrefined fine sea salt

BLACK BEAN FILLING

1 teaspoon cumin seeds

2 teaspoons coriander seeds

1 teaspoon unrefined coarse sea salt

¼ cup sun-dried tomato tapenade

1¼ cups cooked black beans, drained and mashed

About ¼ cup olive oil, for brushing

Canola oil, for brushing the grill

1.   To make the dough: In a bowl, dissolve the honey in 1½ cups of the warm water. With a stand mixer fitted with the dough hook attachment, mix the yeast, flours, and buttermilk powder on low speed for 2 minutes. With the mixer running, gradually add in the honey-water mixture. Increase the speed to medium and mix for 5 minutes, and then return to low speed for another 2 minutes (this starts the creation of gluten, which will add structure to the final dough). Add up to ⅓ cup more water, as needed, to make dough that pulls away from the walls of the mixer bowl and is smooth yet slightly tacky to the touch. (The ambient humidity will affect how much water is needed.) Let the dough rest in the mixer bowl for 5 minutes. Then beat the dough on medium-high speed for another 3 minutes, adding in the salt and letting the dough vigorously slap against the sides of the bowl, creating more gluten and structure to the dough. Lightly oil a large bowl.

2. Place the dough in the oiled bowl and turn to coat in the oil. Cover with a damp cloth or plastic wrap and let the dough rise in a warm place until doubled in bulk, about 1½ hours. Note: For additional flavor, put the dough in a sealed container and let it bulk-ferment overnight in the refrigerator. Allow the dough to come to room temperature for about 1 hour (or more) before gently folding the dough and forming into a ball.

3. To make the black bean filling: Toast the cumin and coriander seeds in a small cast-iron skillet over medium-high heat. Combine the seeds and the coarse sea salt and coarsely grind them using a mortar and pestle or minichop. In a bowl, combine the tomato tapenade, mashed beans, and the seed-salt mixture. Set aside.

4. To assemble the flatbread: Turn the dough out onto a floured work surface. Gently pull the dough to create a rectangular surface for the bean mixture. Spoon the bean mixture evenly across the top of the dough and gently press into the dough. Fold the dough into thirds lengthwise, then fold again in thirds widthwise. Using a bench scraper or a sharp knife, cut the dough into 6 equal pieces and form each into a ball. Some of the beans will peak through the dough.

5. Gently roll the ball on the floured work surface, then set each ball, belly-button side down, on a well-floured baking sheet and lightly brush or spray each top with olive oil. Cover loosely with a towel or plastic wrap and let rise for 30 minutes to relax the dough. (Refrigerate if not using within 1 hour, or place each ball of dough in an oiled self-sealing plastic bag and refrigerate for up to 2 days, or freeze for up to 1 month. Let the refrigerated dough stand at room temperature for 1 hour before using. Thaw frozen dough in the bag at room temperature until the dough warms up and has almost doubled in size.)

6. To grill the flatbreads: While the dough is resting, preheat a wood-fired grill (using lump or hardwood charcoal) or gas grill to medium-high heat (450°F) for about 45 minutes before you are ready to grill the flatbreads. Lightly oil the grill surface with canola oil to prevent sticking

7. If using a cast-iron grill pan (indoors or inside a wood-fired oven), preheat 30 minutes before grilling time. Lightly oil the grill surface just before ready to use.

8. When the dough is ready, form the flatbreads. On a lightly floured surface, press and stretch each ball of dough with your fingertips and heel of your hand to flatten, forming 6 discs that are about ¼ inch thick and 6 inches in diameter each. Place the flatbreads on the backs of baking sheets and lightly brush the tops of the dough with olive oil.

9. Have the baking sheet with the flatbreads directly next to the grill. Moving quickly, gently pick up each flatbread from the baking sheet and flip it over, and place it oiled-side down over direct heat on the grill. Close the lid and cook until the breads puff up, about 5 to 7 minutes. Check the cooked side for good grill marks on the bottom. Flip the flatbread over and move onto indirect heat. Close the lid and cook until the bottom has good grill marks. Remove from the grill, place on a cutting board, and let cool for 5 minutes.

10. Cut into wedges and serve warm.

Sprouted Lentil Dosas

YIELD: 8 to 10 dosas
START TO FINISH: 6 to 12 hours soaking + 20 minutes blending + 12 hours fermenting + 20 minutes mixing + 20 minutes cooking

Dosas are Indian crepes or thin pancakes made with fermented lentils and basmati rice, served with a variety of fillings or sides. These have a slightly chunky texture due to the added mashed sprouted lentils. Another tasty additive is sprouted fenugreek. Don't skip the spiral movement used to smear the batter in the pan: it's a defining characteristic of a dosa.

½ cup red lentils (massor dal) or white lentils (urad dal)

1 cup basmati rice

Filtered water

1¼ teaspoons unrefined fine sea salt

1 teaspoon ground cumin

¼ cup dried brown lentils, sprouted and mashed (see page 7)

¼ cup clarified unsalted butter or ghee, for brushing the pan (see opposite)

1. In separate bowls, soak the red lentils and the rice in filtered water to cover by 1 inch for 6 hours or overnight. Drain the lentils, place in a blender along with 1 tablespoon or so of water—just enough to be able to puree it to a smooth consistency. Transfer to a bowl. Repeat the process with the rice. Combine the lentils and rice, cover with plastic wrap and then a terry towel, and place under the hood light of a stove or in another warm spot where you would proof bread dough. Allow to ferment overnight.

2. Stir in the salt, cumin, and mashed, sprouted dried brown lentils. Add more water (up to 1½ cups) to thin the batter to the consistency it was before fermenting.

3. Heat a 10-inch crepe pan, flared-sided omelet pan, or flat cast-iron griddle over medium-high heat. Once the surface is very hot, brush with some clarified butter and ladle about 3 ounces (slightly less than ¼ cup) of batter into the pan. Using the back of the ladle, smear the batter around in a spiral pattern to cover the bottom of the pan. Cook until the edges start to look dry and air holes appear on the surface. Using an offset spatula, check the underside of the pancake for a golden color and doneness. Flip the pancake over and cook until the underside is golden, about 30 seconds. Remove from the pan and set aside on a plate. Repeat until all the batter is used, stacking the dosas as you go.

4. Fill each dosa with a small amount of Cauliflower, Potato, and Onion Curry (page 200), any delicious chutney, curry, or crumbled panir cheese drizzled with honey. Roll up, and serve hot.

5. Dosas can be made a day ahead, stacked, portioned, and refrigerated or kept frozen in a ziplock bag for about 1 month. Warm through to use.

CLARIFIED BUTTER

Clarified butter (clear butter fat) is simply melted (unsalted) butter that has had the milk solids and liquid whey removed. It is the solids that burn when butter is heated to high temperatures. Once the solids have been removed, the clear butter fat can be heated, even at high temperatures for frying, without burning or creating off flavors.

To clarify, slowly and completely melt the butter in a saucepan over low heat. Once melted, remove from the heat and remove the foam from the surface. Carefully pour off the butter fat, leaving the milk solids and liquid whey at the bottom behind. Strain any remaining butter fat through a coffee filter into a container. Discard the solids. Gravy separators are also useful for separating the butter fat from the solids. Clarified butter can be refrigerated and stored for a few months.

Ghee is a form of clarified butter used in India. Due to the lack of refrigeration in that region, the butter is heated in the same manner described but for a longer period of time, until all of the water in the butter is boiled off and the solids have settled to the bottom and browned. The result is a stable, nutty-flavored clarified fat that requires little or no refrigeration. In contemporary kitchens, ghee can be covered and refrigerated or stored in a cool location for a few months.

Rosemary-Lemon Dutch Oven Bread

YIELD: One 1½-pound loaf
START TO FINISH: 20 minutes mixing + 12 to 18 hours fermenting + 30 minutes shaping + 2 hours first rise + 45 minutes baking

This cultured bread is inspired by my favorite bread from my friends at Della Fattoria Bakery in Petaluma, California. Their Rosemary–Meyer Lemon wild yeast bread is baked to a deep, smoky brown perfection in their wood-fired ovens. I've chosen to make this version with yogurt, which acts as a tenderizer and gives some tang to the dough, though not quite as prominent as the flavor of sourdough. This is an easy, no-knead Dutch oven bread that can be made in a conventional home oven, in a wood-fired oven, or on a campfire.

3 cups all-purpose flour, plus ½ cup for dusting
½ cup whole wheat flour
2 teaspoons active dry yeast
1½ teaspoons unrefined fine sea salt
½ cup whole or low-fat yogurt
1¼ cups plus 2 tablespoons water
4 teaspoons coarsely chopped fresh rosemary
Grated zest from 1 lemon (preferably Meyer)
1 tablespoon fleur de sel or other coarse sea salt, for finishing
3 tablespoons lemon olive oil (preferably The Olive Press's Limonato Olive Oil; see Resources, page 241)
1 teaspoon fine cornmeal or rice flour, for dusting (optional)

1. Oil a large, covered container. In a large bowl, combine the 3 cups all-purpose flour, wheat flour, yeast, and fine sea salt. Whisk the yogurt with the water, then fold into the flour mixture until blended (add another tablespoon of water if the dough is dry). The dough should look rough and a bit sticky. Place in the oiled container, cover, and ferment for 12 to 18 hours at 70°F to 72°F. The dough is ready when gas bubbles appear on the surface.

2. In a small bowl, combine the chopped rosemary, lemon zest, and coarse sea salt.

3. Gently empty the dough out onto a lightly floured work surface and dust the dough with flour. Using a bowl scraper or bench scraper, gently fold the dough over on itself twice. Before the second fold, sprinkle half of the rosemary–lemon zest mixture over the surface, and then fold. Cover with a kitchen towel and let rest for 15 minutes. Line a bowl large enough to hold the risen dough with a flour sack or linen kitchen towel. Generously coat the bowl portion of the towel with all-purpose flour or a combination of all-purpose flour and rice flour.

4. Lightly flour your hands and the work surface (if needed) and gently shape the dough into a ball, being careful not to deflate the dough. Quickly place it, seam side down, in the floured bowl. Cover the dough with the ends of the towel and set aside to rest until doubled in size, about 2 hours.

5. The baking temperature for the bread must be 500°F. At least 40 minutes before baking, preheat a 4-quart cast-iron, ceramic, or clay baking pot and lid in the hot wood-fired oven or over hot coals of a live fire. The pot must be very hot when the dough is placed in it. If using a conventional oven, place the baking pot in a cold oven 1½ hours into the dough rise and preheat to 500°F with the empty pot in place.

6. When the dough is ready, carefully remove the very hot pot from the oven. Lift the dough from the bowl using the towel that lined the bowl. Hold one hand under the towel and gently invert the dough into the pot, seam side up (ragged edges are fine). With a serrated knife, quickly cut a ½-inch deep starburst (6 to 8 slashes) in the center of the dough surface to expose some of the zest and rosemary. Brush the entire top with lemon olive oil and dust with the remainder of the rosemary–lemon zest mixture, getting some into the cuts. The cuts will pull back in baking and become crispy and crunchy.

7. Carefully (protect your hands), place the heated lid on the pot and return to the oven to bake for 30 minutes. Remove the lid and bake until the crust is a deep golden color and crispy, and the bread sounds hollow when you gently knock on it (the thump test), another 15 minutes or more.

8. Slide out of the pot and cool on a rack. It tastes best if left to rest for at least 1 hour before cutting.

100% Sprouted Grain Bread

MAKES 1 loaf
START TO FINISH: 5 to 10 minutes grinding sprouts +
12 to 15 minutes mixing + 2½ to 3½ hours fermenting,
shaping, and proofing + 40 to 60 minutes baking

This is one of my favorite breads from Peter Reinhart that always reminds me of his days operating Brother Juniper's Bakery in Sonoma County, California. It is a wonderfully dense, moist, slightly sweet bread made with no flour, only sprouted grains. It makes a great, nourishing breakfast toast, slathered with Toasted Nut Butter (page 78). The bread is simple to make, requiring no biga (a type of starter used in Italian baking) or starter because the sprouted grains function as such. Because the grains lose some gluten in the sprouting process, as Peter notes, if you want a more airy result you'll need to add some vital wheat gluten (see Resources, page 241). You can bake the dough as a rustic hand-shaped loaf or in a greased 8½ by 4-inch loaf pan.

Note: Sprout grains according to the directions on page 7. When measuring the amount of grains to be sprouted, remember that they will approximately double in weight and more in volume in the sprouting process. If you have more sprouts than needed for this recipe, put them to good use in salads, on sandwiches, or combined with cooked legumes in a hummuslike spread.

About 4 cups (24 ounces) sprouted wheat kernels, other sprouted grains, or a combination (see page 7)

½ cup plus 2 tablespoons (2.4 ounces) vital wheat gluten (optional)

1⅛ teaspoons (.32 ounces) salt

2¼ teaspoons (.25 ounces) instant yeast

1½ tablespoons (1 ounce) unrefined raw honey or agave nectar, or 2 tablespoons (1 ounce) raw sugar

½ cup (4 ounces) water, at room temperature

1. Using a food processor, pulse the sprouted grains to as fine a pulp as possible, but not to the point of generating a lot of heat. If the pulp begins to feel warm to the touch, stop processing it and let it sit for about 10 minutes to cool off before continuing. A manual meat grinder, or *mocajete* (Latino mortar and pestle) works even better than a food processor and does not generate heat.

2. If mixing by hand, combine the sprout pulp, wheat gluten, salt, yeast, honey, and ¼ cup of the water in a bowl and stir vigorously with a mixing spoon or knead with wet hands for about 2 minutes, until all of the ingredients are evenly integrated and distributed into the dough. The dough should be soft and slightly sticky; if not, add more of the water to form a sticky ball of dough. If using a stand mixer, combine the sprout pulp, wheat gluten, salt, yeast, honey, and ¼ cup of the water in the bowl. Mix on slow speed with the dough hook for 1 minute to bring the ingredients together into a ball, adding additional water as needed. Continue mixing at medium-low speed for 2 to 3 minutes, occasionally scraping down the bowl. The dough should form a sticky ball.

3. Mist a work surface with a spray of water, place the dough on the work surface, and knead with wet hands for 1 to 2 minutes. Although the dough will be

sticky on the surface, it should have the strength and feel of normal bread dough. Form the dough into a ball and let it rest on the work surface for 5 minutes while you prepare a clean, lightly oiled bowl.

4. Resume kneading the dough for 1 minute with wet hands to strengthen it. The dough should have strength, yet still feel soft, supple, and very tacky. Form the dough into a ball and place it in the prepared bowl, rolling to coat with oil. Cover loosely with plastic wrap and let rise at room temperature for approximately 45 to 60 minutes, until it is about $1\frac{1}{2}$ times its original size.

5. Transfer the dough to a lightly floured work surface and form it into either a loaf pan shape or a freestanding hand-shaped rustic loaf. For loaf pan bread, place the dough in a greased $8\frac{1}{2}$ by 4-inch bread pan. For a hand-shaped rustic loaf, place it on a proofing cloth or on a sheet pan lined with parchment paper and, if you like, dusted with flour. Mist the top of the dough with pan spray (optional), cover loosely with plastic wrap, and let rise at room temperature for approximately 45 to 60 minutes, until it has grown to $1\frac{1}{2}$ times its original size.

6. Preheat the oven to 425°F and, if baking a freestanding loaf, prepare the oven for hearth baking, including a steam pan (steaming is optional for a loaf pan bread). Note: Optimum hearth baking takes place directly on baking stones (the thicker the better for accumulated heat) preheated in the oven for 1 hour or longer before baking. The surface temperature of the stone is as important as the ambient temperature of the oven. Check the temperature of the stone before baking. A laser point-and-shoot thermometer works well for reading the surface temperature. Bread baked in loaf pans do not need to be baked on stones.

7. If you do not have a baking stone, use an inverted baking sheet as a baking shelf. Dough can also be raised and baked on a parchment-lined sheet pan, then placed on the baking sheet shelf. The baking time for this method will take longer due to the insulation from the baking shelf.

8. To create steam (to enhance spring and crisp the crust), place a cast-iron baking pan or rimmed baking sheet on the shelf immediately above or below the baking shelf before preheating the oven. When the dough is ready to bake, place it in the oven, pour 1 cup of hot water into the steam pan, lower the temperature to 350°F, and bake for 20 minutes. Rotate the loaf 180 degrees, mist the oven to create steam, and continue baking for another 20 to 30 minutes, until the loaf is a rich brown on all sides, sounds hollow when thumped on the bottom, and registers at least 200°F in the center.

9. Transfer the bread to a cooling rack and allow it to cool for at least 1 hour before serving.

How to Make a Sourdough Starter: *Capturing Wild Yeast*

YIELD: About 1 quart usable starter
START TO FINISH: 10 minutes prepping + 3 days yeast growth + 11 days developing + 1 day feeding

Vibrant wild-yeast starters are used to add flavor and volume to breads, flatbreads, pancakes, crepes, and sweet or savory baked goods. Since wild yeast is everywhere, it can be made anywhere. The process is quite simple: all you need is flour and water (sometimes inoculated with yeast-covered raisins or grapes, and perhaps a bit of honey to activate the yeast), and a glass or other food-grade container to house the ingredients.

Different recipes and bakers will adamantly state it has to be made with a specific ratio for a certain number of days before using. Some say use only whole wheat flour throughout; others insist on using whole wheat to start, then feeding with unbleached bread flour. Some call for equal parts flour and water; others prefer different ratios based on the desired hydration of the bread they are making with the starter. The number of days to feed before using also varies from 7 to 10 days. The truth is, any of these work. Following is my favorite method.

Keeping a sourdough starter active does take a small amount of attention and management, but once developed to the desired acidity and flavor, you can keep this new family member happy with regular additions of flour. Covered, it can be refrigerated or frozen for up to 6 months, needing only a period of revitalization and a return to room temperature before using again.

Note: If you haven't used your starter for 2 weeks or more, discard half of it and feed for 3 days before using. Once you have a regular schedule of use, refresh your starter daily or every other day. The more often you use the starter, the more often it needs food. If you use it daily, refresh it daily.

½ cup dark raisins (preferably organic)
About 11¾ cups filtered nonchlorinated water, at room temperature (70°F)
1 teaspoon raw, unfiltered honey
1 cup whole wheat flour
9 cups unbleached bread flour

1. Three days before making the starter: Place the raisins in a glass or plastic container. Pour over 4 cups of water, cover the container with cheesecloth, secure it with a rubber band, and set the container in a cool location (60°F to 70°F) in your kitchen. After 3 days, the water will be filled with thousands of wild yeast cells from the raisins. There may even be a visible collection of tiny yeast cells afloat on the water. Scoop 1 full cup of this raisin water from the top of the mixture to begin your wild yeast starter. Discard the raisins. (If any mold appears, discard the entire mixture. Wash and sanitize your container. Rinse it well and start again. On the second try, keep the container in the refrigerator, lightly covered. Three days later, you may scoop water from the top of this mixture and use it to begin your wild yeast starter.)

2. Day 1: In a 1-quart plastic or glass container, combine the 1 cup raisin water and honey. Using a clean hand, stir in the whole wheat flour until all

continued

visible flour is moistened. You can feel this best when using your hand to mix and break up clumps. Cover with cheesecloth, then a lid placed ajar so oxygen will feed the yeast, and set in a cool location (60°F to 70°F) away from drafts.

3. Day 2: You'll notice small bubbles in the mixture due to the yeast creating carbon dioxide. There may be a small pool of liquid on the top and perhaps the bottom. This is to be expected.

4. The middle layer contains what you want to use for this batch. Carefully spoon off the top layer and discard. Without disturbing any liquid or sediment at the bottom, scoop and reserve about $1/2$ cup of the middle-layer starter mixture. Transfer this to a clean container. Blend in $3/4$ cup water. Using your hand, blend in 1 cup unbleached bread flour to moisten as before. Cover with cheesecloth, place the lid ajar so oxygen will feed the yeast, and set in a cool location (60°F to 70°F) away from drafts. Discard the unused bottom sediment from the first container.

5. Day 3: The starter probably has reached a volume of 1 full quart. Transfer it to a 2-quart plastic or glass container and blend in $3/4$ cup water and 1 cup bread flour. Cover with cheesecloth, place the lid ajar so oxygen will feed the yeast, and set in a cool location (60°F to 70°F) away from drafts.

6. Day 4: This time discard half of the starter before feeding. By doing this, the volume of finished starter is manageable and enough quantity for home use. Blend in $3/4$ cup water and 1 cup bread flour. Cover with cheesecloth, place the lid ajar so oxygen will feed the yeast, and set in a cool location (60°F to 70°F) away from drafts.

7. Days 5 through 10: Repeat the process from Day 4.

8. Day 11: Your starter will be bubbling and full of living organisms. It is now vibrant enough to leaven doughs. However, a bit more time is required before you can use it. One day before using the starter, feed it 1 cup each water and bread flour and store at room temperature. Now, remove half of the starter (to be used) and feed the remainder (to be the starter for the next time) with equal amounts of water and flour until it returns to its original volume.

9. After feeding the starter, allow 2 more hours at room temperature before refrigerating. This will allow the starter to begin to digest the new flour. Use this system to keep the starter going. If refrigerating, feed every 2 weeks. When the starter has been refrigerated, allow it to sit at room temperature 1 hour before using.

Preparing sourdough starter, mixing sourdough starter

Sourdough Pizza

YIELD: Three 12-inch pizzas
START TO FINISH: 1 to 1½ hours to heat the pizza stone + 30 minutes mixing + 30 minute fermenting + 30 minutes refrigeration + 10 minutes shaping + 10 minutes baking

Everyone loves pizza, and great pizza starts with flavorful dough. This recipe for basic sourdough pizza dough is from Chef Michael Kalanty, baking instructor and author of *How to Bake Bread*.

You can easily mix this dough by hand if you don't have a stand mixer. The toppings are your choice. Remember to top your pizza lightly, with only a few ingredients, so you can distinguish them and so the dough can bake through properly from both the top and the bottom. The flavor development of the dough, demonstrated in this recipe, will result in a delicious crust you want to taste. Don't overload it!

⅝ cup (5 ounces) whole milk or water
1 packet / 2¼ teaspoons (¼ ounce) active dry yeast
⅞ cup (8 ounces) sourdough starter (see page 133)
2 teaspoons raw, unfiltered honey
3 tablespoons olive oil, plus more for coating dough
About 2½ cups (11 ounces) unbleached bread flour
2 teaspoons kosher salt (preferably Diamond Crystal)
Sea salt, for dusting

1. Preheat a wood-fired oven to a floor-temperature of 650°F, or, in a conventional oven, heat a pizza stone to 500°F. A conventional oven is ready when the temperature of the stone is 500°F—approximately 1 to 1½ hours after heating. Lightly oil a food-grade container with a cover and set aside.

2. In a small pan, heat the milk to 110°F over low heat. Remove from the heat, add the dry yeast, and let sit for 5 minutes to hydrate thoroughly; stir to dissolve. Gently break the wild yeast starter into a few smaller pieces by squeezing it through your fingers, then add starter to the milk mixture. Add the honey and then the oil.

3. Place the milk-yeast mixture in the bowl of a stand mixer fitted with the paddle attachment. Thoroughly combine the mixture on low speed. Change to the dough hook and add the flour and salt. On low speed, mix until all of the flour is moistened. On medium speed, knead the dough for 3 minutes. Cover with plastic wrap and rest the dough for 5 minutes. Again, knead the dough on medium speed for 3 minutes more.

4. Place the dough in the oiled container, cover, and ferment for 30 minutes at about 85°F temperature. Line a 12 by 18-inch baking sheet with lightly oiled parchment paper. Dust a wooden pizza peel with rice flour or all-purpose flour.

5. Divide the dough into three 8-ounce balls. Place on the prepared baking sheet. Coat the balls with olive oil and cover with plastic wrap. Refrigerate for 30 minutes or until needed (up to 36 hours). Bring to room temperature before shaping.

6. Working on a lightly floured surface, dust the pizza balls with flour. Using your floured fingertips, gently stretch and shape each to about 14-inch discs on the prepared pizza peel. Bake one at a time, keeping the other 2 disks covered with a flour-dusted kitchen towel until used.

7. Lightly top each pizza with sauce, pesto, or just olive oil, then a condiment (Agrodolce Onion Marmalade, page 52), a cured meat (Dry-Cured Pimenton Salami, page 157), if desired, and finish with a good melting cheese. Brush olive oil on the edge and dust with sea salt.

8. Place each topped pizza directly on the pizza stone (in a conventional oven) or directly on the floor of the wood-fired oven. Bake until the topping is bubbly and the crust is a dark golden on the edge and on the bottom, about 10 minutes in a conventional oven, about 8 minutes in a wood-fired oven.

Panettone Originale

(Babka Panettone)

YIELD: Two 2-pound loaves
START TO FINISH: 5 minutes prepping + 24 hours soaking + 4 hours first rise + 10 minutes mixing + 4 hours resting + 2 hours second rise + 10 minutes mixing + 50 minutes resting + 2 hours third rise + 30 to 35 minutes baking

This delicious sweet bread recipe is another creation from chef Michael Kalanty. It requires planning, but the results are sensational. In Northern Italy, this rich, dried fruit–studded holiday bread is made from a *madre* (mother) or wild yeast starter. The complete process includes three separate risings over a period of almost two days to create the full flavor and tender, yet elastic, texture of the bread. This recipe is a quicker version using a small amount of active dry yeast to shorten the process, but retains three rises because the final texture is worth the effort. Bake in a round cake pan or the traditional paper panettone baking mold for more show and authenticity (see Resources, page 241).

About 1 cup (6 ounces) mixed dried currants, strips of candied orange peel, raisins, and cherries

About 1/2 cup (2 ounces) slivered almonds, lightly toasted

1 tablespoon brandy or rum

1 tablespoon freshly squeezed orange juice

About 3/4 cup (6 ounces) sourdough starter (see page 133)

About 1 cup milk, heated to 100°F

1 packet / 2 1/4 teaspoons (1/4 ounce) active dry yeast

About 1 1/4 cups (5 ounces) unbleached bread flour

12 tablespoons (6 ounces) butter, plus 4 tablespoons (2 ounces) butter, melted and cooled, for brushing the dough

1/2 cup (4 ounces) raw unrefined cane sugar

2 large eggs

Grated zest of 1 small orange

1/4 teaspoon ground nutmeg

2 teaspoons kosher salt (preferably Diamond Crystal)

About 2 1/2 cups (11 ounces) unbleached all-purpose flour

1. Cut the candied orange peel into 1/3-inch long pieces. Coarsely chop the cherries.

2. In a plastic container, combine the dried fruits, almonds, brandy, and orange juice. Cover and let sit, turning once or twice, for 24 hours.

3. Place the starter in a large mixing bowl, add the warmed milk, and sprinkle dry yeast over top. Let rest for 5 minutes for the yeast to dissolve. Add the bread flour, blending together until all of the flour is visibly moistened. Cover and let sit for 4 hours at 70°F temperature (this is the temperature you'll want for all subsequent sittings and rising). This mixture is the "sponge" (first rise).

4. Meanwhile, in a stand mixer fitted with the paddle attachment, beat together the 12 tablespoons of butter and sugar on medium speed for 2 minutes. Scrape

continued

down the sides of the bowl and beat 1 minute more. Add the eggs one at a time, beating well each time, and scraping down the sides of the bowl after each addition. Once the last egg has been incorporated, beat the mixture on medium speed for 2 minutes more. Cover and set aside for 4 hours.

5. Add the creamed butter mixture to the fermented sponge. Beat on medium speed until well combined, about 2 minutes. Scrape down the sides of the bowl halfway through this process. Cover and let sit for 2 hours. This mixture is the "fermented dough" (second rise).

6. Meanwhile, drain the soaked fruit mixture, gently squeezing excess moisture from it. (The drained liquid can be used to make a simple syrup to moisten the cake; see page 38.) Add in the zest and nutmeg, and then add this mixture and the salt to the fermented dough. Blend all together on low speed until the fruit is uniformly distributed, about 2 minutes. In two additions, add the all-purpose flour. Blend together on low speed until incorporated and all flour is visibly moistened. Cover and let rest for 30 minutes.

7. Form the dough into a round loaf. Cover with an inverted bowl or kitchen towel, and let rest 20 minutes. Meanwhile, butter a 9 by 2-inch round cake pan and line the bottom with a parchment paper round. Butter the parchment. Invert the prepared pan and set aside.

8. Form the dough into a smoother round, using gentle pressure. Transfer to the prepared cake pan or paper panettone mold, if using. Brush the top with cooled melted butter, cover with a large bowl, and let rise for $1\frac{1}{2}$ to 2 hours (third rise).

9. After 1 hour, preheat the oven to 360°F. Set an oven rack so that the panettone will bake in the center of the oven. Bake for 10 minutes. Decrease the oven temperature to 325°F and bake 20 to 25 minutes more. The bread is done when its internal temperature reaches 170°F (to get a true reading, use an instant-read thermometer and check in two different spots) or when the crust is a deep golden brown. Remove from the oven and let cool on a rack for 2 hours.

Seeded Sprouted-Grain Crackers

YIELD: 12 to 14 large crackers
START TO FINISH: 20 minutes mixing + 8 to 12 hours fermenting + 30 minutes resting + 40 minutes shaping and resting + 15 to 20 minutes baking

Crackers are fun and easy to make. These are rustic, crunchy, and a bit chewy. You can use any combination of compatible grain or nut flours and ground seeds. Add a sprouted grain or legume for more texture and flavor. Make them round, as described here, or roll out one large, thin sheet and cut into rectangles or diamonds using a pizza cutter. Finish with honey or agave to make sweet crackers, or, for an extra savory kick, brush with smoked or citrus olive oil and dust with finely grated hard cheese in the last few minutes of baking. *See photo on page 51.*

2 tablespoons sesame seeds, toasted
2 tablespoons sunflower seeds, toasted
4 tablespoons raw, unfiltered honey
About ¾ cup filtered water, at room temperature
1¼ cups all-purpose flour
¼ cup whole wheat flour
1 teaspoon unrefined fine sea salt
2 tablespoons sprouted quinoa (see page 7)
2 tablespoons sunflower or grapeseed oil

1. Finely grind the seeds together in a spice grinder. In a small bowl, mix together 2 tablespoons of the honey and half the water. With a stand mixer fitted with the paddle attachment, combine the flours, half of the ground mixed seeds, and the salt. On low speed, mix in the sprouted quinoa, the honey-water mixture, then the oil, to combine. Slowly add the balance of the water, or as much as needed, for the dough to come together.

2. Cover and refrigerate the dough overnight. Allow the dough to sit at room temperature for 30 minutes before continuing.

3. Preheat the oven to 450°F. Lightly flour a baking sheet. Line two baking sheets with parchment paper.

4. Place the dough on a lightly floured work surface and knead for about 3 minutes; cover with a bowl or towel and let rest for 15 minutes. Knead again for a few minutes until the dough is smooth and a bit elastic. Shape into a ball. Divide into 12 to 14 equal pieces and shape each piece into a balls. Place the balls on the floured baking sheet and dust them lightly with flour. Cover lightly with plastic wrap and let rest for 15 minutes.

5. Flatten each ball slightly then roll each out into a very thin circle, flouring the dough lightly, if needed, to prevent sticking. Alternately, using a hand-crank pasta machine on the finest setting, pass the dough through the rollers twice.

6. Transfer the disks onto the parchment-lined baking sheets.

7. Bake the crackers until lightly golden on top, about 6 minutes. Turn over, brush with the remaining 2 tablespoons of the honey, and sprinkle with the remainder of the seeds. Continue to bake until completely crisp and brown, about 10 minutes. Transfer to a rack to cool. Keep in a sealed container for up to 1 week.

CHAPTER 7
CURED MEATS AND FISH

You MAY NOT KNOW that many preserved meats and fish such as handcrafted prosciutto, cured bacon or pancetta, salami, and salted anchovies are also fermented. We refer to them as cured, which they are, but in some of the curing processes, fermentation also takes place.

By fermenting meat or fish, we are improving flavors, adding nutritional value, and extending shelf life. The items here, however, must be refrigerated as directed to remain safe. Vacuum sealing is extremely valuable for protecting products that have begun their fermentation and need a safe environment to ferment slowly.

As with any fermenting, planning is extremely important. Curing meats and fish at home requires dedicated attention and focus. The proper working and aging environments must be in place. Use only the best ingredients. Special attention to basic food safety and sanitation practices is imperative to the safety of those who will ultimately eat the food. Before you begin, review the general safety and sanitation practices discussed in chapter 2. Take note that it is necessary to segregate food categories being aged to prevent cross-contamination. Do not age cheese and cure meat in the same space.

If you are new to the curing realm, you may have the notion that curing meats can happen in any cool environment, using loads of salt. You may have felt that one could merely follow in the traditional footsteps of the Italians or the Spaniards when making prosciutto or jamón, and then just hang the meat it in the cellar or garage until ready. This is incorrect and totally unsafe. The conditions for making those traditional benchmarks are quite different from what we have at home. In Italy and Spain, the environments used for aging have been exclusively used for that purpose for generations, and are filled with friendly, pathogen-fighting bacteria, keeping the product safe. At home, we don't have such an environment available to us, so we must mindfully create a protected one with controlled temperatures, humidity, and air circulation.

As with cheese making, a dedicated repurposed refrigerator makes a good aging cave. Equip it with a hygrometer, an instrument that measures relative humidity and also has a thermometer reading. With this control, you can manage the thermostat control and adjust the humidity by placing a pan of water or a wet towel inside the refrigerator, which can be added or removed to come as close as you can to the desired humidity. Air circulation is important; address it by visiting your aging refrigerator daily. Get in the habit of looking at all your instruments regularly, making any adjustments, and, at the same time, allowing for air to be exchanged.

Consider this chapter a primer, an introduction to the world of meat and fish preservation through fermentation, with a range of styles, flavors, and concepts. Some are condiments and pantry items; many are cuts of meat or fish. Some recipes in this chapter are very simple to make and take little of your time. Others require some specialized equipment and curing ingredients as well as regular attention from you. All include tips to guide you to success.

Equipment and Supplies

The basic equipment and supplies you'll need for nearly all the recipes include the following:

- Disposable vinyl or food-service gloves for handling the meat and fish

- Instant-read kitchen thermometer

For a few of the recipes, you will also need some of the following:

- Cheesecloth (2 yards)

- Draining rack: nonreactive material, to sit inside draining tray

- Draining trays: food-grade plastic trays or rimmed quarter-sheet or half-sheet baking pans

- Hygrometer: a tool for measuring relative humidity

- Meat grinder with specified plates (from The Sausage Maker, see Resources, page 241) or a heavy-duty electric stand mixer with meat grinder attachments

- pH strips or pH meter: used to measure acidity

- Vacuum sealer food saver (optional, but very useful)

- Weights: such as foil-wrapped bricks, heavy skillets, or empty milk containers filled with water

Fish Sauces

Fish-based condiments or sauces have been key components of diets for centuries in parts of the world where fish were abundant. They all stem from the same basic ingredients: local small fish (or the entrails of them) and sea salt. In some regions, the fish and salt were mixed together; in others, the fish was layered into barrels or amphoras, alternating with thick layers of sea salt. In either case, the vessel was then placed in the sun for months to allow the fish to ferment. Once fermented, the resulting liquid (the fish sauce) was strained off or drained into clean vessels, plugged, and stored in the ground or another cool place.

ASIAN FISH SAUCE

YIELD: About 3 cups
START TO FINISH: 20 minutes to make + 3 days resting + 6 to 10 weeks fermenting

The most basic of flavoring staples found in every pantry throughout the countries in Asia, this homemade fish sauce is light in color and far less pungent than any store-bought variety. Because we are using a small amount of whey to jump-start the fermentation, the final product will be slightly cloudy. You might consider making a larger batch (this recipe makes about 3 cups) only once or twice a year so you always have fish sauce at hand.

2 pounds sardines or anchovies (or a combination)
9 tablespoons unrefined fine sea salt
6 cloves garlic, crushed
1 teaspoon ground coriander
2 teaspoons whole black peppercorns, crushed
Grated zest of 1 lemon
2 tablespoons tamarind paste
4 tablespoons basic whey (see page 13)

1. Cut the fish into 1-inch-long pieces and place in a food processor; pulverize into small chunks. In a large bowl, toss the fish in 6 tablespoons of the salt and then add the garlic, coriander, peppercorns, and zest. Combine the tamarind paste with the whey and pour over the fish. Stir to combine.

2. Place in a wide-mouth 1-quart jar. Press down to release some of the fish liquid. Add filtered water, if needed, to bring the level to 1 inch from the top of the jar. Place a weight on the fish to keep it submerged. Cover tightly and leave at room temperature for 3 days.

3. After 3 days, stir in the remaining 3 tablespoons of salt, cover, and allow to ferment for 6 weeks. Taste the sauce at that point and if you'd like it more pungent, continue to age for another 2 to 4 weeks. Strain through a mesh strainer into a fresh jar or bottle and seal. Transfer to refrigeration and keep for up to 6 months.

Note: If you have access to a small barrel used for aging wine or spirits, use one for aging your fish sauce for awesome results.

WORCESTERSHIRE SAUCE

YIELD: About 1½ cups
START TO FINISH: 20 minutes to make + 2 weeks to 6 months fermenting

Ancient Roman *garum*, a very early form of fermented fish, inspired the British to create this famous fermented fish–based liquid condiment thousands of years later based on their exposure to a version of it in India. It is named for the home of its first bottling, Worcester, England. Often used to flavor sauces, salad dressings, meats, and soups, it is probably best known as an essential ingredient in Bloody Marys. Bottle the final product and gift to your favorite mixologist.

½ cup pickled onions (see page 27) or coarsely chopped white onions

2 tablespoons dark raisins

1 teaspoon tamarind paste

1½ teaspoons organic molasses (not blackstrap)

½ teaspoon anchovy paste

2 tablespoons raw unrefined cane sugar

½ teaspoon ground ginger

½ teaspoon mustard powder

½ teaspoon garlic powder

½ teaspoon unrefined fine sea salt

⅓ cup raw, unfiltered apple cider vinegar

¼ cup Soy Sauce (page 71)

¼ cup filtered water

1. Place the onions, raisins, tamarind paste, molasses, and anchovy paste in a blender and puree until smooth. Add the sugar, ginger, mustard, garlic powder, and salt to the mixture in the blender and then blend to incorporate. Blend in the vinegar, soy sauce, and water until the mixture is smooth. Place in a pint jar with an air lock. Ferment at room temperature for 2 weeks to 6 months.

2. Taste after 2 weeks and continue fermenting until it reaches your desired flavor. Strain (if desired) after 3 weeks and rebottle in an airtight vessel. Store at room temperature for up to 3 months. Refrigerate after opening.

SHRIMP PASTE

YIELD: About 3 cups
START TO FINISH: 1 hour to make + 3 days fermenting

What a difference homemade makes! Unlike thick, grayish, store-bought shrimp paste, this one is vibrant in color, flavor, and aroma. Shrimp paste, a staple Asian ingredient made from fermented shrimp, is used in Southeast Asian cooking to flavor soups, sauces, curries, and marinades. The paste can be made into shrimp sauce by adding more stock and straining into a bottle. Dried whole shrimp is available in Latino or Asian markets.

3 ounces whole dried shrimp

3/4 ounce small dried Mexican or Thai chiles, stemmed and seeded

4 cloves garlic, chopped

1 teaspoon raw unrefined cane sugar

1 tablespoon unrefined fine sea salt

1 tablespoon Asian Fish Sauce (page 145)

2 tablespoons basic whey (see page 13)

1. Place the shrimp in a small saucepan and cover with filtered water. Bring to a low boil and cook for 2 minutes, then turn off the heat and steep for 20 minutes. Drain the shrimp and reserve the liquid. Place the chiles in a bowl and cover with about 1 cup of the hot shrimp stock. Allow to rehydrate until soft, about 20 minutes.

2. Place the chiles, garlic, sugar, salt, and fish sauce in a blender and puree into a chunky paste. With the blender running, add half of the shrimp stock and the whey. Combine until smooth, then puree at high speed. Add more stock if needed to create a smooth paste. Press through a mesh strainer if desired to remove larger chile bits. Place in two wide-mouth pint glass jars, cover tightly, and leave at room temperature for 3 days. Transfer to refrigeration. Let sit for 3 days before opening. It is best if used within 2 months after opening.

Gravlax: Basic Fish Curing

YIELD: About 1½ pounds
START TO FINISH: 1 hour to make + 2 to 10 days aging

Briny, salty, dill-spiked gravlax is a Scandinavian delicacy enjoyed around the world. Traditionally, the salmon is cured with only salt and sugar, but this version is taken to a delicious fermented state by being doused with whey as well. The sugar and salt remove moisture while the whey helps transform the texture of the flesh, making it firm enough to be sliced easily. Other flavorings—like the dill used here (although chervil or fennel fronds work nicely, too)—absorb into the fish during the curing process. This basic curing process works with other fatty fish such as cod, arctic char, or mackerel. If the fish is smaller but adding up to the weight listed, reduce the amount of weight when pressing. Since it is weighed down and becomes compressed while curing, choose thick pieces of fillet.

One fun option is to cold tea-smoke the fish (see page 214) after turning it into gravlax. Lay the gravlax on a rack and dry in the refrigerator overnight, or until the surface is slightly tacky. At this point, it is ready to be smoked. The tacky surface will help the smoke adhere to the fish.

This method requires a draining mat and rack-on-baking sheet setup as for draining cheese (see page 84).

2 pounds midsection salmon fillet, skin on (cut into 2 equal pieces)
¼ cup unrefined fine sea salt
¼ cup raw unrefined cane sugar
1 tablespoon whole green peppercorns, crushed
¼ cup basic whey (see page 13)
½ cup fresh dill sprigs

1. Remove the pin bones from the salmon. Rinse the fish and pat dry. Set a draining mat on a rack set inside a baking sheet.

2. Mix the salt, sugar, and peppercorns together in a small bowl. Rub the seasoning mix thoroughly into the flesh side of the fish. It may seem more than you need, but you must use all of it in order to accomplish the desired flavor and texture. Sprinkle the surface with the whey and then place sprigs of the dill on top.

3. Place the pieces of salmon together, flesh sides facing. Place on the draining mat and cover the entire tray tightly with plastic wrap. Top with a second baking sheet. Weigh the fish down with a 5-pound brick or ½-gallon milk bottle filled with water, and set on the top baking sheet directly over the salmon.

4. Refrigerate for 2 to 4 days, turning the fish twice a day until ready to serve. Or wrap each piece of gravlax in plastic wrap and refrigerate for another 4 to 6 days before eating. In any case, it is best when used within 10 days.

5. Unwrap, remove seasonings, rinse off any particles, and pat dry. Cover with cheesecloth and air dry in the refrigerator for 1 hour. While still cold, diagonally slice into thin slices. Serve with Crème Fraîche (page 95), pickled onions (see page 27), sprigs of dill, and capers.

PICKLED SARDINES WITH FENNEL

YIELD: 1 quart
START TO FINISH: 45 minutes to make + 12 hours refrigeration + 3 days fermenting + 1 to 2 weeks aging

This Mediterranean-inspired pickled fish features fresh sardines, although anchovies, mackerel, or trout also work well. The fish is salted and refrigerated overnight to draw out moisture and firm up the flesh before being marinated. Cold smoking the fish before marinating would add wonderful smoky notes. These sardines may be eaten raw after fermenting or drained, lightly dusted with fine cornmeal, and pan-crisped or grilled. Remove the spinal bones before eating.

1½ pounds whole sardines
2 teaspoons unrefined fine sea salt, plus more for the brine
1½ cups cool filtered water
¼ cup basic whey (see page 13)
½ cup raw, unfiltered apple cider vinegar
3 tablespoons raw honey
¼ cup mixed golden and dark raisins
1 cup diced fennel bulb
½ teaspoon fennel seeds
1 bay leaf
¼ teaspoon whole black peppercorns
3 to 4 sprigs fennel fronds, for garnish

1. Set a rack in a baking sheet and have ready. Descale the fish, remove the head and tails, and clean out the belly, or have the fishmonger do this for you. Rinse with water and pat dry. Weigh the fish at this point to determine the amount of salt needed in the brine (4 percent of the weight of the fish). Rub the fish inside and out with the 2 teaspoons of salt and set on the draining rack. Cover loosely with cheesecloth and refrigerate overnight.

2. Drain off any moisture, pat dry, and cut the fish into equal lengths, if needed, to fit into the jar.

3. Weigh out enough sea salt to equal 4 percent of the weight of the prepped fish. Combine the salt, water, whey, vinegar, and honey; stir to dissolve the salt and honey. Place the fish upright in a 1-quart wide-mouth canning jar. Add the raisins, fennel, fennel seeds, bay leaf, and peppercorns, then pour the brine over the top. Weigh down the fish to keep it submerged. Cover the opening with cheesecloth and ferment at room temperature for 24 hours.

4. Add additional brine if needed to bring to within 1 inch of the top of the jar. Put the weight back in place to submerge the fish. Cover the opening with cheesecloth and ferment at room temperature for 2 more days.

5. Remove the cheesecloth and close the lid. Refrigerate for 1 to 2 weeks before consuming. Consume within 1 month.

Spicy Marinated Tuna

YIELD: About 1 pound
START TO FINISH: 30 minutes to make + 8 to 12 hours refrigeration + 1 day fermenting + 1 to 2 weeks refrigeration

Fermenting tuna breaks down the protein and makes for a soft texture, much like albacore sushi. This marinated tuna is wonderful on a salad, coarsely chopped and used to make open-faced sandwiches, or served on an antipasti platter. Other firm fish such as swordfish or cod can also be fermented in this fashion.

1¼ pounds skinless tuna fillets, cut into 1-inch cubes
4 teaspoons unrefined fine sea salt
2 teaspoons Aleppo or other spicy ground red pepper
6 to 8 pearl onions, skinned and halved
3 large cloves garlic
4 or 5 small dried Mexican chiles
¼ teaspoon whole black peppercorns
¼ teaspoon fennel seeds, toasted
1 cup cool filtered water
¼ cup basic whey (see page 13)
1 tablespoon raw honey
3 sprigs fresh oregano
½ cup Tuscan-style olive oil

1.   In a bowl, toss the tuna with 1 teaspoon of the sea salt and all of the ground Aleppo pepper. Cover with cheesecloth and place in the refrigerator for 8 hours or overnight.

2.   Place the chunks of tuna, alternating with the pearl onions and garlic, in a wide-mouth 1-quart jar to within 1 inch of the top. Tuck in the dried chiles and sprinkle in the peppercorns and fennel seeds. Combine the water, whey, the remaining 3 teaspoons of salt, and the honey. Stir to dissolve the salt and then pour the mixture over the tuna. Insert the sprigs of oregano. Add more water as needed to cover the tuna and reach to within 1 inch of the top of the jar. Cover the opening with cheesecloth and ferment at room temperature for 1 day.

3.   Remove the cheesecloth and secure with a lid. Refrigerate for 1 to 2 weeks. Drain off the liquid and discard the flavoring ingredients. Toss the tuna with olive oil, place in a clean jar, and cover with a lid. Refrigerate and consume within 1 month. Bring to room temperature before serving.

4.   Alternate method: Cut the tuna into larger pieces to fit the jar. Make a paste of the Aleppo pepper, fennel seeds, garlic, and oregano, spread between the tuna, and stack in the jar. Cover with the fermenting liquid. Finish as above. Then remove the liquid and cover the contents with olive oil. Refrigerate until ready to serve.

TONNATO TAPENADE OR SAUCE

Tonnato traditionally refers to a dish with a sauce made with tuna, but in current culinary jargon, it also refers to the sauce itself. It can be left chunky as a tapenade or pureed into sauce. Place 8 ounces of Spicy Marinated Tuna or two 10-ounce cans of good-quality tuna packed in olive oil, drained, in a small bowl, and then break up the tuna into small chunks. Add 2 anchovy fillets or 1 teaspoon anchovy paste, 1 tablespoon rinsed salted capers, grated zest and juice of 1 lemon, and a pinch of red pepper flakes; toss to combine. Drizzle a small amount of peppery olive oil over the top to moisten. Serve at room temperature.

Corned Beef

YIELD: 4 pounds
START TO FINISH: 20 minutes to make + 24 hours brining + 4 to 6 weeks aging and curing

Corned beef is a beef brisket cured in a seasoned salt brine before being cooked. This version uses a whey brine to cause partial fermentation, breaking down the fibers of the meat and making it more digestible while also improving its flavor. No nitrites are used in this recipe to keep the meat pink, resulting in a natural color change from fresh red to an aged light gray. This is not a sign of decomposition, but one of natural aging. With the addition of whey, the meat goes through a short fermentation period before being refrigerated and further aged. Vacuum sealing is advised for safely storing the brisket in refrigeration while it ages. Plan the size of the brisket so you can turn some of it into pastrami. Start with a good-quality brisket, preferably grass-fed.

Note: This recipe produces corned beef ready to be cooked. I love using it to make Wood-Smoked Pastrami (page 154), but the traditional poaching or boiling method works great, too. Find other ways of cooking corned beef at www.masteringfermentation.com.

One 4-pound brisket, fat trimmed, and chilled

2 tablespoons raw unrefined cane sugar

4 tablespoons unrefined fine sea salt

2 bay leaves, crumbled

2 teaspoons yellow mustard seeds

2 teaspoons juniper berries, crushed

1 teaspoon whole white peppercorns, crushed

2 cups basic whey (see page 13)

4 cups cool filtered water

1. Pierce the brisket with a carving fork or other piercing tool, such as a metal skewer or meat tenderizer. Piercings should be $1/2$ to $3/4$ inch deep and about the same distance apart.

2. Combine the sugar, salt, bay leaves, mustard seeds, juniper berries, and peppercorns in a bowl and rub into the chilled brisket. Place the meat into a crock, food-storage container, or large heavy-duty food-storage plastic bag just large enough to contain the meat.

continued

3. Combine the whey and water to make a brine and add 3 cups of the brine to the container to cover the meat. Use the remaining brine as needed just to cover the meat.

4. Cover or close the container, keeping the meat submerged, and marinate in a dark area, at room temperature (68°F to 72°F) for 24 hours to start the fermentation process. Turn the meat a few times during this period.

5. Vacuum-seal the meat, if you can, or keep it submerged and contained; refrigerate at 38°F for 4 to 6 weeks. Turn the package twice a week (whether vacuum-sealed or submerged).

6. The meat may be frozen at this point or cooked. When ready to cook: Remove the meat from the brine, wash off the brine, pat dry and cook using your preferred method. Or smoke it to become pastrami (see following recipe)!

WOOD-SMOKED PASTRAMI

YIELD: About 3½ pounds
START TO FINISH: 1 hour soaking + 30 minutes to make + 24 hours refrigeration + 4½ hours or more smoking and cooking

This wood-smoked pastrami begins as corned beef (page 153). Use a brisket that is relatively uniform in size so that it will smoke and cook evenly. Hot smoking is the tastiest cooking method. Use your favorite aromatic smoking wood chips or pellets depending upon the make and style of smoker you are using. This method is adapted from *The Joy of Smoking and Salt Curing*, by Monte Burch. You can adjust the rub ingredients to your taste; however, the typical pastrami has plenty of cracked pepper as its crust. It makes an amazing pastrami sandwich topped with Apple-Caraway Sauerkraut (page 57).

Corned Beef (page 153)
¼ cup cracked black peppercorns
2 tablespoons cracked white peppercorns
2 tablespoons crushed dried oregano
1 tablespoon crushed brown mustard seed
1 teaspoon crushed red pepper flakes
1 teaspoon crushed juniper berries
1 teaspoon garlic powder
¼ cup raw, unfiltered honey, diluted with 1 tablespoon filtered water

continued

Wood-Smoked Pastrami sandwich with Dijon Style Whole-Grain Mustard, Apple-Caraway Sauerkraut, and Hop Stoopid Ale

1. Remove the corned beef from refrigeration and rinse in cool water to wash off any excess rub. Place in a food-grade container and cover with cool filtered water. Weight down the meat to keep it submerged. Keep in a cool (50°F to 55°F) spot for 1 hour. This soaking process removes any excess cure from the meat.

2. Combine the peppercorns, oregano, mustard seed, red pepper flakes, juniper berries, and garlic powder in a bowl to make the rub. Lay out plastic wrap on a rimmed baking sheet. Remove the corned beef from the water and pat it dry. Brush the surfaces of the meat with the diluted honey. Place the meat, fat side up, on the plastic. Sprinkle the rub evenly over the meat and rub it thoroughly into all the surfaces. Wrap tightly in the plastic wrap, place in a plastic food-storage bag to capture any accumulating liquid, and set on the baking sheet. Place in the refrigerator for 24 hours.

3. Remove the meat from the refrigerator, unwrap, and pat the surface dry; you want to remove any condensation that may have accumulated but also keep the crusted rub intact.

4. Following the manufacturer's instructions for your smoker, bring the meat to the required temperature for smoking. Then, place in the smoker either on a smoking tray, screen, or by hanging in your smoker. Smoke for 1 hour at 225°F. Remove the meat and wrap it tightly in one continuous piece of aluminum foil. There will be plenty of juice coming from this process, so be sure there are no holes or openings in the foil for the juices to drain out.

5. Hot-smoke until the internal temperature reaches 155°F, 2 to 3 hours. Remove from the smoker and allow to rest in the foil until the meat is tender, approximately 30 minutes.

6. Place in a clean plastic food-storage bag or container and chill until ready to use. Cut the amount you are going to use into thin slices and serve as sandwich meat or on a charcuterie plate. Heat slightly if serving warm. Store the unused portion, wrapped, in the refrigerator. The pastrami will keep for up to 1 month.

Dry-Cured Pimenton Salami

YIELD: 3¾ pounds sausage
START TO FINISH: 2 hours chilling + 1 hour to make + 45 minutes stuffing + 4 days fermenting + 2 to 3 weeks aging

This recipe is from chef John Toulze, co-owner at the girl & the fig restaurant and its sister properties in Sonoma, California. This salami is seasoned with pimenton, the Spanish smoked paprika. If you like a slightly spicier flavor, you can add a touch of heat with ground Aleppo pepper, piment d'Espelette, or other chile powder. *See photo on page 193.*

4½ pounds pork shoulder, cubed
10½ ounces pork back fat, plus 1¾ ounces pork back fat cut into ¼-inch cubes
1¾ ounces kosher salt
1 teaspoon Insta Cure #2
3½ ounces dextrose
5 teaspoons garlic powder
3¾ ounces smoked paprika
1 teaspoon TSPX starter culture
3 tablespoons distilled water
Hog casings, soaked in tepid water for 30 minutes, then rinsed

1. Place the pork shoulder and 10½ ounces of the fat in separate containers and then freeze until near frozen, about 2 hours. Grind the meat and fat (not including the hand-diced fat) separately through a ⅜-inch die, making sure to keep the meat as cold as possible during handling.

2. Place all of the meat and fat in the bowl of a stand mixer fitted with the paddle attachment, and add the salt, Insta Cure #2, dextrose, garlic powder, and smoked paprika. Mix well until the paste becomes slightly sticky against the side of the bowl. Dissolve the starter culture in the distilled water. Add this to the meat mixture, mixing thoroughly.

3. Stuff the mixture into sausage casings and tie off to the desired length. Weigh the sausages and note their weights.

4. Ferment the sausages for up to 4 days in an area where temperature and humidity can be controlled to 70°F and 80 to 85 percent humidity. Transfer the salami to an aging area where the temperature is relatively consistent, around 60°F and 75 percent humidity.

5. Dry until the salami have lost roughly one-third of their starting weight. This should take 2 to 3 weeks.

DUCK PROSCIUTTO

YIELD: Depending on the original weight of the breasts, 10 to 12 ounces or more
START TO FINISH: 45 minutes to make + 48 hours refrigeration + 3 to 4 days first cure + 6 to 8 weeks final cure

We all know prosciutto as cured Italian Parma ham. Here is an easy version using duck breasts. Use as any classic prosciutto, thinly sliced on an antipasti platter, wrapped around fresh figs or melon, shredded and tossed into hot pasta, or with the breast seared and sliced as the topping on the Warm Potato and Caramelized Endive Salad with Crispy Duck Prosciutto (page 196).

2 halves duck breast, skin on
1 tablespoon plus 2 teaspoons kosher salt (preferably Diamond Crystal) or sel gris
1 tablespoon raw unrefined cane sugar
½ teaspoon whole white peppercorns
1 teaspoon coriander seeds, toasted
1 teaspoon anise seed, toasted
8 ounces rendered duck fat (recipe follows)

1. Weigh the duck breasts and note it down.

2. Place 1 tablespoon of the salt, the sugar, white pepper, coriander, and anise seed in a spice grinder and grind to combine into a spice mix. Rub the flesh sides of the duck breasts with all of the dry mix.

3. Place the breasts face to face, rub the skins with the remaining 2 teaspoons kosher salt, wrap together in plastic wrap, and cure in the refrigerator for 48 hours.

4. Gently scrape the seasonings from the duck, rinse, and pat dry. Wrap each breast in a single layer of cheesecloth. Attach a string to each one and then hang them in the lower part of the refrigerator (40°F or lower), with a tray underneath to capture any moisture than drains off, for 3 days or until they have

reduced in weight by about one-third. Weigh the duck breasts every day until they lose one-third of their original weight. They should also feel firm but not dried out.

5. Unwrap and rub each breast thoroughly (including sealing the edges) with a solid layer of rendered duck fat to retain the remaining moisture; rewrap in a clean layer of cheesecloth and hang in a controlled temperature (55°F) and humidity (70 percent or more) environment for a minimum of 6 weeks; they will be even better at 8 weeks.

6. Carefully remove the cheesecloth and tightly wrap each breast individually in plastic wrap until ready to use. If you have extra rendered duck fat available, bury the breasts in that instead, cover, and refrigerate. The prosciutto can be refrigerated for up to 4 more weeks. Remove the skin and rub off any of the fat coating before using. Thinly slice it on the diagonal while cold and serve cool or at room temperature.

VARIATIONS

DUCK BACON OPTION: Leaving a thin layer of the fat intact, cold-smoke the prosciutto and then cut into 1/8-inch-thick lengthwise slices. Crisp the slices in a skillet with a small amount of duck fat.

SEARED OPTION: Leave the skin on the breasts, place skin side down in a hot dry skillet, and sear over medium-high heat to render out the fat, until the skin is brown and crispy. Remove from the pan and allow to rest for 5 to 10 minutes before cutting into thin slices.

RENDERED DUCK FAT

Rendered duck fat is used in many recipes in French cuisine as a cooking fat, and also as a packing fat for preserving raw (such as Duck Prosciutto, opposite) and cooked duck (such as confit). It is made by rendering (melting) the fat from the fatty sections of the duck (such as the breast) by cooking or by simply melting chunks of duck fat. To make it, cook the cut-up fat or the breast skin side down in a heated skillet over low heat until the fat is melted and renders out into the pan. Spoon off the fat and place in a jar to cool. Cover and refrigerate. Rendered duck fat can also be purchased from quality duck purveyors such as Sonoma County Poultry (see Resources, page 241).

SUMMER SAUSAGE

YIELD: 5 pounds (approximately 18 sausages)
START TO FINISH: 3 hours chilling + 1 hour to make +
2 days refrigeration + 45 minutes stuffing + 2 hours drying
+ 4½ hours smoking

Summer sausage refers to a dried or smoked sausage that can be kept without refrigeration, which makes it perfect for picnics. It is easy to make and may serve to dispel any anxiety you might have for making sausage at home. But in order for sausage to have this level of stability, there are a few special ingredients you will need (all are available from The Sausage Maker, including sausage casings; see Resources, page 241):

- Fermento: a cultured whey and skim milk starter that speeds up fermentation for safety
- Pink salt (sodium nitrite): a curing salt used to prevent growth of unwanted bacteria
- Dextrose (fine-texture glucose): a naturally occurring sugar that is easily converted in fermentation

You will need a stand mixer with a grinder attachment, ⅛-inch and ¼-inch dies, plus the sausage stuffer tube. You can also use a meat grinder equipped with these dies, and a disposable pastry bag and tip in place of a sausage stuffer. In addition, you'll be using a smoker with both cold- and hot-smoking options. You won't need any dedicated aging environment for curing this sausage, just your home refrigerator.

Note: The pork back listed may not be needed if the pork shoulder you're using has that amount of fat as part of it. You can substitute 3 pounds of grass-fed quality ground beef for the boneless lean beef and mix it with the pork, then regrind using only the smaller die.

Be creative with the flavorings for other versions of this sausage. Apple, garlic, chipotle powder, garam masala, mild curry, or ground cumin are all great options. *See photo on page 193.*

3 pounds boneless lean beef (preferably grass-fed),
    fat and sinew removed, cubed
8 ounces pork back fat, diced (see Note above)
1½ pounds pork shoulder, diced
3 tablespoons kosher or unrefined fine sea salt
3 tablespoons dextrose
1 teaspoon pink salt
½ cup Fermento
¼ to ½ cup filtered water
4 teaspoons mustard powder
1½ teaspoons ground coriander
1½ teaspoons sweet paprika
1 teaspoon garlic powder
Hog casings, soaked in tepid water for 30 minutes,
    then rinsed

1. Place the cubed beef and pork back fat in separate containers and then freeze until near frozen. Chill two 6-quart stainless steel bowls in the freezer.

2. In one chilled bowl, combine the partially frozen beef, fat, pork shoulder, salt, dextrose, and pink salt; mix well.

3. Grind the mixture through the large die into a second chilled bowl set in ice.

4. In a bowl, dissolve the Fermento with $\frac{1}{4}$ to $\frac{1}{2}$ cup filtered water to make a paste. Combine with the mustard powder, coriander, paprika, and garlic powder; stir to mix well.

5. Add to the meat mixture and stir for 2 minutes to combine thoroughly. Fold in the chilled fat.

6. Pack into a food-grade container, removing any air pockets. Cover with plastic wrap, with the wrap pressed against the surface of the meat, and refrigerate for 2 days.

7. Regrind the mixture through the small die. (Regrinding the meat makes for a very fine textured sausage that does not have chunks or air pockets.)

8. Do a taste test. In a small skillet, cook a small bite to taste. Adjust the flavorings, if needed.

9. Stuff the sausage into the casings and twist into 6-inch sausages. Hang to dry in your refrigerator for 2 hours.

10. To smoke: Use your favorite wood for smoking. Fruit woods are always a good choice for this style of sausage. Following the manufacturer's instructions for your smoker, cold-smoke at the lowest temperature for 2 hours. Increase the temperature to 180°F and smoke to an internal temperature of 150°F, 20 to 30 minutes more. The sausage will be dark and firm at this point. Remove from the smoker and hang at room temperature for 2 hours to even out the color. Portion into use amounts and refrigerate at this point. The sausage will be good up to 2 to 3 months.

FERMENTED BEVERAGES

I AM ALWAYS EXPERIMENTING with new fermented beverages and using them as ingredients in marinades or vinaigrettes. "Fermented beverages" makes most of us turn our minds to those with alcohol content. While I love those, too, there are many other interesting and delicious nonalcoholic or low-alcohol beverages to consider for making at home.

Some are fizzy, others not. Some are fruit based (ciders and natural sodas), some are grain and herb based (beers), and still others are dairy based (milk kefir) or water based (water kefir and kombucha). Sugar, raw and unrefined, is part of the cast here, but it's not the star ingredient. Through natural lacto- and in some cases acetic fermentation, the conversion of sugar or starch makes these beverages taste good without being very sweet. Many even have probiotic benefits.

For nearly all the recipes in this chapter, I've focused on beverages that are easier or less time consuming to make than wine or more complex beer, with ingredients and equipment that are accessible, and can be made in any region of the country. But I also wanted to include a couple of beer recipes for the many devoted homebrewers out there. Note that these two recipes are best tackled by those with significant previous experience in home brewing. And to not disappoint any other imbibers, you'll find recipes for the popular categories of ciders and mead online at www.masteringfermentation.com. Also note that fermented fruit and vegetable juices, which can be used as ingredients in other fermented beverages, are discussed in chapter 3.

Equipment and Supplies

The basic equipment and supplies you'll need for nearly all the recipes in this chapter include the following:

- Bottle-cleaning brushes (assorted sizes)

- Butter muslin or fine-weave cheesecloth (2 to 3 yards), from cheese making supplier

- Flexible blade rubber or silicone spatulas (no wooden handles)

- Funnels (wide mouth to fill jars and small to fill bottles)

Natural Sodas

Natural sodas are made with real sugar or other natural sweeteners (no high-fructose corn syrup) and unprocessed flavoring ingredients. Flavors are limited only by your imagination and creativity as a mixologist. Take your lead from the latest flavor trends in interesting store-bought versions, or look to ingredient combinations in classic or contemporary cocktails.

You can make natural sodas in a couple of ways: by culturing and fermenting the ingredients, and then bottling to ferment further, building up carbonation; or by adding ferments to carbonated water or water kefir to create the soda. Water Kefir (page 171) is a wonderful, lightly carbonated probiotic base for making natural fermented sodas. You can also use store-bought bottled carbonated water as the base ingredient or purchase a home soda maker for carbonating household water. First, carbonate the water and then flavor as you choose. Using carbonated water does not result in a fermented drink per se, but it is an easy route for making on-demand natural sodas. The recipes

for Water Kefir Coconut-Ginger Soda (page 174) and Root Beer (page 168) include the methods mentioned. Consider them a starting point for your experimentations.

Once armed with a collection of homemade bottled herbal infusions, shrubs, drinking vinegars, bitter and sweet syrups, and fermented juices from your fermentation pantry, you can make amazing fizzy sodas just the way you like them. Keep a selection of dried flower blossoms, teas, herbs, fresh or dried ginger, and fresh or dried citrus handy for additional infusion ingredients. Use bitters in sodas as in cocktails.

Store the finished beverages in refrigeration to maintain the sweetness level and slow down the increasing carbonation. Some sodas are best served chilled and others are delicious served at room temperature. I prefer my water kefir at room temperature. Any fermented beverages left out at room temperature should be burped daily, allowing the developed gases to be released. Carbonation will continue when the vessel is closed.

- Glass and stainless-steel measuring cups

- Glass clamp-top (swing-top, aka Grolsch-style) beverage bottles

- Glass gallon jars and lids

- Glass vinegar or wine bottles with stoppers

- Ladle or slotted spoon (stainless steel or other nonreactive material)

- Mesh strainers (stainless steel and nylon mesh)

- Nonreactive metal (only stainless steel, ceramic on cast iron, or enamel on steel; no aluminum or nonstick) pots and stockpots

- Stainless-steel measuring spoons, including $\frac{1}{8}$ teaspoon and $\frac{1}{16}$ teaspoon

- Tea bags (muslin or mesh)

- Weights (glass coasters, glass votive candle holders, small plates, small glass jars, washed river rocks)

Optional equipment: Kombucha electric warming mat, spouted beverage crocks from Kombucha Kamp (see Resources, page 241)

Herbal Tonics and Digestifs

Many herbal, floral, and botanical tonics (drinks having restorative properties) have been fundamental beverages in numerous cultures for hundreds of years. Often these drinks are better thirst quenchers than water, and in some parts of the world, safer to drink. Traditional beverages designed to stimulate the appetite pre-meal (aperitifs) or stimulate digestion post-meal (digestifs) are still produced in France, Italy, and other parts of the Mediterranean, and served at bars and dinner tables throughout the region as well as in the United States. Though many are alcoholic, having fortified wine or spirits as the carrier ingredient, delicious nonalcoholic lacto-fermented stimulators have also been important components of nutrient-rich diets throughout Europe and Asia.

The brines from fermented vegetables (such as sauerkraut) or fruits can be added to other fermented fruit or vegetable juices (see chapter 3) to make tonic drinks. Drinking vinegars or shrubs (see page 169) added to sparkling or flat water; Kombucha, made from sweetened fermented tea (page 177); and Water and Milk Kefirs (pages 171 and 175) are also tonics containing beneficial restorative properties.

Ginger Beer

YIELD: 1 gallon
START TO FINISH: 20 minutes to make + 5 minutes stirring daily for 3 days + 3 to 5 days fermenting to build carbonation

Ginger beer is not a beer but a naturally fermented soda using a starter. It can be either nonalcoholic or alcoholic, and tastes like a strong, more gingery ginger ale. I love it plain, but it makes a zippy mixer, too. It can even be warmed with spices to make mulled cider. For this fermented version, you first make a wild-yeast ginger starter, known as a "ginger bug." This starter helps ferment the final beverage. It is easy to make, but you'll need to plan ahead because the bug takes a few days to become a useful starter.

Note: Be sure to leave the ginger's thin skin on; it carries desirable bacteria needed for successful fermentation. You'll need a 1-gallon glass jar for brewing, plus swing-top bottles for storage (see Resources, page 241).

14 cups nonchlorinated unfiltered water
1/3 cup freshly squeezed lemon juice
1 1/2 cups raw unrefined cane sugar, plus more as needed
1 cup Ginger Bug starter (opposite)
1/3 cup packed grated organic ginger (skin on)

1. Place the water and the lemon juice in a 1-gallon glass jar and stir in the sugar to dissolve. Add the Ginger Bug and grated ginger and stir for a few minutes to aerate. Cover the jar with cheesecloth and secure with a rubber band.

2. Wrap just the sides of the jar (not the top) with a kitchen towel or place the jar in a mitt pot holder to keep it insulated. Let sit in a warm (75°F to 85°F) area of your kitchen, perhaps on top of the refrigerator or under the stove hood light.

3. Stir the mixture every day for 3 days, tasting each time. If the brew loses its sweetness, add 1/4 cup more sugar. You should see bubbles (sign of carbonation) by the end of the third day; if not, add 1 cup more of the Ginger Bug, stir, and wait 1 to 2 days for bubbles to appear. Once you have bubbles, strain the mixture into a glass measuring cup, then use a funnel to fill the prepared stopper bottles. Leave at room temperature for 3 to 5 days to build up carbonation. When fizzy to your liking, refrigerate until ready to serve. The sweetness diminishes over time, so the beer is best if consumed with a few weeks.

GINGER BUG

YIELD: About 3¼ cups
START TO FINISH: 10 minutes to make + 24 hours fermenting + 10 minutes feeding daily for 3 to 7 days

3⅓ cups nonchlorinated unfiltered water
1 tablespoon raw unrefined cane sugar, plus more for feeding starter
1 tablespoon grated organic ginger (skin on), plus more for feeding starter

1. Place the water in a quart jar and add the sugar. Stir to dissolve and then stir in the grated ginger. Stir for a few minutes to aerate. Cover the jar with cheesecloth and secure with a rubber band.

2. Wrap just the sides of the jar (not the top) with a kitchen towel or place the jar in a mitt pot holder to keep it insulated. Let sit in a warm (75°F to 85°F) area of your kitchen, perhaps on top of the refrigerator or under the stove hood light.

3. After 24 hours, feed the starter with 4 teaspoons sugar and 1 tablespoon grated ginger. Stir in as before. Repeat this process every 24 hours for 3 to 7 days or until obvious fizzing is present. You should see small bubbles at the surface edges after 2 days. Once fizzing is present, stop feeding. The bug is now ready to use. If you don't have bubbles and fizzing after 7 days, discard and start a new batch.

BONUS RECIPE #1

You many have some bug left over in some recipes (as in this one). Use what remains as a starter to ferment compatible fruits and juices. Store any leftover bug for up to 1 week, in a closed jar, and refrigerate. Bring to room temperature 1 day before you are ready to use and give one feed using the same amounts of sugar and ginger as before. Cover with cheesecloth, wrap, and leave in a warm environment to activate. Feed it twice, if needed, to see bubbles. Once you see bubbles around the surface, as you saw before, you can use this starter to ferment as suggested.

BONUS RECIPE #2

If all of the bug is used in the final beverage (resulting in stronger flavor), you can reuse the bug sediment to start a new bug. Discard half of the sediment, add 2 cups of water, 2 teaspoons sugar, and 2 teaspoons grated ginger, and stir to combine. Repeat for 7 days as before.

ROOT BEER

YIELD: About 14 ounces syrup
START TO FINISH: 1½ hours to make + 12 hours at room temperature + 1 day refrigeration

The original root beer was created in the mid-1800s in Philadelphia by a pharmacist, Charles Hines. It was a naturally fermented beverage made with various roots (burdock, sassafras, and ginger being the most prominent), herbs, molasses, and some barks (sarsaparilla, wintergreen, and others) and had low alcohol content. This nonalcoholic version uses a fermented root beer syrup and carbonated water. Play with the proportions to suit your taste. The dried ingredients can be purchased from your local natural foods store or online from Mountain Rose Herbs (see Resources, page 241).

4 cups filtered water
4 cups raw unrefined cane sugar
2 ounces chopped sassafras root
1 ounce chopped burdock root
1 whole star anise
1 ounce (1½-inch piece) fresh ginger, chopped
1 ounce juniper berries
1 whole clove
1 teaspoon coriander seeds
½ teaspoon dried orange zest
¼ teaspoon dried mint leaves
¼ cup unsulphured molasses (not blackstrap)
Carbonated water

1. The syrup begins as a tea—an infusion of the roots, spices, herbs, and sugar. In a nonreactive pot, combine the water and sugar and stir to dissolve. Add the rest of the ingredients except for the molasses and bring to a simmer over medium heat. Simmer for 30 minutes, remove from the heat, and let steep for 15 minutes while the tea cools.

2. Strain the tea through fine-weave cheesecloth or a double mesh strainer into a separate nonreactive pot. Stir in the molasses. Bring the mixture to a low boil over medium heat, decrease the heat, and simmer for 10 minutes to reduce slightly.

3. Cool the mixture and place in a wide-mouth 1-quart glass jar. Securely attach a layer of cheesecloth over the opening and leave at room temperature for 12 hours or overnight. Bottle and refrigerate for 1 day to thicken to a syrupy consistency. The syrup will keep for a few weeks.

4. To use, combine 1 ounce of the syrup with 5 to 6 ounces of carbonated water per serving and serve over ice.

Drinking Vinegars and Shrubs

Drinking vinegars as beverage ingredients have recently garnered attention from mixologists and chefs all over the United States. Drinking raw, unfiltered vinegar (especially apple cider vinegar) puts beneficial vitamins and other nutrients into our systems. Often the terms "drinking vinegar" and "shrub" are used interchangeably. For my pantry, they are developed slightly differently in terms of sweetness. Both are used in a diluted form to create refreshing beverages. Start with a ratio of 5-to-1 water (flat or sparkling) to fruit vinegar (see page 33) or shrub and adjust as your taste dictates.

Herbal versions can be made with basil, mint, lemon verbena, or lovage; floral ones can be made with rose petals or hibiscus. These shrubs require a bit more attention but are wonderful. You can find recipes for these online at www.masteringfermentation.com.

GINGER-MINT SHRUB

YIELD: About 1½ cups
START TO FINISH: 10 minutes preparation + 12 hours fermenting + 1 week at room temperature + 1 week refrigeration

Shrubs date back to colonial America. Use these amazing sweet-sour syrups to make cocktails, sodas, and to flavor Water Kefir (page 171), or even Kombucha (page 177)! They also make great vinaigrettes.

½ cup thinly sliced fresh ginger
½ cup packed fresh mint leaves
¾ cup raw, unfiltered apple cider vinegar
½ cup freshly squeezed lime juice
½ cup raw unrefined cane sugar

1. Place the ginger and mint leaves in a glass jar; bruise them to release some of the juices. Add the vinegar, close the jar tightly, and shake vigorously for 10 seconds. Replace the lid with cheesecloth. Securely attach a layer of cheesecloth over the opening and leave at room temperature for 12 hours or overnight.

2. Replace the cheesecloth with the lid, secure tightly, and repeat the vigorous shaking daily for 1 week. Strain out the ginger and mint and stir in the lime juice and sugar until dissolved. Bottle, add a sprig of mint, close tightly, and shake vigorously for 10 seconds. Refrigerate for 7 days before using. Give the bottle a vigorous shake every day for that week. Refrigerate after opening. Syrup will last for up to 4 months.

Kefir: Water and Milk

Kefir (keh-FEER) is a remarkable, effervescent fermented beverage typically made from whole cow or goat milk, or water, though today it is also made with coconut milk or water, soy, nut, and grain milks. Once fermented into kefir, milk and water take on enormous digestive benefits they lack in their unfermented state since kefir has remarkable beneficial probiotic properties. Kefirs are cultured with special organisms called "grains." These clusters are called grains due to their appearance. They are composed of a symbiotic colony of bacteria and yeast (SCOBY). Though their functions are the same (to ferment the fluid they are placed in), the grains for each have different properties in appearance, texture, and composition. For milk kefir, they are soft, gelatinous white or yellow clusters, whereas the water kefir grains are solid, dry particles resembling enlarged sugar clusters.

The dehydrated water kefir grains (see top photo at right) first need to be hydrated and activated (the first fermentation stage) before being placed in the water to produce a fermented beverage. (See hydrated water kefir grains in the bottom photo at right.) Milk kefir grains do not need to be activated before being placed in the milk. In all cases, after fermenting the beverage, the grains are then removed before the beverage is consumed. The used grains can be immediately used in a new batch of the same fluid or stored (see headnote, opposite) to be used in a future batch. These grains are available online and from a few retail sources. Be aware that not all grains being sold are of premium quality so don't just shop based on price alone. Buy from a reliable source such as Cultures for Health (see Resources, page 241), or secure some healthy grains from a friend's vibrant colony. Once you have a healthy colony of grains, with proper care, they can be used indefinitely.

Top to bottom: Dehydrated water kefir grains, hydrated water kefir grains

WATER KEFIR

YIELD: 2 quarts
START TO FINISH: 2 hours to heat and cool water + 3 to 4 days rehydrating grains at room temperature + 2 hours to heat and cool water + 24 to 48 hours fermenting + 2 days at room temperature before consuming

A mildly effervescent, aromatic fermented beverage, water kefir begins as sugar water cultured with a unique SCOBY (Symbiotic Colony of Bacteria and Yeast). This is used to grow the colony of organism that feeds on the sugar, contributing beneficial organisms to create a fermented fluid. The majority of the sugar is consumed by the colony, leaving about 10 percent in the final beverage. As a result of the SCOBY, water kefir is probiotic. Water kefir is often combined with other juices, fruits, or vinegars to add flavor and carbonation.

Kefir grains require minerals to thrive. Hard, mineral-rich water such as well water or spring water is best. Do not use filtered water because too many of the minerals will have been removed. If using tap water, first bring it to a boil to remove any possible chlorine, and then cool it to room temperature before using. Supplementing with Trace Mineral Drops ($1/8$ teaspoon per quart of water) is a good security measure. These can be purchased from the same source as your grains (see Resources, page 241).

Use kefir as a mixer; add infusions or syrups to it to make sodas (see page 164) or agua frescas. Used in alcoholic beverages, the beneficial bacteria will be inactivated, but the taste is great. I have found that making two separate jars of water kefir works best for my needs. This method allows me to ferment each of them to different levels of sweetness and carbonation. Once transferred to my 1-liter swing-top bottles, I can flavor the sweeter one with fruit or grated fresh ginger, and leave the other plain.

Follow the vendor's directions for hydrating the grains. The quantities you receive may differ from one company to another. In general, the formula and method used at the beginning of this recipe works well.

Unused grains can be fed and stored, covered, in sugar water ($1/4$ cup sugar to 1 quart water), and refrigerated for up to 2 weeks. Bring the mixture to room temperature before using the grains for a new batch of kefir. For longer periods of storage, the grains should be laid out to dehydrate, stored in an airtight container, and refrigerated. This process returns the grains to their original state.

12 cups nonchlorinated water, at room temperature
$3/4$ cup raw unrefined cane sugar or Sucanat
2 teaspoons dehydrated grains (see photo opposite)

1. To hydrate the grains: The first time you use the dehydrated grains (or if they have been stored for an extended period of time), they need to be hydrated to become active. In a small pan, heat 2 cups of the water over medium-high heat to just boiling. Place $1/4$ cup of the raw sugar in a 1-quart glass jar and cover with the hot water. Stir to thoroughly dissolve the sugar. Add enough room-temperature water to bring the level of the liquid to the shoulder of the jar. Cool the mixture to room temperature and then add the grains. Cover the opening with fine-weave cheesecloth or a kitchen towel and secure with a rubber band. Allow the mixture to sit at room temperature for 3 to 4 days until the grains are plump. You are

continued

taking a risk if you let them sit any longer than 5 days, as the grains may start to lose their potency from lack of food (sugar).

2. To make the kefir: In a small pan, heat 2 more cups of the water over medium-high heat to just boiling. Divide the remaining ½ cup sugar between two 1-quart glass jars and cover evenly with the hot water. Stir to thoroughly dissolve the sugar. Add enough room-temperature water to bring the level of the liquid to the shoulder of the jar.

3. Cool the mixture to room temperature, and then add equal amounts of the loose plump grains in each jar. Cover the jar opening with fine-weave cheesecloth or a kitchen towel and secure with a rubber band.

4. Allow the mixture to sit at room temperature for 24 to 48 hours, depending on the level of sweetness you want. Shorter time will result in a sweeter kefir; longer will be less so. Do not exceed 72 hours.

5. About 12 hours before you are ready to strain the kefir, start a new batch of sugar water to prepare for the next batch of kefir. This sugar water will need to be ready to receive the grains once you have strained the kefir.

6. Once it has reached the desired level of sweetness, use a dedicated fine-mesh nylon strainer to strain off the liquid into a spouted glass measuring vessel. Using a funnel, fill two 1-liter swing-top bottles. Place the captured grains in the new batch of sugar water to store.

7. Secure the caps on the bottles and leave at room temperature until ready to consume. In a day or so, tiny bubbles of carbonation will appear. This will increase as time passes and if you add fruit to the kefir. Water kefir does not need to be refrigerated unless you want it chilled. It's best to consume within 10 days after opening a bottle.

ALTERNATIVE KEFIRS

Water kefir grains can be used to make a range of other kefirs. Add rehydrated water kefir grains to 4 to 8 cups coconut milk or water, soy, nut, or grain milks, or fruit or vegetable juices and allow to ferment for 24 to 48 hours depending upon the fizziness and flavor you desire. As with other kefirs, remove the grains before consuming the fermented beverage. Grains can be reused, but only for the same purposes. Do not cross-use the grains. Water kefir beer is discussed at www.masteringfermentation.com.

From left: blueberry water kefir, coconut water kefir, hibiscus-ginger water kefir

Water Kefir Coconut-Ginger Soda

YIELD: About 3½ cups (28 ounces)
START TO FINISH: 30 minutes to make + 1 to 5 days carbonation at room temperature

As with so many homemade items, you get to decide the specifics of this soda: both how sweet and how fizzy it is. Enjoy chilled or at room temperature, make a soda float using homemade Yogurt-Cardamom Ice Cream (page 230), or blend the ingredients together to make a milkshake.

1 quart freshly brewed Water Kefir (page 171)
1¼ cups raw or natural coconut water
3 tablespoons Ginger-Mint Shrub (page 169)
2 strips lime zest

1. Place the kefir in a swing-top glass bottle. Add the coconut water and shrub. Stir to combine. Add the lime zest and secure the top. Set at room temperature for one day before testing for carbonation. You should hear the soft sound of released gases when you open the top.

2. Taste the soda. If you like the flavor at this point, it is good to consume. If it is too sweet, leave for another day so more sugar is consumed by the yeast. The soda will become less sweet and fizzier as time goes on. It can be left at room temperature or refrigerate if you want to slow down the carbonation process. Unrefrigerated, this is best consumed within 5 days; refrigerated, up to 7 days.

Milk Kefir

YIELD: 1 quart
START TO FINISH: 15 minutes to make + 12 to 24 hours fermenting + 1 to 2 weeks refrigeration

A fermented dairy beverage, milk kefir is similar in flavor to yogurt, but a bit more sour. Even though it is often called liquid yogurt, kefir is cultured with a complex network of organisms known as a SCOBY (Symbiotic Colony of Bacteria and Yeast) that are quite different from yogurt cultures. As a result of the SCOBY, milk kefir is probiotic and slightly alcoholic (around $2\frac{1}{2}$ percent) due to alcohol that is produced by the yeast during fermentation. Homemade milk kefir is more potent than store-bought, so drink only small amounts (up to 4 ounces) until your system becomes accustomed to it. Milk kefir usually does not bother those who are lactose intolerant because the bacteria and yeast present in the fermenting process consume most, if not all, of the lactose.

You can adjust the ratio of milk to amount of grains used to your taste. Adjust upward using more grains for a stronger and more tart result, or downward for a mild one. Nonfat milk does not work for milk kefir because it lacks the fat needed by the grains to grow properly. Milk kefir grains are different from water kefir grains; they cannot be used interchangeably.

Unused milk kefir grains can be fed by placing them in fresh milk and stored, covered, and then refrigerated for up to 2 weeks. Bring the mixture to room temperature before using the grains for a new batch of kefir. For longer periods of storage, the grains should be laid out to dehydrate and then stored in powdered milk, in an airtight container, and refrigerated. This process takes the grains back to their original state.

Dedicated fine-mesh nylon strainer

4 cups pasteurized whole milk or 2 percent milk, at room temperature
2 tablespoons hydrated milk kefir grains

1. Place the grains in a 1-quart glass jar and cover with the milk. Cover the jar opening with fine-weave cheesecloth or a kitchen towel and secure with a rubber band.

2. Allow the mixture to sit at room temperature for 12 to 24 hours, depending on the level of tartness you want. Shorter time will result in a milder kefir; longer will be stronger. Do not exceed 72 hours. Stir vigorously for 10 seconds every 8 hours or so. Taste the kefir each time to determine the level of tartness.

3. Once the desired level of tartness has been reached, strain off the milk through a fine-mesh strainer into a spouted glass measuring vessel. Place the captured grains in a new batch of milk, or without rinsing, place directly into a glass jar and refrigerate for up to 2 weeks.

4. Fill a clean 1-quart glass jar or 1-liter bottle with the strained milk. If flavoring the kefir, do so at this point. Secure the lid on the jar or cap on the bottle of kefir and refrigerate. It's best if consumed within 10 days after opening.

BEET KVASS

YIELD: About 1½ quarts
START TO FINISH: 1 hour to make + 4 to 5 days fermenting + 1 week refrigeration + 4 to 6 hours at room temperature

Kvass is a lacto-fermented nonalcoholic beverage from Russia, traditionally made from stale rye bread and beets. This tasty beet and citrus fruit kvass recipe was contributed by Jennifer Harris, an accomplished fermentation enthusiast who organizes fermentation events in Northern California. Mixing 6 ounces of finished Beet Kvass with 12 ounces of basic Kombucha (opposite) makes for a wonderful sparkling tonic. Combine the two in a swing-top bottle and allow to sit at room temperature for 4 to 6 hours. The carbonation will continue to build up; don't leave it for longer than 12 hours at room temperature.

Note that you will need a 2-liter glass jar with an air lock (a white plastic Ball jar lid left loose will work as well) and a 2-inch weight to fit inside of the jar (scrubbing, then boiling a rock from the garden for 10 minutes will sanitize it and makes a nice cheap weight).

2 pounds red or yellow beets
1 lemon, quartered
6 to 8 kumquats (substitute 4 quartered tangerines or 3 medium quartered oranges if kumquats are not available), halved
1- to 2-inch knob fresh ginger
½- to 1-inch knob turmeric root or 1 teaspoon turmeric powder
1 tablespoon unrefined fine sea salt
6 cups spring water or filtered water

1. Wash the outside of the produce with water or vegetable wash, but do not peel the beets or citrus; scrub off any dirt. Chop the beets into 1- to 2-inch pieces and place them in the jar.

2. Squeeze the lemon juice into the jar and drop in the peels. Drop the kumquat halves into the jar, squeezing as you add them. Grate the ginger and turmeric on top of the fruit.

3. In a separate container, dissolve the salt in the water.

4. Pour salted water over the produce to cover. The ginger and turmeric will float to the top, which is fine.

5. Place the weight on top of the contents to keep them submerged.

6. Cover with a lid or air lock and ferment at room temperature for 4 to 5 days. Once a day, open the jar to release any built up gasses (unneeded with an air lock), and gently stir the liquid to submerge the floating ginger and turmeric back into the brine periodically.

7. Strain the liquid from the beets and fruit. Let the liquid sit in the refrigerator or root cellar in a closed container to continue low-temperature (38°F to 40°F) fermentation for 1 week (open the lid once or twice during this week to avoid pressure buildup). As the produce ferments during this stage, the saltiness will continue to soften and the slightest bit of carbonation will build up.

8. After 1 week in the fridge, put the liquid into swing-top bottles and leave at room temperature for 4 to 6 hours. This builds up a nice amount of carbonation. Refrigerate before consuming. It's best if consumed within 10 days after opening a bottle.

KOMBUCHA

YIELD: About 13 cups
START TO FINISH: 2 hours to make + 7 to 10 days fermenting + 30 minutes bottling + 2 days at room temperature

This lightly carbonated tea-based beverage has gained in mainstream popularity over the past few years, though its roots go far back to the Chinese Tsin Dynasty in 221 BCE. It can be made with black, green, or white organic teas or combinations thereof. It uses a mother starter known as a SCOBY (Symbiotic Colony of Bacteria and Yeast), often identified as looking like a gelatinous pancake that floats on the surface of the fermenting tea. This colony of organisms grows thicker over time and can be parceled to friends to start new batches of kombucha. When not in use, the SCOBY should be stored in a covered glass jar, immersed in kombucha or raw apple cider vinegar, and kept in a cool, dark location. It can be stored for a few months in this environment or refrigerated for longer.

Kombucha is both slightly sweet and sour, with a bit of astringency. The shorter the fermentation, the sweeter the kombucha will be; the longer the fermentation, the more sour it becomes. About half of the caffeine from the original tea is left in the kombucha, and very little of the sugar. As with many other fermented beverages, kombucha has many beneficial properties. The yeasts and bacteria in the SCOBY consume the sugar in the tea, thereby producing Vitamin B, lactic acid, acetic acid, and gluconic acid, a valuable but powerful detoxifier. Drink small—1/4 cup or so—portions of it throughout the day, before meals (over time it will reduce the amount of food you'll want to eat at meals), and after your evening meal to assist in digestion. Be sure to replenish your system by also drinking water throughout the day when drinking kombucha to benefit the most from its diuretic properties. After bottling, kombucha can be flavored with fruit, herbs, or roots such as beneficial ginger or turmeric. Do not use decaffeinated tea; instead, to remove any caffeine, soak the caffeinated tea in near-boiling water for 15 seconds before brewing. Molasses can substitute for sugar using a 1-to-1 ratio. It will take longer for the sugars in molasses to convert but you'll get the added benefits of the minerals it contains. Kombucha can even be made with brewed coffee in place of tea.

Kombucha makes a tasty brine or marinade for meats and adds punch to salad dressings.

A SCOBY can be purchased from a reliable retail source or, if you're lucky, you might get one as a gift from a friend's thriving colony. Kits for making basic kombucha are available from Lion Heart Kombucha and Kombucha Kamp (see Resources, page 241). In any case, you'll need a 1-gallon glass jar and a muslin tea bag to make this kombucha.

4 to 6 teaspoons organic loose black tea (such as caffeinated oolong, green, or a combination)
13 cups filtered water
1 cup raw unrefined cane sugar
8 ounces finished plain kombucha from a previous batch to jump-start this batch (optional)
1 SCOBY

1. Place the loose tea in a muslin tea bag. In a saucepan, combine 3 cups of the water with the tea bag and the sugar. Stir to dissolve the sugar and then bring to a boil over medium heat. Take off the heat and steep

continued

for 30 minutes. Remove the tea bag and squeeze out any tea. Add the remaining 10 cups of water. Cool to 98°F. Add the finished plain kombucha, if using.

2.   Place the SCOBY in a clean 1-gallon glass jar and cover with the cooled tea. Cover the opening of the jar with cheesecloth and secure with a rubber band. Store in a warm, dark location for 7 to 10 days. Taste it every few days and when you think it is ready, testing for sweetness, sourness, and carbonation. Bottle in swing-top bottles at this point or leave to ferment longer.

3.   When you are satisfied with the result, save about 1½ cups (12 ounces) of kombucha for storing the SCOBY (which you can use to make another batch of kombucha). Pour the remainder into a glass container; siphon or pour the kombucha into storage bottles or lidded jars, leaving ½ inch of air space at the top. Discard the residual matter.

4.   Using your clean hands or a stainless steel slotted spoon, remove the SCOBY from the primary jar and move to a smaller clean container along with the 1½ cups kombucha. Store as directed in the headnote, until ready to use for the next batch.

5.   Leave the bottled kombucha at room temperature for 1 to 2 days to build up carbonation, and then refrigerate until ready to consume. After bottling, your kombucha can last for up to 3 months or longer. It is best if consumed within 7 days after opening a bottle.

Kombucha SCOBY in jar of brewed tea

Placing kombucha SCOBY into brewed tea

Turmeric-flavored green tea kombucha

Sparkling Fruity Kombucha

YIELD: 2 gallons
START TO FINISH: 2 hours to make + 7 to 16 days fermenting + 30 minutes bottling + 3 to 5 days fermenting

Use fresh fruit juice to make this sparkling kombucha from fermentation expert Jennifer Harris, created through an extended fermentation time. Use freshly squeezed juice or one that is store-bought as long as it is 100 percent juice with no preservatives. Note that you'll need 14 (16-ounce) swing-top bottles or 4 empty plastic 2-liter soda bottles.

1 cup raw unrefined cane sugar
1½ gallons filtered or bottled water
5 bags green or black unflavored tea or 5 teaspoons
    loose tea
1 SCOBY
4 cups pure fruit juice of your choice

1.   In a large pot, dissolve the sugar into the water and boil for 5 minutes over medium-high heat. Turn off the heat, add the tea bags, and steep for 4 minutes. Remove the tea bags, cover the pot with cheesecloth or a clean kitchen towel, and let cool to room temperature.

2.   Once cool, place the SCOBY in the bottom of a wide-mouth 2-gallon glass jar, and pour the cooled sweet tea over it. Cover with doubled layers of cheesecloth, and place in a dark spot indoors at 65°F to 80°F and ferment for 7 days, undisturbed.

3.   After 7 days, check the kombucha each day using a plastic straw to draw up a small sample amount. Allow the kombucha to become as sour as you like. At 7 days, you should begin to taste the sour tang of a kombucha beverage; at 21 days, the beverage will be so tart that it will taste more like apple cider vinegar. Those who appreciate a stronger flavor might allow their kombucha to ferment 14 to 16 days. Those who appreciate a sweeter kombucha flavor might allow their kombucha to ferment 8 to 10 days. I often like mine fermented to 11 days.

4.   Using a stainless steel slotted spoon, remove the SCOBY from the primary jar and move to a smaller clean container along with 3 cups of kombucha. Store as directed for kombucha (see page 177) until ready to use for the next batch.

5.   Pour the fruit juice into the remaining kombucha and stir to combine. Using a measuring cup or stainless steel ladle and funnel, fill each bottle. Leave ½ inch of air space at the top before closing.

6.   Close each bottle and set aside to ferment for 3 to 5 days at room temperature. If using plastic soda bottles, you can squeeze the bottles to detect carbonation. When using glass bottles with a swing-top lid, it is best to check at 3 days and each day afterward by opening the jar to see how the carbonation is building up.

7.   Drink within 1 month of bottling. Chilling bottles in the refrigerator prior to opening will minimize foaming and overspill, but be sure to open them over the sink, since carbonation will increase with time.

Beer

This chapter would not be complete without including a sip or two of the world's most popular (and my favorite) fermented beverage, beer. Though this subject could easily be a book unto itself, the information you'll find here was crafted as a short introduction to whet your appetite for home beer brewing. Home-brew versions of the two classic styles of beer, lager and ale, will start you on a flavor-filled effervescent journey: Black Pepper Pilsner (page 186), a mellow American pilsner-style lager with a peppery finish, and Hop Stoopid Ale (page 188), the notable hop-forward ale made by Lagunitas Brewing Company in Petaluma, California.

What is beer, anyway? The term *beer* covers the full range of fermented grain beverages, encompassing lagers, ales, and wheat beers. Steeped in history, this fermented grain-based beverage is more than five thousand years old, and is made with water, malt (germinated barley or wheat), yeast, and hops. Some scholars say that in ancient times growing grains (barley and wheat) for bread making lead to their use for beer making, the first steps toward creating an agriculturally based civilization. Beer was made by boiling water in which the malt was steeped—there was no yeast or hops in those times. The brewed liquid turned the local, often bacteria-ridden water supply into a nutritional beverage, rendering it safer than the water itself. Once allowed to ferment into a drinkable beverage, it also contributed to the digestion of the daily meals.

In today's world, whether producing a lager (fermented at temperatures of 45°F to 50°F, with bottom-fermenting yeast, then aged for several weeks to several months) or an ale (fermented at temperatures of 65°F to 68°F, with top-fermenting yeast, then

aged for a few weeks), fermentation in terms of beer is the process by which yeast feeds on sugars, producing ethyl alcohol and carbon dioxide (the carbonation) as by-products.

Though the concept of home brewing may seem to be a relatively new trend, it is actually experiencing a renaissance. Much of the beer brewing throughout recent history occurred in the home (usually made by the woman of the household) until the industrialization of this process drove out local small-scale production in favor of centralized large-scale production. Today, craft breweries are proliferating across the American landscape, with creative brewmasters putting their individual and regional spins on classic traditions, brewing up amazing bubbly concoctions for us to enjoy and be inspired by.

Brewing beer at home does not require a special set of skills, though some basic specialized equipment and ingredients and a general understanding of unique brewing terms are needed before you jump into your pot of hot mash. As with other fermentations, safety and sanitation are of premium importance. A list of specialized equipment, supplies, and definitions of brewing terms used in these recipes are included here. Once you are comfortable with the home-brewing and bottling processes, try a few recipes of interest, then mix up a few batches of your own proprietary blends, inspired by your favorite crafted brews. Join your local and national home-brew organizations to share experiences, taste a variety of beers, and keep current on the trends. Your local brewing supplier probably has a brew club worth participating in.

In addition, there are a number of very useful and enjoyable books available on beer and home brewing. A few of my favorites are listed in the Recommended Reading section at www.masteringfermentation.com.

EQUIPMENT

In order to make the beers presented here, you'll need some specialized brewing equipment. Check Resources (page 241), for where to get individual basic brewing items or kits. The Beverage People have a Super Standard Brewing Equipment Kit for 5 gallons that includes a great basic selection of must-have equipment if you are new to beer brewing and bottling. Kegging systems (as an alternative to bottling) are also available. The basic equipment and supplies you'll need include the following:

- Three 5-gallon stainless steel brewing kettles with lids

- Two 8- or 10-gallon stainless steel brewing kettles with lids

- 6.8-gallon plastic fermentor and lid

- 5-gallon PET plastic carboy for secondary storage

- Air lock and drilled rubber stopper

- Siphon assembly

- Bottle filler

- Bottle caps

- Bottle capper

- Stirring spoon

- Bottle brush

- Cleaner

- Sanitizer

- 54 (12-ounce) beer bottles or 30 (22-ounce) beer bottles

- Wort cooler (optional)

INGREDIENTS

As with the other forms of fermenting, when brewing, begin with the best quality ingredients you can find. It is important to know the source of your ingredients. The primary ingredient to source is water—the success of your brew depends on it. Purchase the flavoring ingredients from reliable sources such as the brewing suppliers listed in Resources (see page 241). Once you've tried the beer recipes in this section or at www.masteringfermentation.com, you may choose to explore substituting regional or homegrown hops, or home-toasted grains to experiment and taste how their unique contributions affect your brew.

Water. Water contributes up to 95 percent of the finished product. As with other fermentations, the quality of the water is of utmost importance for success. Reverse osmosis water, which can be purchased at many national grocers in the water section, and in storefront vending machines, is best for consistent results. You can also adjust the hardness or softness of your municipal water to suite the style of beer being brewed. Learn more on how to do this by reading *Brewing Quality Beers*, by Byron Burch.

Malt grains. The primary source of sugar for the yeast to consume and convert. The starches in malted grains have been converted into fermentable sugars through the malting process. Malted grains in various unique combinations give the beer its flavor, body, and mouthfeel (see sidebar on page 185).

Sugar. Serves to raise the alcohol level and add carbonation to the beer. It does little to add flavor. Corn sugar (dextrose) is primarily used in home brewing. Other sugars can be used: honey, maple syrup, molasses, sorghum syrup, cane sugar (sucrose), demerara, and turbinado.

Hops

Hops are the flower cones (whole hops) of the female hop plant and are members of the hemp family; they are an essential ingredient in beer making. Hops contain an essential oil with a very bitter flavor. Hops also contain the chemical compound alpha acid, the amount of which determines the level of bitterness. The percentage of alpha acid (% AA) in the variety of hops being used is valuable to the brewer to determine the desired level of bitterness in the finished beer. Pungent, resiny hops are used in beer making in their papery state as a natural preservative, a flavoring, or an aromatic. Hops can be used whole (fresh), or in pellet or extract form. Their bitterness counters the sweetness of the malt in the brew. The percentage of alpha acid (in other words, the amount of hops by weight that is alpha acid) is listed on the label of the packaged hops. The designation IBU on a finished beer or in a recipe refers to the International Bitterness Units, a universal system used to measure the level of hop bitterness in the beer. Brewmasters work with this sweet malt–bitter hops combination to create the desired balance in their beer. A wide variety of hops grown in regions of the United States and Europe are cultivated to impart their unique bitter or aromatic flavor profiles to the finished beer. Hops are designated as *bittering*, to be added to the wort during boiling, or as *aromatic*, added to the wort at the end of the boiling process. For additional hoppiness, dry hops or wet hops (fresh) can be added before bottling. Hops can be purchased from your beer-making supplier (see Resources, page 241), or you can grow your own.

Hops grow as a hearty vine and can easily be grown at home on fences or arbors with midday sun and little attention from you other than watering. The hop cones will begin to appear in late summer and are harvested once they have turned from bright lime green and sticky to the touch, to lighter in color and papery in texture. Spread the cones out in a single layer to dry, and then bag them in plastic storage bags and store out of UV light, or even better, in refrigeration or freezer. Use within 4 to 6 months in your brews.

Yeast. Active beer yeast makes the fermentation process work. The two basic designations of yeast are ale yeast (top fermenting; used in fermenting above 60°F) and lager yeast (bottom fermenting; used below 55°F). Each strain has its maximum alcohol tolerance.

Hops. These flower cones of the female hop plant, are an essential part of the beer, contributing a balance to the sweetness of the malt. See sidebar on page 183 for more information.

Adjuncts. Any grains or other fermentable sugars other than barley or wheat.

Flavorings. Optional ingredients such as fruits, herbs, spices, or extracts that can be added to enhance the flavor of the brew.

PREPARATION AND TECHNIQUES

Refer to the Preparation and Techniques section of chapter 5 (page 90) for directions on preparing your brewing equipment. An industry iophodor (iodine-based) sanitizer is recommended for preparing brewing equipment, and can also be used for sanitizing cheese-making equipment. In home brewing, the general beer-making process has several components:

Malting. The moist germinating process that converts the grain to a form that has more carbohydrates available for fermentation.

Mashing. Steeping malt in hot water to facilitate enzymatic conversion of starches to sugars. Resulting liquid is the wort.

Brewing. Filtered wort is boiled in separate brew kettle with hops. From there it is strained again and chilled rapidly to proper temperature for fermentation.

Fermentation. Chosen strain of yeast is added to the cooled wort, and then placed in a carboy with air lock to begin its first phase of fermentation; the yeast consumes the sugars, producing carbon dioxide. Once the yeasts die off (after consuming the last of the sugars) and settle to the bottom, the beer is racked (siphoned off, leaving the sludge behind) to another vessel (bottled or kegged) to rest (condition).

Conditioning. Resting period before the beer is ready to consume. Depending on style, the beer is conditioned for a few days up to a few weeks before being filtered (optional) and bottled or kegged.

Consult the Glossary (page 235) for important reference terms regarding home brewing. The following list includes select terms that may prove useful to refer to as you start your beer-making journey.

- **Beer yeasts.** Used in either dry or liquid form, beer yeasts are a class of fungi (*Saccharomyces* spp.) that feed on the sugars to ferment the malt and other sugars, producing ethyl alcohol and carbon dioxide.

- **Boil.** The phase of beer making where all the ingredients except the yeast and the priming sugar come together.

- **Diacetyl rest.** The resting time needed to reduce the level of diacetyl (the compound giving beer its buttery or butterscotchlike flavor) to the proper level for optimum flavor and stability.

- **Distillation.** A process of heating a fluid to remove some component(s) by evaporation, combined with condensing and collecting those components. The most common method for concentrating the ethanol initially produced via fermentation, forming a strong spirit.

- **Gravity.** A measure of the amount of sugar in the wort; using a saccharometer (a hydrometer designed to measure by weight the amount of sugar in a solution), the gravity reading is taken at the beginning, before fermentation (starting gravity), and at the end of fermentation (final gravity). The gravity declines as fermentation progresses and is a useful indicator of the health the fermenting process.

- **Lagering.** The process of cold aging after fermentation.

- **Malting.** The moist germinating process that converts the grain to a form that has more carbohydrates available for fermentation.

- **Mash.** To steep malt in hot water to facilitate enzymatic conversion of starches to sugars.

- **Priming sugar.** Sugar that is used to prime the beer for bottle conditioning. It is added at bottling to supply the yeast with more sugar (fuel) to metabolize while the yeast is active.

- **Rack.** To siphon a clear beverage off of sediment to derive an improved product. The sediments are called lees in winemaking and trub in brewing.

- **Siphon.** Tubing system used to drain off fermented liquid, leaving residual sludge behind.

Malted Grains

Malt grains for beer—usually barley or wheat—are the primary source of sugar (food) for the yeast in the brew to consume and convert. Through the malting process (soaking and sprouting), the starches in malted grains are converted into fermentable, usable malt sugars. Malted grains (aka roasted malt) in various unique combinations give the beer its flavor, body, and mouthfeel. Roasted malt is kiln-dried sprouted grains, which are roasted at various temperatures to determine the color (ranging from pale to dark black) and flavor (ranging from crisp and dry to creamy and robust) of the malt, and therefore the final profile of the beer. Malted grains can be toasted at home using a very simple method as described by Byron Burch in *Brewing Quality Beers*. Experiment with toasting times and temperatures to get fresh-roasted aromas and flavors. Spread some grain malt on a baking sheet at no deeper than 1 inch, and toast in a preheated oven (300°F to 400°F depending on the results you want), for 10 to 45 minutes (based on the depth of flavor you want). The longer the time or higher the temperature, the more color and toasted flavor you'll get. After toasting, allow the grains to cool and rest stored at room temperature for at least a week for the flavors to mellow.

Malted grains are not just for beer making. They are also used in breads in the form of sprouted grains (see recipe, page 130), or sprouted grain flour, and in the form of malted barley flour to enhance many bread flours. Both wheat and barley malt syrup can be added to your sourdough starter to jump start the enzymatic action and keep it well-fed.

- **Sparge.** To rinse a solid material (as grain from mashing for beer) with hot water to transport soluble substances.

- **Wort.** The sugar-containing solution derived from malt that, when fermented, becomes beer.

BLACK PEPPER PILSNER

YIELD: 5 gallons
STARTING GRAVITY: 1.062
FINAL GRAVITY: 1.008–1.012
BITTERNESS: 34.8 IBU
START TO FINISH: 3 to 6 hours brewing + 2 to 3 weeks
fermenting + 2 days resting + 3 to 6 weeks lagering
(making black pepper infusion during the last week)
+ 1 day kegging or bottling + 7 to 10 days carbonation
(bottle-condition only)

This classic American pilsner (a stronger, hoppier version of standard American lager) from Bob Peak, expert teacher of DIY home brewing, winemaking, and cheese making, and a partner at The Beverage People in Santa Rosa, California, is finished with a splash of homemade black peppercorn extract. It placed for a ribbon in the Western Regional competition of the American Homebrewers Association contest in 2010 and went on to be a featured brew at a Northern California brewery. You'll start by making a base beer, then flavoring it with black pepper. *See photo on page 193.*

11 gallons water

3¼ pounds 2-row pale malt

3 pounds 6-row malt

½ pound honey malt

½ pound Carapils malt

1 pound white rice

1 pound corn grits (polenta)

1 pound pearl barley

½ pound additional 6-row malt (mill and keep separate)

¼ teaspoon gypsum (added anytime during the boil)

¼ teaspoon calcium chloride (added anytime during the boil)

½ teaspoon chalk (added anytime during the boil)

½ ounce Cluster hops (bittering; added for all 60 minutes of the boil; 15.8 IBU, 7.9% alpha acid)

½ ounce Cluster hops (flavoring; added during last 30 minutes of the boil; 5.5 IBU, 7.9% alpha acid)

1 ounce Perle hops (flavoring; added during last 30 minutes of the boil; 10.8 IBU, 8.9% alpha acid)

1 tablespoon Irish moss (added during last 15 minutes of the boil)

½ ounce Perle hops (aroma; added during last 5 minutes of the boil; 2.7 IBU, 8.9% alpha acid)

1 pack #2007 St. Louis Lager Yeast

2 tablespoons whole black peppercorns

½ cup vodka

¾ cup corn sugar (for priming if you are bottling; omit if you will keg and force-carbonate your beer)

1. For this all-grain recipe, you need three kettles of 5-gallon capacity or more, made from stainless steel or enameled steel. One is the mash kettle, in which the grain is steeped or "mashed." Another is the boiling kettle, used in this recipe to boil a portion of the grain, and then used to boil the sugar solution (wort) to be fermented later. The third is the "hot liquor" tank; it holds the hot water used to rinse ("sparge") the grain after mashing.

2. In the mash kettle, heat 4 gallons of the water to 125°F. Add all the malts except the separate additional 6-row malt. Stir to combine with a stainless steel spoon, cover, and let rest off heat. Meanwhile, in the boiling kettle, heat 3 gallons of the water to 163°F and stir in the rice, corn, and barley, plus the additional 1/2-pound 6-row malt. Adjust the temperature in this kettle to 158°F and hold at that temperature for 10 minutes. After 10 minutes, heat this kettle to boiling (uncovered) and boil for 20 minutes. Pour the boiled cereal mash into the malt mash that has been resting in the mash kettle. Adjust the temperature as needed to reach 150°F in the newly combined mash, cover, and hold at that temperature for 90 minutes.

3. In the hot liquor kettle, heat 4 gallons of sparge water (water to be used to rinse the mash) to 170°F. Reheat the resting mash to 170°F with stirring, let it settle for 5 to 10 minutes, then rinse ("sparge") with the 170°F water from the hot liquor tank, collecting about 6 gallons of wort. Bring to a boil and continue to boil while stirring for 60 minutes, adding the gypsum, calcium chloride, and chalk in the sequence indicated in the ingredients list. Add the hops and Irish moss to the boil in the sequence indicated in the ingredients list. At the end of the 60-minute boil, cool the wort to 75°F or below and add the yeast.

4. Ferment in a 6.8-gallon carboy or bucket fitted with an air lock at 48°F to 52°F for 1 to 2 weeks (until active bubbling through the air lock stops). Rack (siphon off the clear liquid) to a 5-gallon glass or PET-plastic carboy fitted with a fermentation lock and hold for secondary fermentation at 55°F for 1 week.

At the end of that week, raise the temperature to 70°F and hold for 48 hours (this is a diacetyl rest to allow fermentation byproducts to be reabsorbed by yeast residue). Decrease the temperature to 30°F to 34°F and hold for 3 to 6 weeks (a period known as lagering, during which the beer will become brilliantly clear).

5. During the last week of lagering, prepare the pepper extract. Lightly crush the peppercorns with a mortar and pestle. Place the peppercorns in a glass 1/2-pint jar, and add the vodka. Cover and let stand in a dark, cool location for 1 week. At kegging or bottling time, rack (siphon) the finished beer to the keg or to a bottling bucket. Carefully take your jar of pepper extract out of storage, leaving the peppercorns undisturbed at the bottom of the jar. Scooping the clear brown liquid from above the peppercorns with a measuring spoon, add 1 tablespoon at a time to the beer. Using a sanitized stirring spoon, stir the extract into the beer, and scoop a small amount into a wine glass (the shape of the glass enhances perception of aroma). Taste the sample, and continue adding 1 tablespoon of extract at a time until the flavor profile suits your taste. Most likely the amount will be about 6 tablespoons of extract for 5 gallons of beer.

6. If kegging, chill the keg and force-carbonate. If bottling, boil the priming sugar for 1 minute with 3/4 cup of water and stir into the beer in the bottling bucket; bottle and cap. Store in a cool, dry place. As soon as the beer is carbonated (7 to 10 days), it is ready to drink. Like other aromatically spiced things, it is better young than old, so drink within 6 to 12 months after bottling or kegging. Refrigerate before serving.

Hop Stoopid Ale

YIELD: 5 gallons
STARTING GRAVITY: 1.085
FINAL GRAVITY: 1.014–1.015
BITTERNESS: 119.5 IBU
START TO FINISH: 3 to 7 hours brewing + 7 to 10 days fermenting + 8 days to 4 weeks dry hopping (or 4 days to 2 weeks for one dry-hop addition) + 1 day kegging or bottling + 10 days carbonation (bottle-condition only)

This ale recipe from Lagunitas Brewing Company, in Petaluma, California is not for the faint of heart or palate. This hoppy home-brew version of their popular Hop Stoopid Ale (one of my favorites) is a real treat to have included here.

Making this ale at home takes some previous home-brewing experience and knowledge of the jargon. Thanks to home-brew teacher, competition judge, and recipe tester, Gabe Jackson, the recipe has been adapted for home brewers. If you are new to home brewing, follow the method as presented here and in Black Pepper Pilsner, page 186. Once you are well into home brewing, you'll only need a list of the ingredients and amounts needed to make your brew, and the method will become second nature. Check the Glossary (page 235) for unfamiliar terms.

Note: Reverse osmosis water is readily available on retail shelves, and in many vending dispensing machines. If Magnum hops cannot be found, use Nugget or Simcoe as alternatives. If Simcoe hops cannot be found, use Amarillo as a substitute. Alternatively, Summit, Centennial, Chinook, and Cascade are good options. *See photo on page 155.*

12½ pounds 2-row barley malt (all-grain version) or 8 pounds light dry malt (extract version)

8 ounces Victory malt

1 ounce acidulated malt (or enough to adjust mash pH to 5.4)

5 gallons water (if filtered, unchlorinated drinking water, add ½ teaspoon gypsum in boil; if reverse osmosis water, add 1½ teaspoons gypsum in the mash, ¼ teaspoon calcium chloride in boil, and ½ teaspoon gypsum in the boil with bittering hop addition)

1½ pounds corn sugar (added to the boil)

1 ounce Magnum hops (bittering; added for all 90 minutes of the boil; 52 IBU, 13% alpha acid)

0.6 ounce Cascade hops (flavoring; added for last 10 minutes of the boil; 2.9 IBU, 7% alpha acid)

0.6 ounce Chinook hops (flavoring; added for last 10 minutes of the boil; 5.5 IBU, 13% alpha acid)

1.25 ounces Simcoe hops (aroma; flameout addition; added after 90 minutes at zero/flameout; 11.4 IBU, 13% alpha acid)

3 packs #1028 (#1968 option) London ale yeast

FIRST DRY-HOP ADDITION (AROMA)

3 ounces Columbus hops (27.3 IBU, 13% alpha acid)

0.75 ounce Chinook hops (6.8 IBU, 13% alpha acid)

SECOND DRY-HOP ADDITION (AROMA)

1.5 ounces Simcoe hops (13.6 IBU, 13% alpha acid)

1. In a 6-gallon or larger mash kettle, combine the mash grains (barley malt, Victory malt, and acidulated malt) together in 5 gallons of 150°F prepared water for 1 hour. Sparge with water at 168°F to 170°F.

2. Bring to a boil and then add the corn sugar. Continue to boil for 90 minutes, adding hops in the sequence indicated in the ingredients list.

3. At the end of the 90-minute boil, cool the wort, using a wort chiller, to 68°F to 72°F (into fermentation range to keep yeast alive) and aerate well by vigorously stirring with a stainless steel slotted spoon for 5 minutes before adding your yeast. At home you can also use shaking or splashing and achieve as much as 8 ppm of oxygen. Pour in the yeast, and ferment in the middle of the optimal fermentation range for the yeast (60°F to 72°F for #1028). Primary ferment for 7 to 10 days; you can track the temperature during this time to determine the amount of actual time needed. The warmer the temperature, the faster the sugars are consumed, thereby shortening the fermentation time. The foam should subside as best guide for readiness.

4. For the first dry-hop, add the Columbus hops and Chinook hops to the secondary fermentor before moving the beer to it. The beer will benefit from a long warm rest in the secondary fermentor (68°F to 72°F for a couple days), after yeast removal during racking or siphoning. Leave the beer with dry hops in secondary fermentation for 4 to 7 days. The second dry-hop addition can be accomplished by either racking to a tertiary fermentor, or by temporarily removing some beer from the secondary fermentor, adding the Simcoe hops, then topping the secondary up with sanitary beer or water. Remember that the hops will cause some foaming upon contact with the beer. The beer will be very cloudy from dry hops after secondary and tertiary fermentation.

5. If you can keg the beer instead of bottle, use gelatin to remove the cloudiness and soften the hop astringency. It is recommended for new brewers to bottle rather than keg. Bottled beer will require ¾ cup of boiled corn sugar added to the bottling bucket for carbonation and at least 10 days of bottle conditioning before drinking (10 days at 70°F, cooler temperatures will require longer bottle fermentation time). To increase the clarity of bottled beer, keep it in the refrigerator and clarity will increase as the solids precipitate (generally 3 to 6 weeks for good clarity).

CHAPTER 9

COOKING WITH FERMENTED FOODS

Now that your pantry is brimming with fermented delicacies, you can use them to create fun and diverse dishes. I am constantly inspired by the flavors and textures that fermented foods offer. I weave ferments into everyday dishes and menus to create flavor and texture as well as to add nutritional benefits. In this chapter, I'm sharing a collection of my favorite salad, soup, flatbread, main course, and dessert recipes, along with tips to inspire you and get you started. More are online at www.masteringfermentation.com. Beyond these recipes, be creative. Explore ways you can transform some of your favorite foods by fermenting them for greater flavor, complexity, and nutrition. Add those ferments to your favorite recipes for amazing results. Use as many fermented ingredients as you can when making these (and your) recipes. Some are specified, but when unavailable, use the best-quality store-bought ingredients you can find.

Antipasti Platter

While an array of savory nibbles like this is typically served as the appetizer prelude to the main meal, an antipasti platter can indeed be a meal unto itself. Typically it includes cured meats and fish, olives, roasted peppers, cheeses, and pickled vegetables.

With the bounty of ferments you've created, here's a short list of suggested gems to mound up on your antipasti platter:

Duck Prosciutto (page 158), served sliced, Summer Sausage (page 160), or Dry-Cured Pimenton Salami (page 157)

Spicy Marinated Tuna (page 152) or Pickled Sardines with Fennel (page 150)

Cured Olives (page 19)

Sweet and Salty Pickled Vegetables or Stem and Stalk Pickles (page 27)

Goat Feta Marinated in Herb Olive Oil (page 106)

Rosemary-Lemon Dutch Oven Bread (page 128)

Clockwise from bottom left: oil-cured ripe olives, brined green olives, Summer Sausage, Dry-Cured Pimenton Salami, Goat Feta Marinated in Herb Olive Oil, Black Pepper Pilsner, Stem and Stalk Pickles, Rosemary-Lemon Dutch Oven Bread

Toasted Kale and Spinach Salad

with Sweet Pickled Shallots, Cheese Croutons, and Tomato Vinegar Dressing

SERVES 4

This is a hearty salad, loaded with earthy, toasted flavors. Serve it with grilled fish or slices of steak drizzled with a bit of the tomato dressing and you've got a tasty main course.

You can make many of the components ahead (toasted kale, croutons, roasted shiitakes, toasted walnuts, the dressing, and, of course, the pickled shallots) and compose the salad just before serving. You'll have extra dressing left over—cover and refrigerate it, then use it for a warm potato salad or drizzle it over grilled fish.

½ cup walnut pieces

½ cup coarsely grated cheese (such as Parmesan, Toma, or Asiago)

¼ teaspoon smoked paprika

½ pound plain artisan bread, hard crust removed, and cubed

¼ cup olive oil, plus more for brushing

¾ pound shiitake mushrooms, stemmed and sliced

½ teaspoon unrefined fine sea salt, plus more for seasoning

6 large kale leaves

2 cups packed baby spinach, stemmed

¼ teaspoon ground white pepper

2 sweet pickled shallots (Sweet and Salty Pickled Vegetables, page 27), thinly sliced into wedges

TOMATO VINEGAR DRESSING

½ cup tomato vinegar (see page 36)

2 tablespoons brine from pickled shallots (Sweet and Salty Pickled Vegetables, page 27)

2 teaspoons raw, unfiltered honey

¼ teaspoon ground cumin

Pinch of ground white pepper

2 tablespoons roasted walnut oil

To make the salad: Preheat the oven to 350°F. Spread the walnuts on a baking sheet and toast in the oven until they smell toasty, about 10 minutes. Set them aside to cool and then coarsely chop them.

Line a baking sheet with parchment paper. In a small bowl, combine the grated cheese and smoked paprika. In a large bowl, toss the cubed bread with 1/4 cup of the olive oil and then toss with the cheese mixture. Spread out cubed bread in a single layer on the parchment-lined baking sheet.

Toss the shiitake with 3 tablespoons olive oil and lightly salt. Spread out on a separate unlined baking sheet.

Place both pans in the oven until the croutons are golden and crispy, and the mushrooms are roasted, 30 to 35 minutes. Set both aside to cool.

Lightly brush the kale leaves with olive oil and season lightly with sea salt. On the stovetop, over an open flame, lightly toast the kale leaves until charred and crispy. When cool enough to handle, cut away the large center stem with a knife and tear the leaves into chunks. Toss in a bowl along with the spinach.

To make the dressing: Whisk together the vinegar, brine, honey, cumin, and the pinch of pepper. Whisk in the walnut oil.

To assemble: When ready to serve, toss the kale and spinach mixture with the mushrooms, then add the 1/2 teaspoon salt, pepper, and the shallots. Dress with half of the dressing. Toss in the walnuts and croutons. Adjust seasoning. Toss with more dressing, just to moisten, then serve.

Warm Potato and Caramelized Endive Salad

with Crispy Duck Prosciutto

SERVES 4 to 6 as a side dish

Soaking potatoes in brine for 8 to 12 hours before cooking reduces the glucose and fructose in the potatoes, making them more digestible. The texture and flavor of the potatoes is also so much better than if you don't use a brine. Put the potatoes in the brine in the morning and they will be ready to cook for dinner that evening. Brussels sprouts or radicchio work well in place of, or in addition to, endive. If you don't have Duck Prosciutto (page 158), use the classic Italian ham prosciutto in its place.

3½ teaspoons unrefined fine sea salt, plus more for seasoning

4 cups cool filtered water

1½ pounds small Yukon gold potatoes, skins on

¼ cup olive oil

8 to 10 thin slices Duck Prosciutto (page 158)

2 shallots, thinly sliced

6 heads red and green Belgian endive, root end removed, leaves separated

½ teaspoon raw cane sugar

¾ cup light Belgian-style ale

¼ cup freshly squeezed orange juice

Ground white pepper

2 teaspoons Whole Grain Dijon-Style Mustard (page 63)

¼ cup malt or homemade beer vinegar

Juices from the cooked endive (previous)

¼ teaspoon unrefined fine sea salt

⅛ teaspoon ground white pepper

½ cup olive oil

To make the salad: Dissolve 2 teaspoons of the salt in the water in a bowl. Place the cut potatoes in a strainer to fit the bowl and submerge in the brine. Cover with cheesecloth and move to a cool location to soak for 8 hours or overnight.

Preheat the oven to 350°F. Drain, rinse, and pat dry the brined potatoes, cut into quarters lengthwise, and toss with 3 tablespoons of olive oil, then the remaining 1½ teaspoons salt. Lay the quarters, cut side down, on a baking sheet. Roast in the oven until golden brown and slightly crispy, about 25 to 30 minutes.

Decrease the oven temperature to 300°F, cover the potatoes with aluminum foil, and keep warm in the oven until the other ingredients are ready.

In a lightly oiled ovenproof skillet over medium heat, lightly crisp the prosciutto strips for 2 minutes. Drain the strips, cover the pan with foil, and set aside in the oven to keep warm.

In a large skillet over medium-high heat, heat 2 tablespoons of the olive oil and sauté the shallots until soft, about 2 minutes. Add the endive leaves and sauté until the leaves have just wilted. Sprinkle with the sugar and sauté until the leaves begin to caramelize, about 2 to 3 minutes. Stir in the beer and orange juice, increase the heat to bring the liquid to a boil, and

continued

cook until the sauce reduces by half, about 4 minutes. Season with salt and white pepper and then cool for 10 minutes.

To make the dressing: Combine the mustard, vinegar, endive juices, salt, and pepper; whisk in the olive oil.

To serve: In a large bowl, toss the warm potatoes in half of the dressing. Toss in the endive and add more dressing as needed to coat. You will have extra dressing left over. Arrange on a platter, topped with slices of prosciutto; serve extra dressing on the side.

GRILLED AHI TUNA ON PICKLED VEGETABLES AND RICE SALAD
with Miso Dressing

SERVES 4

The pickled vegetables used here are a delicious, versatile Asian-inspired combination of shredded carrots, shredded radishes, strips of green onions, strips of fresh ginger, and edamame, all pickled in a sweet-salty brine. The brine is also an ingredient in the dressing. Use other fish or no fish; the salad works well on its own, too. The brine is also a terrific marinade for skirt or flank steak, as well as pork chops.

DRESSING

2 tablespoons brine from the Sweet and Salty Pickled Vegetables (page 27) or unflavored rice vinegar

1 tablespoon Soy Sauce (page 71)

1 tablespoon light miso paste

1 teaspoon Chile-Garlic Paste (page 75, optional)

1 tablespoon raw unrefined cane sugar

2 tablespoons finely minced fresh ginger

Juice of 1 lime

1 teaspoon toasted sesame oil

$\frac{1}{3}$ cup canola or grapeseed oil

Kosher or unrefined fine sea salt

Ground white pepper

2 tablespoons brine from the Sweet and Salty Pickled
    Vegetables (page 27)

1 teaspoon toasted sesame oil

3 cups cooked short-grain sweet rice, at room temperature

Grated zest of 2 limes

1½ cups Sweet and Salty Pickled Vegetables (page 27),
    drained and brine reserved

Shredded napa cabbage, for serving

Canola oil, for brushing

1½ pounds fresh 1-inch-thick ahi tuna steaks

Unrefined fine sea salt

Ground white pepper

½ teaspoon powdered wasabi (optional)

To make the dressing: Place the brine, soy sauce, miso paste, chile paste, sugar, ginger, lime juice, and sesame oil in a blender. Pulse to combine the ingredients. With the blender running, slowly drizzle in the grapeseed oil until an emulsion is formed. Season with salt and pepper. Add a small amount of water or lime juice to thin, if necessary. Set aside.

To make the salad: Whisk the brine and sesame oil together. Toss the cooked rice with the mixture. Stir in the lime zest and the pickled vegetables. Set aside.

To grill the tuna: Heat a gas or charcoal grill to high, or heat a stovetop griddle, ribbed side up. Decrease the heat to medium-high. Rub the grilling area with a light coat of canola oil. Brush the tuna steaks with oil and lightly season with salt, pepper, and a light dusting of wasabi, if using. Grill, uncovered, until well marked, turning over once, and keeping the interior pink in center, 5 to 6 minutes total. Remove from the heat, cool for 3 minutes, then break the tuna into large pieces, about 3 inches or so, and set aside.

To assemble: Toss the rice mixture with ¼ cup of the dressing or enough just to moisten, and season to taste with salt. Arrange a bed of finely shredded napa cabbage on a large serving platter or on individual plates. Top with the rice salad. Place chunks of the grilled tuna on top of the rice salad and drizzle more dressing over the tuna.

Cauliflower, Potato, and Onion Curry

with Sprouted Lentil Dosas

SERVES 6 as a side dish

This curry is also delicious over fragrant rice. The sauce is mostly created by the yogurt. You can use low-fat yogurt, Coconut Milk Yogurt (page 40), whole coconut milk, or even coconut milk kefir (see page 172) in its place. Throw in a few golden raisins for additional sweetness. This dish is particularly delicious when kissed with smoke from being cooked in a wood-fired oven or on a grill.

3 tablespoons canola oil

2 medium onions, chopped

1/2 jalapeño chile, stemmed, seeded, and minced

3/4-inch piece of fresh ginger, minced

4 cloves garlic, finely chopped

1 teaspoon brown mustard seeds

1/2 teaspoon cumin seeds

1 1/2 teaspoons coriander seeds

2 whole cloves

4 whole white peppercorns

1 teaspoon unrefined fine sea salt

1/2 teaspoon ground turmeric

1 teaspoon smoked paprika

1 1/2 cups whole yogurt, mixed with 1 1/2 teaspoons cornstarch

1/2 cup filtered water

1 head cauliflower (about 2 pounds), broken into bite-size florets

1 pound mixed red-, yellow-, and purple-skinned potatoes, cubed and roasted

1 large yam, peeled, cubed, and roasted

Sprouted Lentil Dosas (page 126)

Preheat the oven to 325°F. In a skillet, heat 2 tablespoons of the oil and sauté the onions until soft, 5 to 7 minutes. Add the jalapeño and ginger and cook for another 2 minutes. Stir in the garlic and cook for another 2 minutes. Set aside.

In a Dutch oven or heatproof clay pot, heat the remaining 1 tablespoon oil over medium heat; sauté the mustard seeds, cumin, coriander, cloves, and peppercorns until you can smell them toasting. Remove the spices from the pan and reserve the pan (don't clean it).

Combine the onion mixture, the toasted spices, salt, turmeric, and paprika and put in a blender. With the blender running, pour in 1 cup of the yogurt mixture to create a thin paste.

Place the paste in the pan used for the spices (to pick up the oils from the spices) and thin with the water. Stir in the cauliflower, cover, and cook until not quite tender, about 7 minutes. Add the roasted potatoes, yam, and the remaining 1/2 cup of yogurt. Add more water if needed to create a sauce. Cover and place in the oven to continue cooking until tender and the flavors have blended, about 15 minutes. Remove the lid and continue to cook for another 5 minutes. To serve, spoon into Sprouted Lentil Dosas (page 126).

Hot-and-Sour Tofu Soup

with Shrimp and Pickled Vegetables

SERVES 6 as a main course

This soup is simple, quick, delicious, and comforting. Use homemade cabbage kimchi or other spicy fermented leafy vegetable. Adding in other fermented ingredients (soy, vinegar, and tofu) makes it hearty and nutritious.

2 tablespoons toasted sesame oil

6 green onions (including ½ inch of green part), coarsely chopped

1½ cups Kimchi (page 54), coarsely chopped

2 teaspoons Chile-Garlic Paste (page 75)

6 cups mushroom or vegetable stock (see page 72)

1 tablespoon rice vinegar

4 teaspoons Soy Sauce (page 71)

1 teaspoon raw unrefined cane sugar

One 1-inch piece fresh ginger, cut into coins

1 pound extra-jumbo (16–20 count) shrimp, shelled with tail on

½ cup diced soft or firm Tofu (page 75)

1 cup coarsely chopped spinach

Juice of 1 lime

¼ cup chopped fresh cilantro, plus more for garnish (optional)

Sweet and Salty Pickled Vegetables (page 27), as garnish (optional)

In a Dutch oven or other heavy pot, heat the oil over medium heat, add the green onions, and stir for 1 minute. Stir in the kimchi and chile paste, then decrease the heat to medium; add the stock, vinegar, soy sauce, sugar, and ginger, and bring to a low boil. Add the shrimp, cook for 5 minutes, and then add the tofu. Cook until the shrimp are tender and pink, about 3 more minutes, and then add in the spinach and cook until just wilted. Stir in the lime juice and cook for 1 minute, then adjust the seasonings. Just before serving, stir in half of the cilantro.

Serve in warmed bowls, garnished with pickled vegetables and more cilantro, if desired.

Falafel-Stuffed Whey Flatbread

with Pickled Vegetables

MAKES 8 small flatbreads

Here's a great place to use reserved whey. To keep with the Middle Eastern theme, you can replace 1/4 cup of the all-purpose flour with the same amount of garbanzo-fava flour or plain garbanzo (chickpea) flour. Once made, this dough can be portioned and kept frozen in self-sealing plastic freezer storage bags until a few hours before you are ready to use. Bring to room temperature and proceed. This flatbread is grilled while being soft and pliable so that it can be folded in half, then filled with delicious sesame falafel and pickled vegetables.

Note: For additional flavor, put the dough in a sealed container and let it bulk-ferment overnight in the refrigerator. Allow dough to come to room temperature (about 1 hour) before gently folding the dough and forming into a ball.

DOUGH

1 tablespoon raw, unfiltered honey

1 cup warm water (110°F), or more as needed

2 teaspoons active dry yeast

4 cups unbleached all-purpose flour

1 1/2 teaspoons unrefined fine sea salt

1 teaspoon ground cumin, toasted

1/2 cup basic whey (see page 13)

2 tablespoons olive oil, plus more for brushing

FILLING

3 cups Sprouted Chickpea Hummus (page 61)

6 to 8 Sesame Falafel Cakes (page 205), crumbled or cut into slices

Sweet and Salty Pickled Vegetables (page 27)

To make the dough: Dissolve the honey in the warm water. Using a stand mixer fitted with the dough hook attachment, mix the yeast, flour, salt, and cumin on low speed for 2 minutes. With the mixer running, gradually add the honey-water mixture, then the whey, and then drizzle in the olive oil. Increase the speed to medium and beat for 5 minutes. Decrease to low speed and beat for another 2 minutes to start the creation of gluten, which will add structure to the final dough. Add up to 1/3 cup more water as needed to make a dough that pulls away from the walls of the mixer bowl and is smooth yet slightly tacky to the touch. (The ambient humidity will affect how much water is needed.) Let the dough rest in the mixer bowl for 5 minutes then turn the mixer on medium-high speed for another 3 minutes, vigorously slapping the dough against the sides of the bowl, creating more gluten and structure to the dough.

On a lightly floured board, form the dough into a ball. Lightly oil a bowl, add the dough, and turn the dough to coat with oil. Cover with a damp cloth or plastic wrap and let the dough rise in a warm place until doubled in bulk, about 1 1/2 hours (see Note in headnote).

Generously flour a baking sheet. Using a plastic bowl scraper, reach down to the bottom of the bowl and gently stretch and fold the dough onto itself four times. Empty the dough onto a lightly floured board,

continued

form into a ball, and cut into 8 equal pieces. Shape each piece into a ball by gently stretching and tucking the dough to form a "belly button" on the bottom. Gently roll the ball in the palm of your hand or on the floured board and set each ball, belly button side down, on the prepared baking sheet and lightly brush or spray each top with olive oil. Cover loosely with a towel or plastic wrap and let rise until doubled in size, at least 1 hour. Refrigerate if not using within 1 hour, or place each ball of dough in an oiled self-sealing plastic bag and refrigerate for up to 2 days, or freeze for up to 1 month. Allow the refrigerated dough to stand at room temperature for 1 hour before grilling. Thaw the frozen dough in the bag at room temperature until dough warms up and has risen to almost twice its size.

To grill the dough: Preheat a wood-fired grill (using lump or hardwood charcoal) or gas grill to medium-high heat (450°F) about 45 minutes before you are ready to grill the flatbreads. If using charcoal, make sure the coals have burned down to glowing embers before grilling. Lightly oil the grill grate with canola oil to prevent sticking. Lightly flour the backs of two baking sheets.

On a lightly floured surface, form the 8 flatbreads by pressing and stretching the dough rounds with your fingertips until each round is about $\frac{1}{4}$ inch thick and about 8 inches in diameter. Place the flatbreads on the backs of the prepared baking sheets and lightly brush the tops of the dough with olive oil, being careful not to get any onto the baking sheet. Doing so will "glue" the flatbread to the sheet pan, making it very challenging to get off the pan and onto the grill!

With the baking sheet directly next to the grill, and moving quickly, gently pick up each flatbread from the sheet pan and flip it over, placing it, oiled side down, over direct heat on the grill. Close the lid and cook until each puffs up, 3 to 5 minutes. Check the cooked side for good grill marks on the bottom. Flip the flatbread over, brush the grill-marked top with olive oil, and move onto indirect heat. Close the lid to finish cooking until the bottom has good grill marks and the flatbread is still soft and pliable, another 3 minutes. Remove from the grill and keep warm in foil.

To serve: Spread some hummus on one side of each warm flatbreads, top with crumbled falafel and then pickled vegetables. Serve while warm.

SESAME FALAFEL CAKES

MAKES 6 to 8 patties

Falafel is a popular deep-fried delicacy from the Middle East made from ground chickpeas and regional spices. Shaped into balls or patties, falafel is both aromatic and crunchy. Serve as part of a Mediterranean salad, in a pita sandwich, or in a folded flatbread or piadina (soft, folded pizza); it is sometimes accompanied by a tahini dressing.

4 cups Sprouted Chickpea Hummus (page 61)

¼ cup chopped fresh flat-leaf parsley

2 tablespoons garbanzo-fava flour or plain garbanzo (chickpea) flour

½ teaspoon baking soda

¼ cup white sesame seeds

Neutral cooking oil (such as grapeseed oil), for frying

To the hummus, mix in the parsley, flour, and baking soda. Taste and adjust seasoning. Shape into 6 to 8 patties and place on a baking sheet. Cover and chill for 2 hours or overnight before frying. Just before frying, toss each patty in the sesame seeds.

In a large skillet, heat 2 inches of oil to 350°F. Fry 3 or 4 patties at a time, turning once to brown, until they are a deep golden color and crispy, 5 to 7 minutes.

Serve hot.

GRILLED YOGURT NAAN *Stuffed with Herb-Nut Butter*

MAKES 10 flatbreads

This flatbread is a crowd-pleaser. The dough is tender (due to the yogurt), and the filling is aromatic and bursting with flavor. Adjust the combination of herbs to your liking. The flatbreads can be grilled on a stovetop using a cast-iron grill pan. You may want to make a double batch of this filling because it is terrific slathered on grilled fish or chicken, or tossed with hot pasta.

DOUGH

4¼ cups all-purpose flour

1 cup whole wheat flour

2 teaspoons raw unrefined cane sugar

4 teaspoons baking powder

3 teaspoons unrefined fine sea salt

1 large egg, at room temperature

½ cup whole milk yogurt, at room temperature

1½ to 1¾ cups warm water

½ cup peanut oil or canola oil

FILLING

½ cup fresh mint leaves

1 cup coarsely chopped fresh cilantro

¼ cup coarsely chopped fresh basil

2 cloves garlic, chopped

1 tablespoon chopped fresh ginger

½ teaspoon unrefined fine sea salt

½ cup Toasted Nut Butter (page 78), crumbled

⅓ cup Clarified Butter (page 127), for brushing

continued

To make the dough: With a stand mixer fitted with the paddle attachment, combine the flours, sugar, baking powder, and salt. In a large bowl, whisk together the egg and yogurt, then whisk in the water and oil. Change to a dough hook attachment. Add the egg mixture to the flour mixture in the mixer bowl and, on low speed, knead the dough for about 5 minutes. Line a baking sheet with parchment paper or lightly dust with flour.

Turn the dough out onto a lightly floured board and divide it into 10 equal pieces. Form each into a ball, place on the prepared baking sheet, cover with plastic wrap, and let the dough rest at room temperature 1 hour before shaping.

To make the filling: Combine the mint, cilantro, basil, garlic, ginger, and salt in a food processor. Pulse until the ingredients are finely chopped; scrape down the sides. With the processor running, drop in pieces of the nut butter and mix until the ingredients are combined. Place into a small bowl.

To assemble the flatbreads: Line a baking sheet with parchment paper. On a floured board, using a rolling pin, roll a ball of dough into a 5-inch-diameter circle. Spread about 2 teaspoons of the filling in the center, leaving about a ½-inch border. Gather up the edges, pinching them together in the center, to seal in the filling. Turn the pouch over and using very little pressure, with a rolling pin roll it into a 6-inch-diameter circle, being careful not to squeeze out the filling. Transfer to the prepared baking sheet. Continue forming the flatbreads, layering parchment in between the breads if you stack them. Keep them covered with a clean kitchen towel to proof.

To grill the flatbreads: Prepare a medium-hot fire in a charcoal grill. When the coals have burned down to hot embers, place about 3 breads, pinched side down, directly on the grate set 8 or so inches above the coals. Close the lid and cook until the breads look puffy and the undersides brown lightly in places, 1 to 2 minutes. Turn the breads over and finish cooking the top side. Once you get grill marks on this top side, turn the flatbread 45 degrees to create a diamond pattern. Move to indirect heat to finish grilling. Just before taking off the grill, turn top side up and brush lightly with clarified butter. Repeat to cook the remaining breads.

Cut each naan in half diagonally and serve warm.

Potato-Herb Gnocchi

with Creamy Whey Reduction Sauce

SERVES 4 to 6 as a side dish

A few creative restaurant chefs are playing with reserved whey as an ingredient in their repertoires with amazing results, including my friend chef Michael Easton, proprietor of Il Corvo Pasta in Seattle, Washington, who shared this dish. Use fresh or frozen whey reserved from yogurt, fresh cheeses (ricotta), basic chèvre, or even tomme. You'll want to avoid whey that contains molds such as *P. roqueforti*, used in making blue cheeses, or *B. linens*, used in washed-rind cheeses, for this dish, as they may negatively influence the final sauce.

1¼ pounds russet potatoes, skin on
¼ cup plus 2 teaspoons kosher salt
1 heaping tablespoon finely chopped fresh dill
1 heaping tablespoon finely chopped fresh mint leaves
1 heaping tablespoon finely chopped fresh flat-leaf
  parsley leaves
2 large eggs, at room temperature
1¾ cups all-purpose flour, sifted, plus more for shaping
  the dough
12 ounces whey (see headnote)
6 tablespoons butter, at room temperature
1 lemon
½ teaspoon ground white pepper
½ cup grated Parmigiano-Reggiano (optional)

To prepare the potatoes: Put the whole potatoes in a large, wide, shallow pot of cold unsalted water, and heat over medium heat. This will ensure that the potatoes cook in a single layer at a slow and even heat, allowing them to cook fully and keep their shape. The potatoes are done when they pierce easily with a knife, 20 to 30 minutes.

While the potatoes boil, ready a separate large pot of water for the gnocchi: fill the pot with at least 1 gallon of water mixed with ¼ cup kosher salt and set over medium heat.

When the potatoes are done, remove them from the pot with a slotted spoon, drain them, and let cool for 5 minutes. Remove their skins by lifting up a corner with a paring knife and peeling away.

As soon as the potatoes are cool enough to handle, force the potatoes through a food mill or ricer onto a cookie sheet, spreading the milled potatoes out evenly as you work to let the potatoes release steam and dry out slightly. Excess water makes gnocchi dense and heavy.

Once you have milled all the potatoes, sprinkle the chopped herbs over the top to warm them and enhance their flavor, then let everything cool to room temperature. The milled potatoes can be stored in refrigeration at this point but will need to come to room temperature before forming the gnocchi.

To form the gnocchi: Into a large bowl, weigh out 1 pound of the cooled, milled potatoes and herbs. Add the eggs and the remaining 2 teaspoons salt, and mix with a wooden spoon until incorporated. Add the

continued

flour, and mix with a wooden spoon until it is incorporated and the dough feels slightly stiff.

Turn the dough out onto a lightly floured work surface to knead with your hands. With floured hands, knead the dough gently, just until it has come together. It should be very soft but not stick to your fingers. Flatten the dough on your work surface, and shape into a square roughly $\frac{1}{2}$ inch thick.

Cut off $\frac{1}{2}$-inch-wide strips, lightly flour, and gently roll out into a long rope, about $\frac{1}{2}$ inch thick. Cut each rope into $\frac{1}{2}$-inch-long pillows, toss with flour, and set aside on a baking sheet.

Warm the whey over low heat, just until it has heated through. Turn off the heat, keeping the pan on the burner to stay warm from the retained heat.

To cook the gnocchi: Oil a baking sheet and have nearby. Add the gnocchi to the pot of reserved boiling salty water. Once the water has returned to a boil, boil the gnocchi for 3 minutes, then remove them with a slotted spoon, allowing some of the water to drain off, and set on the oiled baking sheet to rest.

Add 2 tablespoons of the butter to a large slopped-sided skillet over medium-high heat. Once the butter begins to brown, add the gnocchi and sauté until they are browned. Add the warm whey to the pan, scraping the bottom of the pan with a spatula to deglaze. Keep on the heat, reducing the whey by one-fourth. Once the whey is reduced by one-fourth, finish with the remaining 4 tablespoons of butter, a light squeeze of lemon, white pepper, and salt to taste.

Serve immediately in warmed pasta bowls, garnished with the Parmesan if desired, or without and let the taste of the whey shine through.

CIDER-BRAISED DUCK *with Apple-Caraway Sauerkraut and Potatoes*

SERVES 4

This is a contemporary take on a classic Alsatian combination. My duck of choice comes from Sonoma County Poultry in Northern California (see Resources, page 241). Owner Jim Reichert, a fourth-generation duck farmer, has been raising his Liberty Ducks, a strain of a meatier Pekin, since 1992, delivering them to appreciative chefs all across the country. A heavy-duty pot that holds heat well, like a cast-iron or ceramic-coated Dutch oven, gives the best results with this dish.

1 tablespoon unrefined fine sea salt

1/4 teaspoon ground white pepper

2 whole duck legs (leg-thigh combo), trimmed of excess skin and fat

2 tablespoons Rendered Duck Fat (page 159), plus any duck skin trimmings

6 large shallots, cut into thin wedges

1 pound small whole red and yellow potatoes, halved

2 teaspoons Basic Dijon-Style Mustard (page 63)

3 cups raw apple cider

3 fresh sage leaves

3 cups Apple-Caraway Sauerkraut (page 57), drained

1 tablespoon raw, unfiltered apple cider vinegar

Lightly salt and pepper the duck. In a skillet over medium-high heat, heat the duck fat until hot, then sear the skin side of the duck legs to brown. Remove the duck from the pan and set aside.

Bring the duck fat back on high heat and render the fat out of any duck skin trimmings. Remove the crisped skin. Sauté the shallots in the fat until tender, salting lightly. Add the potatoes to the pan and cook for 5 minutes to coat and flavor. Lightly season with salt and pepper.

Decrease the heat to medium, and set the duck, skin side up, on top of the potatoes. Mix the mustard and cider together and then add just enough to cover the duck, 2 1/2 to 3 cups. Stick in the sage leaves, cover, and slow-cook over low heat for 1 hour.

Layer on the sauerkraut, cover, and continue to cook until the duck is very tender, about 30 minutes. Remove the duck and continue to cook, uncovered, until the liquid is reduced by half or just enough to have a sauce. Place the duck back in the pot to heat through. Remove the duck and cut into serving pieces. Add a splash (about 1 tablespoon) of apple cider vinegar to the sauerkraut-potato mixture, and then serve.

ROASTED COD ON SHREDDED GREENS

with Ponzu Onion Jam

SERVES 4

It takes little time to make this fantastic dish when you use fermented Agrodolce Onion Marmalade (page 52) from your pantry. When doing so, add the ponzu sauce to the jam. Save the chard stems for making easy Stem and Stalk Pickles (page 27). Use drained fermented chard, brussels sprouts, or kale in place of fresh if you have them.

ONION JAM

¼ cup olive oil

1½ pounds white onions, cut into ¼-inch-thick wedges

½ pound red onions, cut into ¼-inch-thick-wedges

¾ cup Champagne vinegar

2 tablespoons Ponzu Sauce (page 72)

Ground white pepper

1½ teaspoons raw unrefined cane sugar

1½ teaspoons cumin seeds

½ teaspoon unrefined fine sea salt

4 (6-ounce) cod fillets

4 tablespoons Ponzu Sauce (page 72)

1 tablespoon mirin

¼ teaspoon ground white pepper

1 tablespoon toasted sesame oil

2 tablespoons olive oil

2 cups shredded brussels sprouts

2 cups chopped or julienned red Swiss chard leaves or kale leaves

4 cloves Roasted Garlic (recipe follows), mashed

1 teaspoon unrefined fine sea salt

¼ teaspoon red pepper flakes

To make the jam: In a large skillet, heat the olive oil over medium heat and sauté the onions until translucent, about 5 to 6 minutes. Add the vinegar, ponzu, and a pinch of white pepper. Bring to a slow boil and decrease the heat. Add the sugar and cumin seeds, and cook until the liquid is almost completely reduced and the onions have "melted" into a jam, 30 to 35 minutes. Remove from the heat. Add salt to taste. Transfer the jam to a bowl and let cool slightly.

To prepare the fish: Preheat the oven to 350°F. In a small bowl, combine the ponzu, mirin, and pepper, and then whisk in the sesame oil. Rub the fish with the mixture and set aside in a dish to marinate for 30 minutes.

Heat a dry skillet over medium-high heat, put the fish in the skillet, and roast in the oven until tender, 8 to 10 minutes. While the fish is roasting, heat a separate skillet and quickly sauté the shredded brussels sprouts and chard in olive oil just to wilt, 3 to 4 minutes. Stir in the garlic and season with salt and pepper flakes. Remove from the heat.

Serve the roasted fish on a bed of the sautéed greens. Top with a generous dollop of jam and garnish with any pan juices.

continued

ROASTED GARLIC AND SHALLOTS

Preheat the oven to 350°F. Cut off the top end of a whole head of garlic just to expose the garlic cloves. Place root end down on a flat piece of foil large enough to completely encase the head. Drizzle about 1 teaspoon of olive oil into the cut area. Wrap and twist the foil to enclose the head and place in the oven to roast until the cloves of garlic are soft to the touch when squeezed, 30 to 35 minutes. Let the garlic cool, remove the foil, and place the head in a small jar. Cover and refrigerate for up to 1 week. Pull off cloves as needed and squeeze the softened paste out of the end of the clove.

Follow this procedure for shallots, cutting into each shallot individually. Shallots can be grouped in foil to roast.

GRILLED LAMB

Stuffed with Apricot-Date Chutney and Saffron Yogurt Sauce

SERVES 8

The combination of lamb with dates and apricots is often found in the Mediterranean. Tangy yogurt shows up twice: first as a gentle tenderizer and flavor contributor for the meat; second, as a saffron-infused warm sauce. Also enjoy this chutney as a companion to Saffron Yogurt Cheese (page 99).

3 pounds butterflied leg of lamb (or other cut suitable for stuffing and grilling)
2 cloves garlic, thinly sliced lengthwise

MARINADE
½ cup chopped white onion
½ cup plain yogurt
½ cup apricot nectar
1 teaspoon raw, unfiltered honey
½ teaspoon mustard powder
1 teaspoon ground white pepper
1 teaspoon unrefined fine sea salt

1 cup Apricot-Date Chutney (page 50)

SAUCE
4 cups plain yogurt, drained
14 saffron threads
4 teaspoons cornstarch
½ cup apricot nectar
¼ teaspoon ground coriander
1½ teaspoons unrefined fine sea salt

Canola oil, for brushing

Trim any excess fat from the lamb. Cut 1-inch-deep slits in the lamb and insert garlic slices in the slits.

To make the marinade: In a food processor or blender, puree all of the ingredients until smooth.

To prepare the lamb: Place the lamb, open, in a shallow dish, generously coat with half of the marinade, cover, and let stand at room temperature for 3 hours or refrigerate overnight. Reserve the other half of the marinade to use as a glaze while grilling the meat. If the marinated lamb was chilled, let the meat sit at room temperature for 1 to 2 hours before cooking.

Drain off any marinade and then spread the chutney over the meat. Roll up and secure closed with kitchen twine. Place on a rack in a roasting pan.

Preheat a hardwood charcoal or gas grill to medium-high heat.

While the grill heats, make the sauce: Combine the yogurt and saffron in a bowl and allow to steep while the grill heats up. Whisk the cornstarch into the yogurt mixture, and then stir in the apricot nectar, coriander, and salt. Set aside at room temperature while the meat cooks.

continued

Lightly brush the heated grate with canola oil to keep the meat from sticking. Grill over medium-high direct heat until seared and a crust is formed by the rub, approximately 3 minutes per side, turning until well marked.

Mop with the remaining marinade to glaze the meat, and move to indirect heat; cook until the internal temperature reaches 155°F to 160°F for medium doneness, 15 to 20 minutes. Remove the lamb to a cutting board and let rest for 10 minutes. While the meat rests, heat the yogurt sauce in a saucepan over medium heat, and bring to a low boil to heat through and thicken slightly.

To serve, cut into ½-inch-thick slices across the grain of the meat and top with the sauce.

TEA-SMOKED TROUT
with Walnuts and Crème Fraîche Lentils

MAKES 4 main course servings or 8 appetizer servings

Aromatic smoked trout is a tasty treat. This version is tea-smoked, adding both sweetness and smokiness to the succulent fish. You can use the stovetop tea-smoking method here on other fish such as fillets of salmon, cod, or other fatty fish. Cut the fish into portions (about 4 ounces per person) before smoking to get even flavoring on each serving. You can also preserve tea-smoked fish by storing in olive oil in a covered jar.

3 cups cooked Le Puy green lentils

5 teaspoons Soy Sauce (page 71)

2 tablespoons unseasoned rice vinegar

1 teaspoon unrefined fine sea salt

½ teaspoon ground white pepper

1 teaspoon dried dill

2 tablespoons walnut oil

1 cup walnut pieces, toasted and finely chopped

¾ cup Crème Fraîche (page 95), whipped to soft peaks

4 (8-ounce) filleted or butterflied trout, heads, tails, and fins removed

BRINE

1 tablespoon brown sugar

1 tablespoon unrefined fine sea salt

⅓ cup mirin

⅔ cup chilled filtered water

½-inch piece fresh ginger, chopped

½ cup brown sugar

½ cup white rice

¼ cup black or oolong tea leaves

2 whole star anise

Pickled onions (see Sweet and Salty Pickled Vegetables, page 27), for garnish

In a bowl, combine the lentils with the soy sauce, vinegar, salt, pepper, and dill. Drizzle in the walnut oil and stir to combine. Stir in the walnuts and then fold in the crème fraîche to combine. Taste and add a splash more of vinegar to taste. Set aside.

Cut the fish into thirds and set aside.

For the brine, combine the sugar, salt, mirin, water, and ginger in a bowl and stir until the sugar and salt are dissolved.

Place the fish in a single layer in a shallow baking dish and cover with the brine. Cover with plastic wrap and refrigerate for 1 hour, and then let sit at room temperature for 30 minutes before smoking.

Line a wok snugly with aluminum foil. Combine the sugar, rice, tea, and star anise for the tea-smoking mixture and add them to the wok.

Remove the fish from the brine, remove any pieces of ginger that cling to the fish, and pat the pieces dry. Place two pieces at a time in a bamboo steamer basket or on a mesh pizza rack sized to fit the wok, raising the fish at least 2 inches above the smoking mixture. Leave room between the pieces of fish so the smoke will cover all surfaces evenly.

With the fish in place, heat the wok over moderate heat until the tea mixture begins to smoke.

Cover, decrease the heat to low, and smoke for 10 to 12 minutes. Turn off the heat and allow to smoke for another 3 to 5 minutes. Test for doneness; the trout should be done to medium at this point. If needed, smoke a few minutes longer. Wrap up the smoking ingredients in the foil and discard.

Serve the fish warm or at room temperature on a bed of room-temperature lentil mixture, accompanied with a small pile of pickled onions.

GRILLED SPICE-RUBBED SKIRT STEAK

with Sourdough Walnut-Parsley Sauce

SERVES 6

This grilled steak recipe always pleases my guests. As a counterpoint to the pomegranate glaze, serve it topped with Sourdough Walnut-Parsley Sauce (see opposite).

SPICE RUB

1 teaspoon ground fennel

1 teaspoon garlic powder

1 teaspoon brown sugar

½ teaspoon ground white pepper

½ teaspoon unrefined fine sea salt

1 (2½- to 3-pound) skirt steak

GLAZE

¼ cup robust red wine (such as Zinfandel or Cabernet Sauvignon)

2 tablespoons Pomegranate Molasses (page 38)

2 tablespoons raw, unfiltered honey

4 cloves Roasted Garlic (page 212), mashed

1 teaspoon freshly ground black pepper

½ teaspoon unrefined fine sea salt

2 tablespoons olive oil

Sourdough Walnut-Parsley Sauce (opposite)

To make the rub, combine all of the ingredients and then use the rub to coat all sides of the steak. Let the meat come to room temperature for 30 minutes. In the meantime, preheat a hardwood charcoal or gas grill to medium-high and make the glaze.

For the glaze: Combine the wine, molasses, and honey in a food processor and process until the honey is dissolved. Add the garlic, black pepper, and salt and pulse for a few minutes until blended. With the food processor running, drizzle in the olive oil until blended. Adjust the seasoning to taste.

Lightly brush the heated grate (or cast-iron griddle pan if cooking indoors) with canola oil to prevent sticking. Grill the steak over medium-high direct heat (450°F) or on the stovetop until seared and a crust is formed by the rub, approximately 3 minutes per side, turning until well marked.

Mop with half of the glaze and move to indirect heat for another 3 minutes. Turn the steak over and mop once more while cooking. The internal temperature should be 130°F to 135°F for medium-rare, or 140°F to 145°F for medium doneness.

Allow the steak to rest for 5 minutes, then slice across the grain and serve topped with Sourdough Walnut-Parsley Sauce.

SOURDOUGH WALNUT-PARSLEY SAUCE

MAKES about 4 cups

True to the traditional Italian cooking style of not wasting anything, this no-cook sauce is flavored and thickened with leftover bread and pulverized nuts. It's absolutely delicious!

The nuts are first toasted—either in the oven, on stovetop, or for a smoky flavor, in a wood-fired oven or over indirect heat on the grill. Almonds or hazelnuts may be substituted for the walnuts. Almond milk may be used in place of whole milk. Use the sauce on grilled beef, pork, pasta, fish, or as a spread, made with less milk, on crusty garlic toast.

2 slices day-old plain artisan sourdough bread

2 to 3 cups whole milk

8 ounces toasted walnut halves or pieces

4 cloves fresh garlic or Roasted Garlic (page 212)

¼ cup flat-leaf parsley leaves

Juice of 1 lemon

½ teaspoon unrefined fine sea salt

¼ teaspoon ground white pepper

⅓ cup olive oil

1 tablespoon walnut oil

Red pepper flakes (optional)

In a bowl, soak the bread in enough milk to cover. Place chunks of soaked bread in a food processor along with the walnuts, garlic, and parsley. Pulse together into a paste. Add the lemon juice and taste. Add the salt and white pepper. With the processor running, drizzle in the olive oil and then the walnut oil. Add the red pepper flakes to taste, and more milk if the mixture is too thick to be used as a sauce. Place in a food container with a lid and refrigerate. The sauce will keep for 1 week.

Slow-Roasted Pork in Adobo

SERVES 6 to 8

This pork is rubbed with cumin and orange zest, slow-roasted to melted perfection, shredded, and then tossed with a spicy sauce made with adobo paste from Smoky Chipotle in Adobo (page 73). Serve with Grilled Buttermilk–Black Bean Flatbread (page 124) or Sprouted Corn Tortillas (page 123) and Sweet Tomato-Jalapeño Salsa (page 49), or add it to slow-cooked beans. To guarantee a moist roast, first brine the meat before cooking. If cooking a larger roast of 6 pounds or so, brine it overnight. The pork is also delicious slow-roasted overnight at 250°F.

BRINE

8 cups cool filtered water
1/3 cup brown sugar
1/2 cup kosher salt

1 (3- to 4-pound) pork shoulder or butt

CUMIN-ORANGE RUB

2 tablespoons ground cumin
1 teaspoon raw unrefined cane sugar
1/2 teaspoon garlic powder
2 teaspoons unrefined fine sea salt
Grated zest of 1 orange

Olive oil

ADOBO SAUCE

2 tablespoons adobo paste from Smoky Chipotle in Adobo (page 73)
Juice of 1 orange
1 1/2 cups unsalted tomato juice
1 tablespoon raw, unfiltered honey
1 teaspoon dried oregano
1 teaspoon unrefined fine sea salt

To make the brine: Combine all of the ingredients in a food-grade container large enough to hold the water and the pork, considering the level of brine once the pork is added. Stir to dissolve the salt and sugar. Place the pork in the brine and top with a plate or other weight to keep the meat submerged. Cover and refrigerate at a temperature no greater than 40°F. Brine for 6 to 8 hours.

Combine all the ingredients for the rub and set aside. Combine all the ingredients for the adobo sauce and set aside. Refrigerate if holding for more than 3 hours before cooking.

Preheat the oven to 325°F (or 250°F if slow-roasting overnight). Remove the pork from the brine, rinse with water, and pat dry. Rub the pork with olive oil then coat with the rub by rolling the pork in it. Set aside for 10 minutes while heating the oven.

Place pork on a rack in a roasting pan, uncovered, then into the oven. Cover with aluminum foil after 1 hour and continue to cook 3 to 4 hours at 325°F or overnight at 250°F, until the roast is evenly caramelized on the surface and the meat easily falls away. Transfer the meat to a cutting board, tent with foil, and let rest for 15 minutes.

To serve, warm the sauce. Pull the pork apart into chunks or shred and toss with the sauce to moisten.

FETA-STUFFED CHICKEN *with Tzatziki*

SERVES 8

Delicious briny feta and its companions make a sensational stuffing for chicken breasts, rolled skirt steaks, turkey breasts, omelets, or eggplants. Once stuffed, the chicken breast featured here can be grilled with fantastic results. Brining keeps the chicken moist and flavorful. Tzatziki, a Greek cucumber-yogurt sauce with a refreshing tang, is a cooling counterpoint to the robust, salty flavor of the feta stuffing. Save some time and improve the flavor by making the tzatziki ahead. Crumbled Feta in Grape Leaves (page 108) makes a great accompaniment to this dish.

BRINE
8 cups filtered water
2/3 cup kosher salt
1/2 cup brown sugar

8 (1/4-pound) boneless, skinless chicken breasts
Freshly ground black pepper

STUFFING
1/2 cup oil-packed sun-dried tomatoes
10 ounces Crumbly Feta (page 105)
2 tablespoons Greek whole milk yogurt
1/2 teaspoon dried mint
1/2 teaspoon dried oregano
Grated zest of 1 lemon
Pinch of red pepper flakes
Kosher salt

4 cloves garlic, thinly sliced lengthwise
6 tablespoons olive oil
1 teaspoon kosher salt
1 teaspoon freshly ground black pepper
1 lemon, thinly sliced into 10 rounds
Tzatziki (opposite), for accompaniment

To make the brine: Combine all of the brine ingredients in a plastic tub with a lid large enough to hold the brine when displaced by the chicken. Stir until the salt and sugar are dissolved. Add the chicken, fully submerge, and refrigerate for 2 to 4 hours to brine. Remove chicken from the brine, rinse with cool water, and pat dry. Lightly dust with ground pepper and set aside.

To make the stuffing: Drain the sun-dried tomatoes and coarsely chop. In a bowl, combine them with the feta, yogurt, mint, oregano, lemon zest, and red pepper flakes. Salt to taste. Chill until ready to use.

Preheat the oven to 375°F.

To prepare the chicken: Create a pocket in the flesh of the breasts by cutting a 3-inch-long and 2-inch-deep slit to contain a portion of the feta mixture. Spread an equal amount of the feta mixture in the pocket of each breast. Lay a few garlic slices over the mixture and close the pockets, securing with skewers. Rub the chicken with 2 tablespoons olive oil and lightly salt and pepper.

To cook the chicken: In two cast-iron skillets or other heavy ovenproof skillets over medium-high heat, divide the remaining 4 tablespoons of olive oil between the two pans. Working in batches, sear the chicken on one side to create a golden color. Turn over and cook the other side until lightly golden, 3 to 5 minutes. Place the seared pieces on a baking sheet to hold while you sear the rest. Once all the chicken has been browned, return the pieces to the skillets, place slices of lemon on top of each piece, and roast in the heated oven until done (170°F to 175°F internal temperature) and juices run clear, 15 to 20 minutes. Set aside to rest for 5 minutes, then cut into halves or slices and serve topped with tzatziki.

TZATZIKI

MAKES about 2 cups

1½ cups Nonfat Greek-Style Yogurt (page 98)
1¼ cups diced or coarsely grated English cucumber (skin on)
3 green onions (white and light green parts), thinly sliced
1 tablespoon minced fresh garlic
1 tablespoon chopped fresh dill leaves
1 tablespoon chopped fresh mint leaves
½ teaspoon unrefined fine sea salt
Pinch of sugar
Pinch of ground white pepper

In two fine-mesh strainers set in separate bowls, drain both the yogurt and the cucumber. Combine the remaining ingredients in a bowl and adjust salt and pepper to taste. Chill for 30 minutes, drain a second time, and then bring to room temperature to serve with the chicken.

Beer-Batter Fish and Chips *with Two Ketchups*

SERVES 4 to 6

Include a little lead time when making the chips because they are soaked in salted water for 8 hours or overnight before frying, and the fish is seasoned and chilled for 1 hour before frying. Soak the potatoes ahead, season and chill the fish, fry the chips, and then fry the fish. The soak transforms the potatoes, making them crisper and more delicious than any you've ever had. You can substitute yams or sweet potatoes, if you like. I serve this pub-style dish with two homemade ketchups: tomato and mushroom, along with a drizzle of vinegar over the fish. Heavenly!

CHIPS

3 teaspoons unrefined fine sea salt, plus more for sprinkling

4 cups cool filtered water

$1\frac{1}{2}$ pounds large Yukon gold potatoes (skin on), cut lengthwise into $\frac{1}{2}$-inch matchsticks

2 tablespoons all-purpose flour

$\frac{1}{2}$ teaspoon cayenne pepper

1 teaspoon ground cumin

$\frac{1}{4}$ cup olive oil

Canola oil, for frying

FISH

2 pounds skinless cod, rockfish, or halibut fillets, cut into 2-ounce portions

$\frac{1}{3}$ cup mayonnaise

$1\frac{3}{4}$ cups all-purpose flour

2 teaspoons baking powder

1 teaspoon Old Bay seasoning

$\frac{1}{4}$ teaspoon cayenne pepper

1 cup filtered water

$\frac{1}{2}$ cup ale of choice, at room temperature

1 large egg

1 cup panko (Japanese) bread crumbs, lightly crumbled

$\frac{1}{2}$ teaspoon unrefined fine sea salt, plus more for sprinkling

Canola oil, for frying

Tomato Ketchup (page 24), for accompaniment

Mushroom Ketchup (page 25), for accompaniment

Maple-Port Vinegar (page 37), for accompaniment

To make the chips: In a large bowl, make a brine by dissolving 2 teaspoons of salt in the water. Place the potatoes in a strainer to fit the bowl and submerge in the brine. Cover loosely with cheesecloth, and move to a cool location to soak for 8 hours or overnight.

Drain the potatoes and lay out on a baking sheet. Chill in the refrigerator for 1 hour before frying.

Combine the flour, cayenne, cumin, and remaining teaspoon of salt in a bowl. In a separate bowl, toss the potato matchsticks with the olive oil. Dredge in the flour mixture and put on a baking sheet.

Preheat the oven to 250°F. Set a rack on a baking sheet for the potatoes to drain. Heat 2 inches of canola oil in a skillet or wok to 350°F. Carefully place a few strips of the potato (four at a time) into the hot oil, making sure they stay separated while cooking. Toss with a slotted spoon to cook evenly, until dark golden in color and crispy, 3 to 4 minutes. Using a slotted spoon or bird's-nest strainer, remove the potatoes from the oil and transfer to the rack to drain. Lightly salt while hot. Keep warm in the oven until ready to serve.

To make the fish: Lay the fish on a platter or baking sheet, coat with mayonnaise, and set aside to chill for 1 hour. Combine the flour, baking powder, Old Bay seasoning, and cayenne in a bowl. In a separate bowl, whisk together the water, ale, and egg. Whisk together the dry and the wet mixtures. Set aside to chill for 10 minutes. Combine the panko and salt and spread on a baking sheet.

Set a rack on a baking sheet for the fish to drain. Over medium-high heat, heat 2 inches of canola oil in a skillet or wok to 350°F. Dip the mayonnaise-rubbed fillets into the batter and then dredge in the panko mixture. Carefully place each piece of the fish (two or three at a time) into the hot oil. Toss and cook on both sides until dark golden in color and crispy, 5 to 7 minutes. Using a slotted spoon or bird's-nest strainer, remove the crispy fish and place on a rack in a baking sheet to drain. Lightly salt each side of the fish while hot.

Serve immediately or keep warm in a 250°F oven until ready to serve with the chips and the two ketchups.

CHOCOLATE SOURDOUGH CUPCAKES

with Coconut-Pecan Cream Cheese Frosting

MAKES 24 cupcakes

These cupcakes are my nod to my grandmother's German chocolate cake. Two talented chefs collaborated independently to bring this recipe to life. Michael Kalanty created the sourdough cupcake recipe based on a popular chocolate cake recipe from his collection. To be true to the German chocolate cake tradition, there had to be a coconut-pecan frosting, and because I felt the fat needed to be fermented, Farmhouse Cream Cheese (page 102) was used. If you use store-bought cream cheese, make sure it is the real deal, without stabilizers. My assistant, Annie Simmons, stepped up to the challenge and created this frosting. It's good enough to eat by the spoonful!

CUPCAKES

$3/8$ cup whole milk

1 cup semisweet chocolate chunks

2 teaspoons pure vanilla extract

$1/8$ teaspoon balsamic vinegar

$3/4$ cup unsalted butter, at room temperature

$1^1/2$ cups raw unrefined cane sugar

4 large eggs, separated

$1^1/2$ cups sourdough starter (see page 133)

$1^1/2$ cups all-purpose flour

1 teaspoon unrefined fine sea salt

1 tablespoon baking powder

1 teaspoon baking soda

FROSTING

$1/2$ cup unsalted butter, cut into pieces

$3/4$ cup packed dark brown sugar

8 ounces Farmhouse Cream Cheese (page 102) or other natural cream cheese

1 cup unsweetened shredded coconut, toasted

$1/2$ cup pecan pieces, toasted

To make the cupcakes: Line 24 standard cupcake molds with paper liners and set aside.

Preheat the oven to 375°F. Adjust the oven racks so that the cupcakes will bake in the middle of the oven.

In a small saucepan, heat the milk over medium-low heat. Add the chocolate pieces and let heat for 5 minutes to begin to melt. Stir to melt completely and then add the vanilla and vinegar. Remove from the heat and let cool.

In a stand mixer fitted with the paddle attachment, cream the butter and sugar together on medium speed until light and fluffy, about 2 minutes. On low speed, beat in the egg yolks, two at a time. Beat in the

continued

sourdough starter to combine, then beat the cooled chocolate mixture into the sugar-starter mixture and set aside.

In a separate bowl, sift together the flour, salt, baking powder, and baking soda; set aside.

In a clean, dry stand-mixer bowl fitted with the whisk attachment, whip the egg whites on high speed to a firm peak.

Fold one-third of the flour mixture into the chocolate mixture. Gently fold in half of the egg whites. Continue with another one-third of the dry mixture, the remaining egg whites, and then the final one-third of the dry ingredients.

Spoon or pipe the batter into the cupcake papers, filling them three-fourths full. Place the pan(s) on a baking sheet and transfer to the oven. Bake until a toothpick comes out clean, 16 to 18 minutes.

Let the cupcakes cool in the pan for 5 minutes, and then transfer to a rack to cool for 30 minutes before frosting. They will deflate slightly in cooling, but that gives more space for frosting!

To make the frosting: Combine half of the butter and the brown sugar in a small saucepan. Cook over medium heat, stirring occasionally, until the butter melts and the sugar begins to bubble. Continue to cook until the mixture is smooth and thoroughly combined, 2 to 3 minutes. Remove from the heat.

Place the cream cheese in a medium bowl and pour the hot sugar mixture over it. Using a stand mixer with a paddle attachment or with beaters, blend the cream cheese and sugar together until smooth (you may still see little bits of brown sugar in the frosting; these are fine). Add the remaining half of the butter and continue to beat until the butter is completely incorporated into the warm frosting.

Fold the coconut and pecans into the frosting, cover, and allow to sit for 30 minutes before using. Frosting may be made ahead and refrigerated. It will keep, refrigerated, for up to 1 week.

To frost the cupcakes: Bring the frosting to room temperature, if chilled, then spread on the cooled cupcakes. Store frosted cupcakes in a covered container in the refrigerator for up to 1 week.

Seasonal Fruit Tart *with Cream Cheese Crust*

SERVES 8

This not-too-sweet dessert has the perfect components: soft, juicy fruit and a crispy, tender crust. As with any fat, the cheese adds flavor as well as tenderizes the dough. You can make one large tart or multiple individual tarts, a free-form galette, or a 10-inch tart in a pan. Any seasonal firm, ripe fruit or even homemade preserves work well for filling this tart. Add toasted nuts or shredded coconut to the top of the filling, if desired: apricots or nectarines are wonderful with almonds or pistachios; plums are great with walnuts. You can also substitute chèvre for the cream cheese—Basic Fresh Goat Chèvre (page 101) or store-bought—it will work beautifully. This crust is great for a savory tart as well. In that case, you may opt to add ½ teaspoon of dried or fresh finely minced herbs to the dough. This dough can be frozen for up to 1 month.

CRUST

1 cup all-purpose flour

¼ teaspoon unrefined fine sea salt

¼ teaspoon baking powder

2 tablespoons cold unsalted butter, cubed

2 tablespoons cold Farmhouse Cream Cheese (page 102), cut into pieces

1 teaspoon raw, unfiltered apple cider vinegar

1 tablespoon ice water, plus more if needed

FILLING

4 large firm, ripe stone fruit (such as plums, apricots, nectarines, or peaches)

Juice of 1 orange, for brushing

1½ cups unsalted butter

¾ cup raw unrefined cane sugar

2 tablespoons unbleached all-purpose flour

Grated zest of 1 orange

Crème Fraîche (page 95), optional

To make the crust: With a food processor, combine the flour, salt, and baking powder; process for 5 to 10 seconds to mix thoroughly. Add the cold butter pieces and cream cheese to the flour, and pulse several times until both butter and cream cheese are almost fully incorporated and the flour looks grainy.

Combine the vinegar and ice water in a small bowl and sprinkle over the top of the flour mixture. Pulse until the mixture comes together into a rough ball of dough, 10 to 12 times. Slowly drizzle in another small amount of ice water, if needed. Flatten the dough into a disk, wrap in plastic wrap, and refrigerate for 15 to 20 minutes to relax the dough before rolling.

Preheat the oven to 375°F.

continued

To make the filling: Blanch the stone fruit in a 2-quart pot of simmering water for about 30 seconds, and then place in a water bath to cool slightly. Remove the peel from the fruit, cut into quarters, and remove the pit. Brush the fruit with orange juice so they do not brown. Put the fruit in a bowl.

Melt the butter and the sugar together in a saucepan and slowly cook together until the sugar dissolves. Cook over a low to medium heat until the sugar has begun to caramelize, about 20 minutes Whisk in the flour to dissolve then stir in the zest. Toss the fruit in the mixture and cook for 5 minutes. Remove from the heat and let the mixture cool for 20 minutes.

To assemble the tart: On a lightly floured surface, roll out the dough into a 13-inch round. If making a tart, gently drape and press into the tart pan. Dock by pricking with a fork and prebake for 10 minutes. If making a free-form galette, place the dough round on a parchment-lined baking sheet.

If making a tart, fill the tart pan with the cooled fruit. If making a galette, spoon and spread the cooled fruit onto the rolled-out crust, up to $1\frac{1}{2}$ inches from the edge. Place the tart on a baking sheet. Bake the tart or galette until the pastry is golden brown, 20 to 25 minutes. Let cool on a rack.

Cut into wedges and serve each slice topped with a dollop of lightly sweetened crème fraîche.

ALMOND-CRUSTED CHÈVRE CHEESECAKES

SERVES 8

This style of cheesecake, based on Italian ricotta cheesecake, is one that I love. It is rustic and not too rich or too sweet. Almonds and oranges are often combined in Mediterranean desserts. Here almond meal and orange blossom water make the cakes both fragrant and delectable.

Unsalted butter, for greasing ramekins

1/2 cup ground almond meal, plus more for topping

2 1/2 tablespoons raw turbinado sugar

1 cup raw unrefined cane sugar

1/3 cup all-purpose flour

1/8 cup golden raisins, finely chopped

1/2 teaspoon unrefined fine sea salt

14 ounces Basic Fresh Goat Chèvre (page 101) or store-bought chèvre, at room temperature

6 large eggs, lightly beaten

1/8 teaspoon ground anise seed

1/8 teaspoon ground ginger

2 teaspoons pure vanilla extract

1/2 teaspoon orange blossom water

Grated zest of 2 oranges

Fruit preserves, for topping

Preheat the oven to 325°F. Generously butter 8 ovenproof 4 1/2-ounce ramekins. Combine 1/2 cup of the almond meal and the turbinado sugar and dust the inside of the ramekins. Tap out any excess. Set the ramekins aside.

Mix together the cane sugar, flour, raisins, and salt. In a stand mixer fitted with the paddle attachment (or whisk by hand), beat the chèvre at low speed until smooth. Slowly add the beaten eggs, then add the sugar-flour mixture and gently mix to blend. Add the anise seed, ginger, vanilla, orange blossom water, and zest. Mix thoroughly. Pour the batter into the prepared ramekins, leaving about 1/2 inch unfilled at the top.

Place the ramekins on a baking sheet and set on the center rack of the oven. Bake until the cheesecakes are lightly golden, fairly firm in the center, and a toothpick comes out clean, 30 to 35 minutes. Transfer to a rack to cool for 5 to 10 minutes.

To serve, tap the cheesecakes out of the ramekins into the palm of your hand, turn right side (top) up, and place on individual serving plates.

Top each cheesecake with a spoonful of seasonal fruit preserves and dust with ground almond meal.

Yogurt-Cardamom Ice Cream *with Goat Crème*
Fraîche Caramel Sauce

MAKES about 1 quart

Tangy yogurt paired with aromatic cardamom makes this ice cream glorious! Drizzle Goat Crème Fraîche Caramel Sauce (page 232) over the top, and then garnish with chopped candied orange rind and chopped pistachios. Try another tasty version topped with Ginger-Mint Shrub (page 169).

2 cups whole milk

2 cups heavy cream

10 to 12 cardamom pods, crushed

½ vanilla bean, split, or 1 teaspoon pure vanilla extract

9 large egg yolks

¾ cup raw unrefined cane sugar

1 cup Greek-style whole milk yogurt (not low fat)

Seasonal fruit, fruit preserves, chopped candied orange, Goat Crème Fraîche Caramel Sauce (recipe follows), or Ginger-Mint Shrub (page 169), for accompaniment

¼ cup finely chopped pistachios, for garnish

Place the milk and cream in a nonreactive saucepan. Warm over medium-low heat, stirring occasionally, to just below boiling point. Turn off the heat and add the cardamom pods (and vanilla bean, if using), cover the pan, and allow the mixture to steep for 50 minutes. Pour the mixture through a fine-mesh strainer into a bowl, pressing firmly against the pods to release their flavor. Discard the pods. Prepare an ice bath. Return the flavored cream to the saucepan.

Place the pan over medium-low heat and reheat the mixture to just below the boiling point. In a small bowl, whisk the egg yolks together with the sugar. Whisking constantly, slowly add about 1 cup of the hot cream to the yolks, tempering the eggs. Pour the yolk mixture back into the saucepan and cook over medium-low, stirring constantly with a wooden spoon until the custard thickens and coats the back of a wooden spoon (about 170°F on a thermometer). Do not let the mixture boil, as the eggs will curdle. Remove from the heat and immediately pour the mixture through a fine-mesh strainer into a large stainless steel bowl. Set in the ice bath and stir the custard gently for a few minutes to cool slightly. Whisk in the yogurt and, if not using the vanilla bean, the vanilla extract. Remove from the ice bath and cover with plastic wrap directly on the custard surface and refrigerate until ready to serve. At this point it can be served as a sauce—known as crème anglaise.

Chill thoroughly for about 2 to 3 hours or overnight, and then freeze in your ice cream maker according to the manufacturer's directions. Immediately transfer the ice cream to a storage container, cover, and place in the freezer. Serve within 1 hour of freezing or the

continued

ice cream will become too hard to scoop. If it does get too hard, leave in the refrigerator to soften a bit.

Serve with seasonal fruit, fruit preserves, or drizzled with Goat Crème Fraîche Caramel Sauce or Ginger-Mint Shrub and garnished with chopped pistachios.

GOAT CRÈME FRAÎCHE CARAMEL SAUCE

MAKES 1 pint

This delectable sauce, similar to the popular dulce de leche from Mexico, is made from Goat Milk Crème Fraîche, which is then caramelized to become a creamy sauce. This sauce can also be made with cow milk crème fraîche. Use it as a topping on ice cream, or on cakes or tarts. You can even serve it warm as a dipping sauce for fruit fondue.

2 cups raw unrefined cane sugar

½ cup water

Pinch of cream of tartar

4 tablespoons Cultured Butter (page 96)

1½ cups Goat Milk Crème Fraîche (page 95), at room temperature

¼ teaspoon unrefined fine sea salt

In a medium heavy saucepan, whisk the sugar and water with the cream of tartar to combine. Cook over medium-low heat until the sugar dissolves. Increase the heat to medium-high; boil, without stirring, until the syrup becomes a deep amber color, occasionally brushing down the sides of the pan with a wet (with water) pastry brush, if needed, and swirling the pan. Remove from the heat.

Add the butter and swirl until the butter is melted and the caramel is bubbly. Whisk in the crème fraîche and salt, and place over low heat, stirring until the sauce is smooth. Allow the sauce to simmer until slightly thickened, 15 to 20 minutes. Remove from the heat. Let stand until cool and pourable, about 20 minutes. Store in a plastic squeeze bottle and use immediately to drizzle over ice cream or other dessert, or refrigerate for later use. This will keep for up to 2 months.

ACKNOWLEDGMENTS

THE CREATION OF THIS BOOK has taken me down many diverse, exciting, and sometimes unfamiliar paths that I could not have anticipated at the beginning of the journey. Exploration is a good thing. The personal benefits gained by crafting a book are enormously rewarding—far beyond words. I am grateful for the opportunity to write, teach, and share. Numerous generous people have played important roles in this book.

Thank you to these talented friends who contributed recipes and valuable information to this book and its companion website: Michael Easton, Steve Garner, Jennifer Harris, Kuba Hemmerling and the Giacomini Family, Michael Kalanty, Ron Lindenbusch, Tony Magee and Lagunitas Brewing Company, Andrea Nguyen, Bob Peak, Peter Reinhart, Steve Sando, John Toulze, Nancy Vineyard, and The Beverage People.

A special nod to Paul Bertolli for generously sharing his knowledge, and for encouraging me to ask lots of questions.

To my team of testers: team leaders Jennifer Luttrell, Susan Pruett, and Annie Simmons. And testers Rachael Burke, Melissa Fenton, Suzy Foster, Jennifer Harris, Terri Hughes, Gabe Jackson, Krysta Kasternakis, Patrick Laherty, Sally McComas, and Nicole Ryan. Thank you for your expertise and enthusiastic palates in testing, tasting, and sharing the fruits of your labor.

A special shout-out to Patrick Laherty for his humor and willingness to dive into unfamiliar territories with me. And to Gabe Jackson for bringing his expertise and collaborative spirit to this project. You nailed those recipes!

Thank you to Bob Peak and his daughter Charlotte for studiously shaping the glossary.

Jars full of thanks to two special helpers: my awesome assistant for this book, Annie Simmons, for enthusiastically joining me and lending her culinary expertise at every point. And to my steady supporter, Susan Pruett, for the endless hours of assistance in classes, and involvement in this book. Thank you both for your friendship and for rescuing me when I needed a break.

Hugs to my partner Bert Archer and special friends Bud and Lorrie Polley for years of love and encouragement.

Mille grazie to the Weber Family and Yunker for giving me the needed sanctuary and workshop for writing this book. Also to Ginger, Gouda, Bird, Mac, Rudy, and Zoe who enthusiastically greet me and remind me every day of what's really important in life.

Hugs to Diane Phillips and Dr. Chuck for your friendship, hospitality, and generosity.

Heartfelt thanks to Great News!, Ramekins, Santa Rosa Junior College Community Ed, The Cheese School of San Francisco, The Fork at Point Reyes

Farmstead Cheese, and the other cooking schools and venues that allow me a platform to teach and encourage enthusiasts. To the savvy folks at Craftsy.com who recognize a growing interest in DIY topics, thank you for inviting me to join your stable of food craft instructors.

To my terrific Ten Speed team: my editor, Sara Golski; designer Katy Brown; art director Betsy Stromberg; editor Melissa Moore; and head wizard Aaron Wehner, who have embraced my areas of passionate interest over the years. Thank you for the encouragement to write about timely, interesting topics and then manifest them in enticing packages.

Special thanks to my extraordinary photographer Ed Anderson, who has once again captured images and light in ways that few others can. Thanks, my friend, for the tip on the cottage. And to Molly Watson, who worked closely with me to fine-tune my voice, present it with clarity, and skillfully craft a worthy manuscript.

Thank you to Sally Fallon for sharing her knowledge, and to Sandor Katz for being an inspirational fermentation revivalist. And my love and gratitude to my late mother, who introduced me to the world of nutrition and Adele Davis many moons ago.

GLOSSARY

ABV. Common measure of alcohol strength in beer and other alcoholic beverages. Refers to "Alcohol by Volume;" listed in percentage on the label of the beverage. Beers in the United States range from 4 percent up to 9 percent or more; the higher the ABV, the stronger the beer.

Acidification. The development of acid (and corresponding drop in pH) in milk or cheese as lactic bacteria convert lactose to lactic acid.

Acidifier. An organism that releases hydrogen ion (acid) during its life process in a fermentation. Also, a food acid added directly to a ferment to lower the pH.

Adjuncts. Grains and other sources of fermentable sugars (other than the barley or wheat), such as cane sugar, corn sugar, and rice.

Aerobic. Requiring oxygen for metabolism. Used to describe yeasts or bacteria that depend upon the presence of air to live and grow.

Air lock. A device that allows carbon dioxide from an active fermentation to escape from the fermentation vessel, but prevents the entry of air or contaminants. Commonly either filled with water or equipped with a one-way silicone valve.

Ale. A beer (fermented alcoholic beverage made from grain) that is top-fermented with an ale yeast strain. Usually produced at warmer temperatures than lager beers.

Alkaline. Having a pH greater than neutral (>7.0). Basic; opposite of acidic.

Anaerobic. Able to thrive in the absence of oxygen; used to describe bacteria or molds that do not need air for their metabolism.

Antinutrients. Compounds found in foods that interfere with absorption of necessary nutrients during digestion.

Autolyse. To destroy a cell (or single-cell organism) through the action of its own enzymes.

Backslopping. Initiating a fermentation by adding back a portion of a previous production.

Bacteria. Autonomous microscopic organisms that reproduce asexually; in fermentation, the most important group is the lactic bacteria that convert sugars to lactic acid.

Beer yeasts. Used in either dry or liquid form, beer yeasts are a class of fungi (*Saccharomyces* spp.), which feed on the sugars to ferment the malt and other sugars, producing ethyl alcohol and carbon dioxide.

Boil. The phase of beer making where all the ingredients except the yeast and the priming sugar come together.

Botulism. A serious paralytic infection caused by consuming botulinum toxin, produced by the bacterium *Clostridium botulinum* under anaerobic conditions.

Brine. A usually strong solution of salts, most often sodium chloride (table salt), sometimes including calcium chloride as well. Used to preserve foods and promote desirable bacterial development for safe fermentation.

Carbonation. Production of carbon dioxide in a beverage through the action of yeast on sugars; also, the introduction of carbon dioxide from an external source, as compressed carbon dioxide.

Cheese mold. Fungal organisms that grow on or in cheese. Alternatively, may refer to the perforated vessel in which a cheese is shaped or pressed.

Cider. The fermented juice of fruits other than grapes, most commonly apples or pears.

Coagulation. In cheese making, the solidification of proteins forming curd.

Culture. A colony of microorganisms developed or maintained for initiating fermentation.

Curd. The solid part of cheese making, as compared with the liquid whey. Curd structure is formed from protein and it contains fat, moisture, salts, and other milk components.

Curing. Food preservation by the addition of salts or sugar. Sometimes includes dehydration, smoking, cooking, fermentation, or some combination of processes.

Dextrose. Glucose; a simple monosaccharide (sugar) found in plants and fruits.

Diacetyl rest. The resting time needed to reduce the level of diacetyl (the compound giving beer its buttery or butterscotchlike flavor) to the proper level for optimum flavor and stability.

Digestif. An alcoholic beverage traditionally served after a meal, theoretically to aid digestion.

Distillation. A process of heating a fluid to remove some component(s) by evaporation, combined with condensing and collecting those components. The most common method for concentrating the ethanol initially produced via fermentation, forming a strong spirit.

Dry-cured. Refers to meat that has been rubbed with dry salts, rather than soaked in brine.

Dry hopping. Process of adding dried or pellet aromatic hops after the alcohol is formed to extract fresh flavor and aroma prior to, and removed before, the beer is kegged or bottled.

Dry-salting. Rubbing or embedding in salt, rather than brining.

Enzymes. Biologically active proteins that break or form chemical bonds in specific substrates (as the action of rennet on casein in milk).

Ethyl alcohol. Ethanol, C_2H_5OH; beverage alcohol.

Fatty acids. Carboxylic acids with a long aliphatic component; essential dietary components usually derived from consumed fats.

Fermentation. Conversion by microorganisms of a specific substrate into a desired product, as alcohol from fruit sugar or lactic acid from milk sugar.

Fermento. A proprietary product containing cultured whey protein and skim milk, used to quickly impart a tangy flavor in semidry sausages; substitute for lactic fermentation of such sausages.

Flameout. The point at which the flame under the wort is turned off. It is also a designated time (flameout addition) for hops additions in some recipes.

Flora. In fermentation, descriptive of the entire population of microorganisms involved (bacteria, molds, and yeasts). Also, the microbial population in a mammal's digestive system.

Ghee. A form of clarified butter, used in Indian cooking, which can withstand high cooking temperatures.

Glucose. A simple hexose (6-carbon) sugar or monosaccharide; also called dextrose or corn sugar.

Gravity. The density of a solution in relation to pure distilled water at a given temperature. Also a measure of the amount of sugar in the wort; using a saccharometer (a hydrometer designed to measure by weight the amount of sugar in a solution), the gravity reading is taken at the beginning, before fermentation (starting gravity) and at the end of fermentation (final gravity). The gravity declines as fermentation progresses and is a useful indicator of the health the fermenting process.

Gut. The digestive tract of an animal.

Gut flora. The microbial population of the gut.

Homogenization. The mechanical reduction of fat particle size in milk to make it form a stable emulsion.

Hop bill. The ingredient list of hops varieties used in the recipe, including the sequence in which they are added and their function.

Hops. An essential ingredient in beer making. Hops are the flower cones (whole hops) of the female hop plant (*Humulus lupulus*), used in beer making as a preservative, a flavoring, and an aromatic. Used as whole hops or in pellet or extract form. A wide variety of hops exists to impart their unique bitter or aromatic characteristics. Hops are designated as *bittering*, to be added to the wort during boiling, or as *aromatic*, added to the wort at the end of the boiling process.

IBU. International Bitterness Units; a scale of bitterness in beer, measured in a laboratory as mg/L (parts per million) dissolved alpha acids of hops.

Incubate. To store at a controlled temperature, generally to facilitate the growth of desired microorganisms.

Infusion. A solution produced by steeping a solid material in water at a temperature below the boiling point.

Inoculate. To introduce microbes to a substrate for fermentation.

Kefir. Milk fermented with lactic bacteria and yeasts.

Kegging. Placing beer in a stainless steel pressure vessel and carbonating it (through fermentation of sugar or by adding compressed carbon dioxide). An alternative to bottling.

Lactic acid. A naturally occurring carboxylic acid of formula $C_3H_6O_3$. The fermentation product of lactic acid bacteria.

Lactic acid bacteria. Microorganisms that produce lactic acid as the primary metabolic product of carbohydrate fermentation.

Lacto-fermentation. Microbial conversion of glucose into either two lactic acid molecules or one lactic acid molecule plus one ethanol molecule and one carbon dioxide molecule.

Lactose. The sugar of milk; a disaccharide (12-carbon sugar) consisting of the two monosaccharides, glucose and galactose.

Lager. Refers to beers produced with lager yeast strains (commonly *Saccharomyces pastorianus*) at cool temperatures. Such beers are referred to as bottom fermented and are usually subjected to cold storage after fermentation to improve clarity. The word is from the German for "storage."

Lagering. The process of cold aging after fermentation.

Leaven. To cause a dough to rise through the production of carbon dioxide.

Lipase. An enzyme from the gut of a juvenile milk-producing mammal that breaks down fat into aromatic short-chain fatty acids.

Live culture. Living organisms, usually lactic acid bacteria, in a fermented dairy product.

Malt. Barley (sometimes wheat, rye, or other grains) that has been sprouted and kilned or dried to initiate enzymatic conversion of starches to sugar. Sometimes refers to a liquid or dry extract of such grains, although those products are more properly called *malt extract*.

Malting. The moist germinating process that converts the grain to a form that has more carbohydrates available for fermentation.

Mash. To steep malt in hot water to facilitate enzymatic conversion of starches to sugars.

Mesophilic. Refers to microorganisms that thrive on "middle" temperatures; generally from about 70°F to 90°F.

Metabolism. The life process of an organism.

Minerals. Naturally occurring, nonorganic (not containing carbon) elements and compounds. In the diet, usually refers to chemical elements other than carbon, hydrogen, oxygen, and nitrogen that are essential to nutrition.

Mold. A form of perforated plastic or stainless steel used for draining and shaping a cheese; also, fungal microorganisms that grow in multicellular filaments.

Mother culture. A substrate harboring a desired microbial population that is used to inoculate new batches of a fermented food or beverage.

Oxidation. Chemically, loss of electrons. In practice, this generally refers to the reaction of organic matter with oxygen producing certain oxidized by-products. By-products are often brown and undesirable, although oxidation is deliberate in some fermented foods and beverages.

Pasteurization. Heat treatment of milk to reduce the population of viable microorganisms, intended to eliminate pathogens.

Pickling. Placing food in brine and fostering lactic fermentation to achieve acidic preservation along with a salty and sour taste. Also, the processing of foods directly in acid solution (such as vinegar) with salt to achieve similar preservation and flavors without fermentation.

Pink salt. A mixture of table salt (sodium chloride) and sodium nitrite, sometimes containing sodium nitrate as well. Nitrites and nitrates inhibit spoilage bacteria (specifically *Clostridium botulinum*) to help prevent botulism from cured meats. The salt is dyed pink to avoid its accidental consumption as table salt.

Priming sugar. Sugar that is used to prime the beer for bottle conditioning. It is added at bottling to supply the yeast with more sugar (fuel) to metabolize while the yeast is active.

Probiotics. Living microorganisms that are considered to confer health benefits to the host when introduced to the gut.

Racking. Siphoning a clear beverage off of sediment to derive an improved product. The sediments are called lees in winemaking and trub in brewing.

Raw food. Foods that are not heated above temperatures that would inactivate native enzymes; about 100°F to 120°F. Fermented, sprouted, dehydrated, and frozen foods may still be considered raw, as long as they have not been cooked.

Reverse osmosis water. Water than has been purified by reverse osmosis; desirable for brewing beer. Reverse osmosis drinking water is available on retail shelves and in dispensing machines nationwide.

Roasted malt. Dried sprouted grains, roasted at various temperatures to determine the color and flavor of the malt and the final beer.

Room temperature. In scientific practice, 68°F. For common purposes, any temperature within a few degrees of this target temperature.

Salinity. The concentration of salt(s) in a water solution.

SCOBY. An acronym for Symbiotic Colony of Bacteria and Yeast; describes the "mother culture" of fermented preparations such as kombucha.

Secondary cultures. Additional microorganisms present in or added to a fermentation to achieve additional results beyond the primary product. These may include mold spores for bloomy cheeses, lactic bacteria for beer, yeasts for dairy beverages, and others.

Siphon. Tubing system used to drain off fermented liquid, leaving residual sludge behind.

Sparge. To rinse a solid material (as grain from mashing for beer) with hot water to transport soluble substances.

Starter. A substrate that contains, harbors, or captures microorganisms for use in fermented products.

Starter culture. A preparation of living organisms suitable for inoculating milk to develop cheese or inoculating other foods or beverages to induce fermentation.

Sucanat. A brand of natural whole cane sugar that can be substituted for raw cane sugar.

Sucrose. Table sugar; a disaccharide (two hexoses) sugar of formula $C_{12}H_{22}O_{11}$. Structurally, it is the combination of a glucose molecule and a fructose molecule. Commercially, sugar cane and sugar beets are the dominant sources of sucrose.

Thermophilic. Refers to microorganisms that thrive at warmer temperatures, usually 104°F to 122°F.

Tonic. A preparation or beverage, often of herbal origin, intended to stimulate, rejuvenate, or otherwise confer health benefits on the person who consumes it.

Tun. Kettle.

Ultra-pasteurization. Treatment at very high temperature to produce long-life milk; generally not suitable for cheese making due to protein damage during the process.

Vitamins. Organic compounds essential to healthy metabolism that are not produced in sufficient quantities by the body and must be included in the diet. Distinguished from nutrients primarily by their effectiveness in very small amounts.

Wet hopping. Process of adding fresh aromatic hops after the alcohol is formed to extract fresh flavor and aroma prior to, and removed before, the beer is kegged or bottled.

Whey. The watery solution that is drained from curds during cheese production; the part of milk that does not become cheese.

Wild fermentation. Conversion of foods or beverages by organisms that are captured from the environment or are present on the substrate to start with, rather than added as a deliberate culture.

Wort. The sugar-containing solution derived from malt that, when fermented, becomes beer.

Yeast. Fungal microorganisms employed to produce carbon dioxide for baking and ethanol in beverages, as well as other fermentation products.

RESOURCES

FERMENTING SUPPLIES

Cultures for Health (starter cultures, kefir grains, nigari flakes, tofu supplies, mineral drops, yogurt maker)
www.culturesforhealth.com

Pickl-It (starter cultures) • www.pickl-it.com

Respectfully Green (vinegar mother cultures)
www.respectfullygreen.org

The Sausage Maker (sausage-making supplies)
www.sausagemaker.com

Victorio Kitchen Products (sprouter)
www.victoriokitchenproducts.com

CHEESE-MAKING SUPPLIES

The Beverage People • www.thebeveragepeople.com

The Cheese Connection • www.cheeseconnection.net

The Cheesemaker • www.thecheesemaker.com

Glengarry Cheesemaking and Dairy Supply
www.glengarrycheesemaking.on.ca

New England Cheesemaking Supply
www.cheesemaking.com

BREWING SUPPLIES

The Beverage People • www.thebeveragepeople.com

Kombucha Kamp • www.kombuchakamp.com

Lion Heart Kombucha • www.lionheartkombucha.com

INGREDIENTS

Bob's Red Mill (assorted flours, wheat gluten)
www.bobsredmill.com

Bulk Foods (pickling lime) • www.bulkfoods.com

Frontier Natural Products Co-Op (mustard seeds and powder) • www.frontiercoop.com

King Arthur Flour (flours, candied fruit)
www.kingarthurflour.com

Local Harvest • www.localharvest.org

The Meadow (gourmet and artisan salts)
www.atthemeadow.com

Mountain Rose Herbs • www.mountainroseherbs.com

The Olive Press (Limonato olive oil)
www.theolivepress.com

Purcell Mountain Farms (lentils)
www.purcellmountainfarms.com

Rancho Gordo New World Specialty Food (beans, piloncillo sugar) • www.ranchogordo.com

The Smoked Olive (smoked olive oil and sugar)
www.thesmokedolive.com

Sonoma County Poultry (Liberty Ducks and rendered duck fat) • www.libertyducks.com

Sun Organic Farm • www.sunorganicfarm.com

To Your Health Sprouted Flour
www.organicsproutedflour.net

Whole Spice Inc. • www.wholespice.com

BOTTLES, JARS, AND CROCKS

The Beverage People • www.the beveragepeople.com

Bram Clay Cookware • www.bramcookware.com

Cultures for Health (air lock jars, crocks)
www.culturesforhealth.com

Pickl-It (air lock jars, glass weights)
www.pickl-it.com

Weck Canning Products • www.weckjars.com

MISCELLANEOUS

The Beverage People (cheese wrapping paper)
www.thebeveragepeople.com

Campaign for Real Milk (raw milk laws, cow shares)
www.realmilk.com and www.realmilk.com/
cowfarmshare.html

Kitchen Supply Company (Panettone paper baking
molds) • www.kitchensupply.com

SodaStream (carbonated water maker)
www.sodastreamusa.com

Weston A. Price Foundation ("Real Milk" information,
cow shares, and general nutrition)
www.westonaprice.org

PUBLICATIONS

Culture magazine • www.culturecheesemag.com

Imbibe magazine • www.imbibemagazine.com

FERMENTATION AND CHEESE-MAKING CLASSES

The Cheese School of San Francisco
San Francisco, CA • www.cheeseschoolsf.com

The Fork, Point Reyes Farmstead Cheese Company
Point Reyes Station, CA
www.theforkatpointreyes.com

Great News! Cooking School • San Diego, CA
www.great-news.com

The Pantry at Delancey • Seattle, WA
www.thepantryatdelancey.com

Ramekins Culinary School • Sonoma, CA
www.ramekins.com

Santa Rosa Junior College, Community
Education • Santa Rosa, CA
www.santarosa.edu/communityed

Recommended Reading sources are posted at
www.masteringfermentation.com

Author's websites: www.artisancheesemaking
athome.com; www.masteringfermentation.com

BIBLIOGRAPHY

Alford, Jeffrey and Naomi Duguid. *Flatbreads & Flavors*. New York: William Morrow, 1995.

Bertolli, Paul. *Cooking by Hand*. New York: Clarkson Potter, 2003.

Bitterman, Mark. *Salted*. Berkeley, CA: Ten Speed Press, 2010.

Bittman, Mark. *How to Cook Everything Vegetarian*. Hoboken, NJ: Wiley Publishing, 2007.

Brennan, Jennifer. *The Cuisines of Asia*. New York: St. Martin's Press, 1984.

Burch, Monte. *The Joy of Smoking and Salt Curing*. New York: Skyhorse Publishing, 2011.

Campbell-Platt, Geoffrey. *Fermented Foods of the World*. Kent, England: Butterworths, 1987.

Ciletti, Barbara. *Creative Pickling at Home*. New York: Lark Books, 2000.

Civitello, Linda. *Cuisine & Culture*. Hoboken, NJ: John Wiley & Sons, 2011.

Harmon, Wardeh. *The Complete Idiot's Guide to Fermenting Foods*. New York: Alpha Books, 2004.

Kamozawa, Aki and H. Alexander Talbott. *Ideas in Food*. New York: Clarkson Potter, 2010.

Katz, Sandor Ellix. *Wild Fermentation*. White River Junction, VT: Chelsea Green Publishing, 2003.

Madison, Deborah. *Vegetarian Cooking for Everyone*. New York: Broadway Books, 1997.

McGee, Harold. *On Food and Cooking*. New York: Scribner (Simon & Schuster), 2004.

Morell, Sally Fallon and Mary G. Enig, PhD. *Nourishing Traditions*. Washington, DC: New Trends Publishing, 1999, 2001.

Ngyuen, Andrea. *Asian Tofu*. Berkeley, CA: Ten Speed Press, 2012.

Reinhart, Peter. *Peter Reinhart's Whole Grain Breads*. Berkeley, CA: Ten Speed Press, 2007.

Ruhlman, Michael, and Brian Polcyn. *Charcuterie*. New York: W.W. Norton & Co, 2005.

Sandler, Nick and Johnny Acton. *Preserved*. London, England: Kyle Books, 2004.

Shephard, Sue. *Pickled, Potted, and Canned*. New York: Simon & Schuster, 2000.

Symons, Michael. *A History of Cooks and Cooking*. Champaign, IL: University of Illinois Press, 2004.

Tamang, Jyoti Prakash. *Fermented Foods and Beverages of the World*. Boca Raton, FL: CRC Press, 2010.

Wildsmith, Lindy. *Cured*. Iola, WI: Krause Publications, 2010.

ABOUT THE AUTHOR

MARY KARLIN is a passionate cook, cooking teacher, cookbook author, and freelance food writer. She was a founding staff member and is currently a visiting chef-instructor at the award-winning Ramekins Culinary School in Sonoma, CA, where she has taught wood-fired cooking, cheese making, fermentation, and Mediterranean-themed cooking classes for more than ten years.

Mary is also a guest instructor at The Fork at Point Reyes Farmstead Cheese in Point Reyes, CA, and The Cheese School of San Francisco, as well as at other prominent culinary venues around the United States. She teaches an online cheese making course entitled "Artisan Cheese Making" on Craftsy.com. Mary is the author of two previous acclaimed cookbooks: *Wood-Fired Cooking* (2009) and *Artisan Cheese Making at Home* (2011).

When not teaching, Mary splits her time between Northern California and Arizona where she makes cheese, fills her pantry full of fermented food, and cooks at her wood-fired oven.

www.marykarlin.com
www.artisancheesemakingathome.com
www.masteringfermentation.com

MEASUREMENT CONVERSION CHARTS

VOLUME

U.S.	IMPERIAL	METRIC
1 tablespoon	½ fl oz	15 ml
2 tablespoons	1 fl oz	30 ml
¼ cup	2 fl oz	60 ml
⅓ cup	3 fl oz	90 ml
½ cup	4 fl oz	120 ml
⅔ cup	5 fl oz (¼ pint)	150 ml
¾ cup	6 fl oz	180 ml
1 cup	8 fl oz (⅓ pint)	240 ml
1¼ cups	10 fl oz (½ pint)	300 ml
2 cups (1 pint)	16 fl oz (⅔ pint)	480 ml
2½ cups	20 fl oz (1 pint)	600 ml
1 quart	32 fl oz (1⅔ pints)	1 l

LENGTH

INCH	METRIC
¼ inch	6 mm
½ inch	1.25 cm
¾ inch	2 cm
1 inch	2.5 cm
6 inches (½ foot)	15 cm
12 inches (1 foot)	30 cm

TEMPERATURE

FAHRENHEIT	CELSIUS/GAS MARK
250°F	120°C/gas mark ½
275°F	135°C/gas mark 1
300°F	150°C/gas mark 2
325°F	160°C/gas mark 3
350°F	180 or 175°C/gas mark 4
375°F	190°C/gas mark 5
400°F	200°C/gas mark 6
425°F	220°C/gas mark 7
450°F	230°C/gas mark 8
475°F	245°C/gas mark 9
500°F	260°C

WEIGHT

U.S./IMPERIAL	METRIC
½ oz	15 g
1 oz	30 g
2 oz	60 g
¼ lb	115 g
⅓ lb	150 g
½ lb	225 g
¾ lb	350 g
1 lb	450 g

INDEX